Understanding Effective Writing in the Federal Government

Third Edition

Michael J. O'Bannon

This publication is the exclusive intellectual property of The EOP Foundation.

Without limiting the rights under copyright reserved below, no part of this publication may be reproduced, stored in or introduced into an electronic retrieval system, or transmitted by any means without the prior written permission of the copyright owner and publisher; The EOP Foundation.

The EOP Foundation has published numerous titles, each exploring a facet of our Government process, including: *Understanding the Budget Policies and Processes of the United States Government, Understanding the Interface between Political & Career Executives in the United States Government, Understanding the United States Government's Regulatory Process, Understanding the Presidential Transition Process, Understanding the Diversity Policy of the United States Government,* and *Understanding the Ethics Policy of the United States Government.* All of these titles are integral to training public and private sector officials in these areas.

For more information on the Foundation's training assistance program or to order copies of the publications at a discount for training purposes, contact the Foundation:

Ryan Martin
The EOP Foundation
819 7th Street, N.W.
Washington, D.C. 20001
(202) 833-8940

ii

Table of Contents

Acknowledgments

There are many textbooks, style manuals, and grammar workbooks for those learning and enhancing their writing skills in the public domain. There are also Federal publications which were written to standardize rules of grammar, format, and style for Federal Departments and Agencies. The Foundation staff used many Government publications as source documents for this volume. As a result, integrating the reasons for highlighting routine grammatical rules/style considerations, with why the Government has so many types of documents (or instruments), and explaining the differing applications for those instruments is important. This volume provides a perspective unique to the Government, given current technological advances, to enhance your Government writing skills.

We have been meticulous in citing and footnoting the publications which contributed to the preparation of *Understanding Effective Writing in the Federal Government*. However, we want to acknowledge the authors of those publications here as well.

We are again proud to acknowledge the hard work of the entire Foundation staff, especially the efforts of Shawn Delaney and Ryan Martin who re-edited, and prepared updates and new material for this Third Edition.

It is also important to acknowledge our spouses. Both are named Joyce. They put up with the hours we spent reviewing, editing and seeking their counsel and assistance as we brainstormed topics to be discussed in the book.

Finally, we acknowledge the many Federal Officials who contributed their ideas and expertise to the content of this volume. It is the contributing Federal officials that permitted us to integrate their experience with academic source material and the rules associated with practical writing.

Michael J. O'Bannon
Joseph S. Hezir

Preface

Understanding Effective Writing in the Federal Government is a reference guide and style manual for Government officials. It conveys accepted formats, style considerations, substantive information, and other writing techniques that are unique to the Federal Government. The first two editions of this book have been used extensively by federal departments and agencies as a training tool in Government writing courses.

The EOP Foundation has produced several other publications, including: *Understanding the Budgetary Policies and Processes of the United States Government, Understanding the Interface between Political & Career Executives in the United States Government, Understanding the United States Government's Regulatory Process, Understanding the Presidential Transition Process, Understanding the Diversity Policy of the United States Government, and Understanding the Ethics Policy of the United States Government.* While effective writing is not the focus of our other publications, additional perspectives associated with how effective writing enhances performance in these areas is a learning outcome.

In recent years, federal officials, including career civil servants and non-career appointees, have been more focused on the quality and effectiveness of written material. This new focus includes the full range of written materials prepared for stakeholder consumption. Government writing must be grammatically correct, stylistically consistent, and objective, but it must also be accurate, clear, and concise.

The Clinton Administration's plain language initiative was an inspiration to enhancing writing skill at every level of Government. The basis of the initiative was to establish a requirement for plain and simple language to improve the clarity and reading ease of the Government's written product. The initiative's implementing criteria was to: organize the material to focus on the needs of stakeholders; write in the active voice; and use short sentences to facilitate the audience's understanding of the subject matter.

The EOP Foundation shares its expertise with the Government and the private sector by conducting specialized seminars and lectures. The Foundation also distributes its publications to Government and private sector officials. Our seminar's faculty is composed of current and former Government and private sector officials with extensive knowledge, skills, and experience writing for the Government.

This publication references key grammatical rules and style-related considerations detailed in the *Chicago Manual of Style*,[1] *The Elements of Style*,[2] the *United States Government Printing Style Manual*,[3] the *Department of Defense Manual for Written*

---

[1] The *Chicago Manual of Style 15th ed.,* Chicago: The University of Chicago, 2003.
[2] William Strunk Jr. and E.B. White, *The Elements of Style 4th Ed.,* Boston, Allyn and Bacon, 2000.
[3] *United States Government Printing Office Style Manual,* Washington, DC, 2000.

Material,[4] *the DOJ Bureau of Justice Statistics Guide,*[5] *The National Oceanic and Atmospheric Administration Correspondence Handbook,*[6] *AFS Publication Style - Shorter Version,*[7] *OPM's Guide for Managers, Supervisors and Telework Coordinators,*[8] *and Bureau of Reclamation Correspondence Handbook.*[9] These publications provide guidance associated with content, style, and grammatical structure for Government writing.

A significant benefit of this publication is that the unique instruments and requirements associated with Government writing are targeted and explained.

This text is organized into five major categories: Government decision-making focus, congressional focus, inter-agency focus, good governance writing policy focus, and government writing exercises.

Chapter Overview

Chapters in this book are organized by topic. A general guide to this book follows:

Government Decision-Making Focus (Chapters 1 through 7)

The first section of the book focuses on the decision-making documents of the Executive Branch. This section of the book focuses on interagency deliberations associated with policy alternatives articulated through government written instruments. (Chapter 1) discusses the entire flow of government written instruments that are integral to effective decision-making. The chapter includes a "decision wheel" that outlines, in order, the flow of government written instruments that educate the Executive Branch. Next, the content required to prepare a base program document (BPD) (chapter 2) is discussed. Within Government, this instrument is the most significant tool to any official managing an issue as it serves as an authentication source for written materials. Within the Executive Branch, base program documents incorporate information in all government written instruments (Chapter 3). The aforementioned instruments lay out the factual basis for the range of policy choices to be considered for any issue. The most important drafting principle is eliminating policy choices which are not supported by statutory authority, the administration's feasibility analysis, or are beyond Executive Branch capability to implement. An effective issue paper (Chapter 4) is an important step in the Executive Branch decision-making process. The primary purpose of an issue paper is to examine an issue and discuss approaches associated with addressing that issue. Once a policy has been established it is important to examine the issues associated with

---

[4] *Department of Defense Manual For Written Material,* Washington, DC, 2001.

[5] *U.S. Department of Justice, Bureau of Justice Statistics Style Guide,* Washington, DC, 1997.

[6] *The National Oceanic and Atmospheric Administration Correspondence Handbook,* Washington, DC, 2000.

[7] *AFS Publication Style - Shoter Version,* American Fisheries Society, http:www//www.anacat.ca/dl/AFS_Styleguide_ short_version.pdf.b

[8] *U.S. Department of Personal Management. Telework: A Management Priority. A Guide for Managers, Supervisors and Telework Coordinators,* Washington, DC, 2003.

[9] *U.S. Department of the Interior: Bureau of Reclamation. "Reclamation; Managing Water in the West" Correspondence Handbook,* Washington, DC, 2006.

its effectiveness. These issues must be identified and clearly stated. Then, alternatives must be articulated, analyzed, and compared prior to proposing next steps. The next instrument is the decision document (Chapter 5). The decision document it is used to consider viable alternatives, weigh expected impacts, and document all aspects of the logic and reasoning behind major decisions made by the Federal Government. The decision document typically outlines three options and recommends one of them with an analytical summary. Obviously, writing effective appeal documents (Chapter 6) is the most important instrument to facilitate reconsideration of decisions which have been made that the institution believes could result in unintentional consequences. The appeal process results in another, more targeted review of a decision the institution believes the administration should reconsider. The last chapter in the decision-making section explains effective briefing memoranda (Chapter 7). Briefing memoranda are intended and discuss decisions the Government has made and the key reasons supporting the decision. The memorandum is an important communication tool that is used primarily to share information between employees within the Federal Government.

Congressional Focus (Chapters 8 through 12)

This section focuses on drafting congressional testimony (Chapter 8) which formally conveys the Administration's position on many of the issues that Congress addresses. Congressional testimony is often written in response to Congressional investigations, inquiries, or oversight of federal programs and policies. Chapter 9 provides tips and rules for drafting authorizing legislation and committee directives. Authorizing legislation establishes, continues, or modifies agencies' programs and establishes the baseline for funding. The next chapter of the section examines legal drafting (Chapter 10). In the Government, both lawyers and non-lawyers draft legal documents. Examples include regulations, contracts, and compliance related materials. Chapter 11 focuses on instruments that originate within the department/agency decisions with emphasis on drafting and commenting on regulations. The Executive Branch interprets and implements public law, as passed by Congress, through the promulgation of regulations and issuance of associated program guidance documents so it is imperative that they be written in a clear and concise manner. Drafting budget-related materials and justifications (Chapter 12) is the focus. Government programs depend on obtaining funding through the budget process. Consequently, among the most important written materials produced by Government employees are those associated with the budget. These include the justification materials relied on during the formulation, presentation, and execution phases of the annual budget process.

Inter-Agency Focus (Chapters 13 through 20)

This section is focused on intra-agency communications including e-mails (Chapter 13). It is the efficiency associated with email communication that has made it an essential tool in Government writing notwithstanding its effeciency there are opportunities for missteps. This chapter will discuss ways to avoid these missteps and provides tips for writing effective emails. Writing effective PowerPoint presentations is discussed in (Chapter 14). Tips for effective formatting and styling are discussed along with how to write a PowerPoint presentation that flows properly. Writing effective performance appraisals is discussed in (Chapter 15). The performance appraisal is the method that federal organizations use to measure the performance of the staff within their organization. The metrics used to measure include quality, quantity, time, and the cost associated with their output. There is a strong focus on writing an effective performance appraisal. Executive Summaries are outlined in (Chapter 16). All Government reports, including strategic plans, white papers, scientific/technical reports, and annual performance accountability reports, have an Executive Summary. The summary provides the context and summary of the subject matter discussed, and conclusions inclusive of recommendations/next steps and give the report's target audience a clear understanding of the substance of the report.

Preparation of Effective Procurement Documents (Chapter 17) outlines the steps required to write an effective request for proposal (RFP) and other procurement related documents used in the Federal Government. The chapter discusses how to write acquisition authorization requests, program announcements, selection criteria and other components in order to receive the highest quality goods and services from private contractors. Methodologies and processes associated with effective procurement writing are a major focus of the chapter.

The preparation of correspondence is discussed in (Chapter 18). For the government official, the majority of controlled correspondence is received from members of Congress and congressional committees and subcommittees. Effective writing of interim correspondence, procedural correspondence, policy correspondence, and FOIA requests are examined. Advocacy documents are the focus of (Chapter 19). Advocacy documents are meant to affect or influence a decision-makers viewpoint on an issue so clear and concise writing techniques are articulated in this chapter. The use of media instruments, e.g. Facebook, Twitter, blogs, press releases, and other social media is discussed in (Chapter 20). The media relies on the accuracy and credibility of their government sources so techniques associated with the effective preparation of media instruments are the focus of this chapter.

Good Governance Writing Policy Focus (Chapters 21 through 24)

The basic elements of Government writing are addressed first in this section (Chapter 21). Neutral competence is the administrative objective of a merit-based bureaucracy and is a major focus of this chapter. Beyond an understanding of how to write effectively, one must also consider the audience that will read that writing (Chapter 22). Each federal department and agency prepares its written instruments for different audiences. A clear understanding of who your audience is makes writing clear and effective. The chapter focuses on who the key players are and the role they play within each power cluster as related to both policy and operational activities. It is also important to understand the comprehension level of your stakeholders, and this chapter closes with how to write to those various comprehensive levels.

Sources of government resource information are detailed in (Chapter 23). This chapter discusses specific social media applications in the government, web portals for more detailed government writing, and other government resources to aid with writing. This online information will enhance the quality of written instruments and articulates how social networks can expand outreach to stakeholders. Acronyms have become more common in all forms of Government writing, particularly regulations, budget justifications, and legislation. Using them properly is integral in government writing (Chapter 24).

Government Writing Exercises (Chapters 25)

(Chapter 25) is a robust chapter that includes: practical government writing exercises; writing instructions and exercises; a sample base program document; and a sample of written instruments.

Lastly, the book concludes with a glossary of terms which target legal and grammatical terminology (Glossary).

Chapter 1

The Flow of Government Instruments

The government decision-making process is different than decision-making in the private sector. The government's job is to provide goods and services to the American public. The private sector is motivated to profit from the provision of goods and services. Career professionals in the public sector are defined by their success in communicating with stakeholders throughout the decision-making process and later governance itself.

Government policy and operations are interpreted by constitutional scholars and other stakeholders who rely on the carity of the written word shaped with the Executive Branch.

Every President has their own interpretation of congressional intent, whether there is a cost effective approach to implement various programs and the determination of what it is on is not the government's responsibility.

The Executive Branch is responsible for assisting with analytic approaches and process es to ensure that the President has their best efforts to affect public policy. The medium to discharge their responsibilities relies on the institutional memory and neutral competence of government executives. The decision-making process and communication of those decisions to stakeholders are driven by written instruments. The flow of government written instruments is the basis for gaining the best result.

Chapter 1: The Flow of Government Instruments

The figure below illustrates the flow of documents in the Executive Branch decision-making process and shows that all written materials are traced back to the base document. A brief discussion of each of these instruments follows:

Figure 1.1 – Flow of Documents in Executive Branch Decision-Making Process

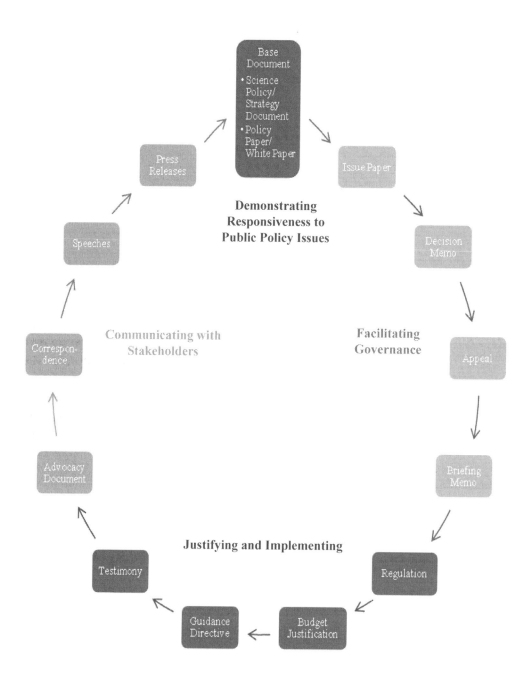

- **The Base Program Document** – This instrument is a comprehensive tool for maintaining the agency program manager's institutional memory on a particular issue including stakeholder perspectives. It is an internal document that is a comprehensive reference and is used to generate any written instrument in a timely manner.

- **Scientific Report** – This instrument is used by researchers to convey findings consistent with the Governments best research to support the decision-making process. Technical reports similarly provide a summary and analysis of the science and engineering information that are integral to the Government decision-making process.

- **Policy Paper/White Paper** – This instrument is a comprehensive analysis used to educate and discuss perspectives about new scientific or technological advances, or changes in policy. The information in these documents is used to facilitate discussion of alternative policy choices and to establish the parameters of policy debate.

Facilitating Governance

- **Issue Paper** – This instrument examines a narrow and clearly defined issue. It also evaluates alternative approaches associated with issue resolution. Within the decision-making process, preparation of issue papers follows consideration of white papers and policy papers. Following the evaluation of alternative approaches, a comparative evaluation of the alternatives is conducted. The final requirement is to propose the next steps – not recommendations.

- **Decision Memo** – This instrument articulates the decision required prior to taking a certain action. It describes the background, logic, reasoning, and impact associated with alternative decisions and choices. These internal documents may be associated with the budget, regulation, management, or policy decisions. This is the instrument which includes the institution's recommendation to political management.

- **Appeal** – This instrument lays out options (not alternatives) and analyses which eliminate the unintended consequences of a decision that the institution believes should be reconsidered prior to taking action.

- **Briefing Memorandum** – This instrument is used to share information between the Federal Government and other stakeholders on program, policy, or operational decision being implemented. These documents use charts and graphs to describe expected performance/results.

Justifying and Implementing

- **Regulation** – This instrument interprets and implements public law through the development of the methods and associated guidance documents to implement the statute's requirements. Regulations set forth the procedures governing the operations of Federal agencies and departments, finance related issues, and requirements imposed on industry and state/local Governments.

- **Budget Justification** – This instrument is used to explain the program logic associated with budgetary requests, the pricing methodology, and the relationship of performance metrics to anticipated results. These justification materials include that data relied upon during the formulation, presentation, and execution phases of the annual budget process.

- **Guidance Directive** – This instrument provides specific guidance for implementing a program that does not have the enforcement component found in regulations.

- **Testimony** – This instrument provides the administration's position to members of Congress at formal committee hearings. Testimony includes a written statement from which an oral statement is presented. Written statements represent the administration's formal position on an issue.

Communicating with Stakeholders

- **Advocacy Document** – This instrument is used to influence stakeholders on issues, proposals, and solutions considered in the decision-making process. Government advocacy is the provision of education on a particular issue, policy, or program – not lobbying. Branches and divisions within agencies use this instrument to educate and seek support for a particular decision or approach to an issue.

- **Correspondence** – This instrument answers stakeholder inquiries (e.g. Congressional committees, trade associations, NGO, etc.) about Government policies and programs.

- **Speeches** – This instrument explains to the public and principle stakeholder groups, the purpose of the program and the rationale that lead the Government to propose funding the program.

- **Press Releases** – This instrument disseminates the facts about a policy, program, or decision. There is an expectation that the media will find the subject newsworthy.

Chapter 2

Writing a Base Program Document Concept

Base Program Document

Government policy, program, and management officials should invest in the preparation of base program documents (BPDs). A BPD is a comprehensive up-to-date analysis of each program under the supervision of a Government career executive. The base document includes the program's history, budget, personnel, stakeholder positions, relevant data, congressional and judicial precedents, and political considerations. In short, the base document is the key to increased program knowledge, efficiency, and productivity for Government managers.

Many Government managers do not invest in the preparation of a base program document. Other managers do not keep the document current or fail to rely on the document to facilitate the preparation of other written Government instruments.

All Government actions are based on written instruments. Government actions rely on political and program-related analysis. Decisions are made following policy consideration of alternatives. Program strategies and operations are codified through regulations and guidance. Budgets must be justified in any forums. Government positions must be communicated to all program stakeholders whether they represent different points of view or not. Written materials also report on Government performance. The nature and natural instinct of the Government's career bureaucracy is to maintain their *records* of events that take place during their tenure in the federal service.

Effective Government writing begins with creating a single base document. The base document should then be used to generate all future written instruments the Government prepares to support its actions.

Very few issues the Government addresses are new. Quite often, materials touching on the issue have already been written. The materials address the various perspectives and their relationship to the positions of outside stakeholders. Frequently, scientific reports or white papers have been written on the program or issue. These materials can and should be used to formulate the development of the base document. Both white papers and scientific reports are explored in detail in Chapter 2.

The base document should compare and contrast the factual support for and against all of these positions. It should also be updated as often as needed to reflect current facts and changing points of view. It should not be generated from scratch, but it will require scouring the *old files* of career staff that were or are currently working in the program. Information should also be requested from various sources within the agency to insure that data filling the gaps in the document are included.

The base document is the Government's *institutional memory* for the addressed issue.[1]

In summary, the base document delineates:

- The historic position or positions the agency or department has taken, inclusive of analyses and decision criteria generated in the past;
- The agency's or department's current position on the issue;
- The up-to-date data and analysis associated with the issue;
- The political and policy position of the agency or department head, which may or may not differ dramatically from the institutional position;
- The position taken by the major stakeholders involved in the issue, both those who support the agency's institutional and political positions and those who oppose them.

As an example, the Environmental Protection Agency's (EPA) investment in preparing a base document on coal ash demonstrates the effectiveness of using a base document. Coal ash is a byproduct of the burning of coal at power plants and is typically disposed of either in solid form in non-hazardous landfills or in liquid form at surface impoundments. It contains contaminants, such as mercury and arsenic, which are associated with negative human health effects, particularly if they leach into drinking water supplies. In 2008, the structural failure of a surface impoundment

---

[1] Institutional memory is defined as collective set of facts, concepts, and experiences held by a group of people.

near Kingston, Tennessee led to the contamination of two rivers and several hundred acres of land and prompted EPA to examine its regulatory options and management practices. Because EPA's historic position concerning coal ash was that it was waste exempt from regulation, the new interest triggered economic, scientific, interagency, and state and local studies of sufficient enough harm to warrant Government action. After Kingston's accident, the agency's position shifted to one of concern that coal ash was of a sufficient concern to human health and that action was now warranted. Issue stakeholders became active, including environmentalists who favor strict regulation of coal ash, the coal-ash industry, energy companies and other industry groups who warned of the potential job losses and increased costs to be borne by consumers if regulations were promulgated.

By exploring the factual bases for each stakeholder's position within a base document, the benefits of that document become clear. The Government official managing this issue has a Government confidential document that is exempt from Freedom of Information Act (FOIA) that:

- Allows for ability to react quickly to comments or concerns as raised by the media or the public;
- Provides ready knowledge as new issues emerge;
- Allows for consistency and uniformity in message from all Government officials who may be writing or speaking on the issue;
- Documents the justifications for the decisions made around the issue; and
- Can be supplemented by public comments to update stakeholder positions.

Government officials make a costly mistake by failing to generate a base document. While the upfront time to prepare it is significant, the performance and efficiency benefits are demonstrated in the long term. Correspondence can be generated far more quickly as a result of the information in the base document. Policy, regulatory, and issue analysis are generated with consistent and uniform data that could not otherwise be prepared in a timely manner.

The BPD for the California Condor should be used as both a sample of a good BPD and as the basis for condor dependent working exercises found in Chapter 25.

Chapter 3

Writing Effective White Papers and Scientific Reports

White Papers

The standard Government method to discuss a subject is the *white paper*. A white paper is a comprehensive, authoritative report that addresses an issue and instructs the reader on the alternative approaches for solving it. It is used to inform the target audience about the issue and to provide the tools necessary for effective decision-making. The term, white paper, was initially used to refer to an official report articulating a Government position. Circulation and consumption of white papers originally occurred only in the Government sector.

White papers serve one of four main purposes, to:

- Educate the reader;
- Discuss a technical advance;
- Provide the data and analysis required as a precursor to a policy shift; or
- Provide a detailed explanation of past events.

Chapter 3: Writing Effective White Paper and Scientific Reports

White papers can take one of two forms:

- Active persuasion where the document represents an attempt to set the agenda for a particular issue, or
- Passive persuasion where policy considerations are captured for later use.

White papers are useful to policymakers because they:

- Are written plainly and clearly and not in *"Government-ise"*;
- Do not contain technical *jargon*;
- Assume the reader has *limited* technical knowledge;
- Serve as a useful *issue primer*;
- Are persuasive because they represent the Government's *neutral competence*; and
- Contain the *links* between the status quo and potential policy recommendations.

Generally, white papers are prepared when their is a transition in leadership, a need for informal agenda control, to facilitate cooperation among different agencies/ departments, to set parameters for policy debates, and to provide a basis for congressional/presidential briefings, among others.

Steps for Writing an Effective White Paper

1. **Clarify the topic:** Narrow your subject and start with a specific topic in mind.
2. **Identify your ideal reader:** Accurately identify your model audience. Pinpoint your audience's industry and general disposition. Always focus on this audience as you write the white paper.
3. **Decide on an objective:** Decide what your overarching objective for the paper is before you start writing. Do you want to inform or differentiate? Be sure to stay on topic throughout the entire white paper.
4. **Develop an outline:** An outline will force you to break the paper into manageable pieces and will keep you on a focused track. In general, the outline should include the following areas:

    a. Abstract – a description of what the paper contains within and the purpose of the paper.
    b. The Problem – define what the problem is and provide some background pertaining to the problem.
    c. Understanding The Product's/Program's Design – a description of how the product/program works in general terms. This and the following section will make up the bulk of the white paper.
    d. How the Product/Program Solves the Problem – a description of how the application of the product/program, or the proposed change in the product/program, solves the problem. Provide evidence why the proposal is the best solution available.

    e.   Conclusion – A summary of why the product/program is the best solution to the problem including the logic chain that inexorably leads from the problem to your preferred solution. This is the appropriate time to offer the next steps.

5. **Speak with the experts:** If you are not the lone content expert in your agency, interview an expert in the subject area you're writing about to gain additional perspective.

6. **Research:** Read as much as you can about the topic of your paper. If your agency has a base program document, read it until you understand the topic. Always seek industry analysis, talk to a trade association involved in your subject area, and review your agency's internal documents.

7. **Write the first page first:** Lay your white paper's foundation and then build on it. The first page will set the stage for the rest of your paper. Carefully craft and refine it to perfection. The rest of your white paper will be an extension of those first words.

8. **Write the title:** First impressions always matter. Create a relevant and compelling title that will encourage your audience to keep reading. Make sure your title is straightforward and focuses on the benefits that the paper will bring your audience.

9. **Write the core of the paper:** Break the paper into manageable components. Continue to repeatedly refine, streamline, redraft and fine-tune your messaging. Come back to your paper after a few days to make sure it conveys the same message you were writing. Always stay focused on your topic, your objective, and your model audience.

10.   **Have someone edit your paper:** A coworker can provide an objective safety net for correcting obvious errors and can ensure that your words are well written.

Examples of white papers can be found online at:

- EPA Nanotechnology White Paper: http://www.epa.gov/OSA/pdfs/nanotech/epa-nanotechnology-whitepaper-0207.pdf
- Critical Infrastructure Protection: http://www.fas.org/irp/offdocs/paper598.htm
- Genomics Task Force White Paper: http://www.oecd.org/dataoecd/32/61/34706973.pdf
- U.S. Foreign Aid: http://www.usaid.gov/policy/pdabz3221.pdf

Scientific Reports

This section provides a general guide for Government science officials who draft reports associated with their research. In addition to describing the conventional rules about the format and content of such reports, it discusses why these rules result in a clearer, more dependable approach to the drafting of scientific documents.

Generally speaking, researchers investigating some scientific hypothesis have a responsibility to the rest of the scientific community to report their findings, particularly if these findings add to or contradict previous ideas. Communication is a necessity if science is to progress, as their findings must be repeatable, critiqued, and advanced.

The two primary goals for those preparing these reports are to:

- Compile the information presented; and
- Establish that the findings are legitimate.

How to Write a Scientific Report

Scientific papers generally follow a conventional format that includes a title, an abstract, a reference (or literature cited) section and the components of the IMRAD structure:

- **I**ntroduction – which answers "why?" and states your hypothesis.
- **M**ethods – which answers "when, where, how, how much?"
- **R**esults – which answers "what?"
- **A**nd
- **D**iscussion – which answers "so what?"

Depending on the intended audience and/or the discipline, the IMRAD structure may take on an entirely different form; some may ask you to include an abstract or separate section for the hypothesis, or call the Discussion section "Conclusions," or change the order of the sections (some professional and academic journals require the Methods section to appear last). Overall, however, the IMRAD format was devised to represent a textual version of the scientific method. The scientific method involves developing a hypothesis, testing it, and deciding whether your findings support the hypothesis.

Drafting a scientific report applying these rules will ensure that the audience's expectations are achieved successfully. This chapter takes each section in the order in which it appears in the report under the IMRAD structure. This does not preclude composing sections in another order for practical reasons. For example, many writers find that composing their Methods and Results before the other sections helps to clarify the experiment or study as a whole.

Writing the Introduction

The introduction provides the audience with the general information required to understand the more detailed information discussed within the report. It will introduce the reader to the subject so that the paper will be comprehensible even if the reader has not done any work in the field. In general, an introduction will move from the broader issues to the specific issue. The introduction contains four elements:

- The purpose;
- The hypothesis;
- The scientific literature relevant to the subject; and
- The reasons for believing that the hypothesis is viable.

The four elements are to introduce the subject, the reason for the writing, the scope, and the way the writer/creator plans to develop the logic of the report. Next, we examine each element of the Introduction to clarify what it covers and why it's important.

Purpose

Perhaps the biggest misconception is that the purpose is the same as the hypothesis. The purpose provides the reader with an indication of the problem you are addressing and why – it is broader than the hypothesis and deals more with what is to be learned through the experiment. In a professional setting, the hypothesis might test which federal agency would react to a certain kind of terrorist attack while the purpose of the writing is to explore further possible uses of biological chemicals as weapons of mass destruction.

Hypothesis

A hypothesis is a tentative statement that proposes a possible explanation to some phenomenon or event. It is a testable statement which may include a prediction. A hypothesis should not be confused with a theory. A theory is a general explanation based on a large amount of data. For example, the theory of evolution is based on a wide range of observations of animal development and explains change of inherit traits over successive generations. However, there are many things about evolution that are not fully understood, such as gaps in the fossil record. A hypothesis would be used to offer a possible explanation for those fossil gaps. Clarity is best when developing a hypothesis. Be as specific as you can about the relationship between the different objects of your study. In other words, explain that when term A changes, term B changes in this particular way. The audience for scientific writing is not content with the idea that a relationship between two terms exists, they want to know what that relationship entails.

Example:

- **Not a hypothesis**: "There is a significant relationship between the atmospheric temperature during the dispersement of an aerosolized biological weapon and the rate at which it is effective."

- **Hypothesis**: "If the temperature of the atmosphere increases, then the efficacy rate of a dispersement of a biological weapon will decrease."

Put more technically, hypotheses contain both an independent and a dependent variable. The independent variable is what you manipulate to test the reaction; the dependent variable is what changes as a result of your manipulation. In the example above, the independent variable is the temperature of the atmosphere, and the dependent variable is the efficacy rate. It is critical that your hypothesis includes both variables.

Background/Previous Research

As the introduction is a brief section to present the topic and discuss its relevance to your audience, a short history or relevant background that leads to a statement of the problem being addressed is key. As such, introductions should follow a funnel style approach, starting very broadly, then narrowing; from the known to something unknown and finally to the question the paper is asking.

Methods and Materials

Writing a Strong Methods and Materials Section

As with any piece of writing, your Methods section will only succeed if it fulfills its readers' expectations. Again, the purpose can be described as how the hypothesis was tested and developed and also to clarify the rationale for the researcher's procedure. However in science, it's not sufficient merely to design and carry out an experiment. Ultimately, others must be able to verify your findings, so the experiment must be reproducible to the extent that other researchers can follow the same procedure and obtain the same (or similar) results.

An example of the importance of reproducibility is as follows. In 1989, physicists Stanley Pons and Martin Fleischman announced that they had discovered "cold fusion," a way of producing excess heat and power without the nuclear radiation that accompanies "hot fusion." Such a discovery could have great ramifications for the industrial production of energy, so these findings created a great deal of interest. When other scientists tried to duplicate the experiment, they didn't achieve the same results, and as a result many wrote off the conclusions as unjustified (or worse, a hoax). To this day, the viability of cold fusion is debated within the scientific community, even though an increasing number of researchers believe it possible. So when writing a Methods section, keep in mind that you need to describe your experiment well enough to allow others to replicate it exactly.

Content

Sometimes the hardest thing about writing a Methods section is not what you should talk about, but what you shouldn't talk about. Writers often want to include the results of their experiment, because they measured and recorded the results during the course of the experiment. But such data should be reserved for the Results section. In the

Methods section, you can write that you recorded the results, or how you recorded the results (e.g., in a table), but you should not write what the results were—not yet. Here, you're merely stating exactly how you went about testing your hypothesis. Most experiments will include a control, which is a means of comparing experimental results. (Sometimes you'll need to have more than one control, depending on the number of hypotheses you want to test). The control is exactly the same as the other items you're testing, except that you don't manipulate the independent variable – the condition you're altering to check the effect on the dependent variable. For example, if you're testing solubility rates at increased temperatures, your control would be a solution that you didn't heat at all; that way, you'll see how quickly the solute dissolves "naturally" (e.g. without manipulation), and you'll have a point of reference against which to compare the solutions you did heat.

Describe the control in the Methods section. Two things are especially important in writing about the control: identify the control as a control, and explain what you're controlling for. Example: "As a control for the temperature change, we placed the same amount of solute in the same amount of solvent and let the solution stand for five minutes without heating it."

Structure and Style

Structure is the most difficult part of writing, no matter whether you are writing a novel, a play, a poem, a Government report, or a scientific paper. If the structure is right then the rest can follow fairly easily, but no amount of clever language can compensate for a weak structure. Structure is important so that readers don't become lost. A strong structure also allows readers to know where to look for particular information and makes it more likely that all important information will be included.

Readers of scientific papers in medical journals are accustomed to the IMRAD structure (Introduction, Methods, Results, and Discussion) and either consciously or unconsciously know the function of each section. Readers have also become used to structured abstracts, which have been shown to include more important information than unstructured summaries. Journals are now introducing specific structures for particular types of papers – such as the Consolidated Standards of Reporting Trials (CONSORT) structure for reporting randomized trials.

Earlier written papers often comprised small amounts of new data—perhaps a case report—with extensive discussion. The function of the discussion seemed to be to convince readers of the rightness of the author's interpretation of data and speculation and was not a dispassionate examination of the evidence. Today there is a far greater emphasis placed on methods and results, particularly as methods have become more complicated and scientifically valid. Richard Horton, editor of the *Lancet*, as well as others, have described how authors use rhetoric in the discussion of papers. They describe and use extensive text without subheadings; expansion of reports with comment relating more to the generalities than to the specifics of the study; the introduction of bias by emphasizing the strengths of the study more than its weaknesses, reiterating selected results, and inflating the importance of the findings. Commonly, authors go beyond the evidence they have gathered and draw unjustified conclusions.

Suggested Structure for Discussion in Scientific Papers

1. Statement of Principal Findings
2. Strengths and Weaknesses of the Study
3. Strengths and Weaknesses in Relation to Other Studies and Presenting any Differences in Results
4. Meaning of the Study, Including Implications for Policymakers
5. Unanswered Questions and Recommended Future Research

The discussion should begin with a restatement of the principal finding – ideally, no more than one sentence. This should be followed by a comprehensive examination of the strengths and weaknesses of the study, with equal emphasis given to both. Indeed, editors and readers are likely to be most interested in the weaknesses of the study: all medical studies have them. If editors and readers identify weaknesses that are not discussed, then their trust in the paper will be shaken: what other weaknesses might there be that neither they nor the authors have identified? Next, the author should relate this study to work that has been done before. The task here is not to show how your study is better than previous studies but rather to compare strengths and weaknesses. Again, hiding the weaknesses of your study will bring a lack of trust in the validity of your effort. Importantly, you should discuss why you might have reached different conclusions from others; but go easy on the speculation. If you don't know why your results are different from those of others, you should not assume that your results are right and the others wrong. Now you should begin the difficult study of discussing what your study might "mean." What might be the explanation of your findings and what might they mean for clinicians or policymakers? Here you are on dangerous ground, and most editors and readers will appreciate your being cautious, not moving beyond what is often limited evidence.

Leave readers to make up their own minds on meaning – they will anyway. You might even emphasize what your evidence does not mean, keeping your readers from reaching overdramatic, unjustified conclusions. Finally, you should discuss what questions remain unanswered and what further work is needed. Again, editors and readers will enjoy restraint. Indeed, this is the part of the paper where authors often run amok, but don't corrupt your evidence with speculation.

Other subheadings might sometimes be needed, but we think that this suggested structure should fit most studies. Although some may find uniform structuring difficult and even restrictive, we believe that our proposed structure should reduce overall length; prevent unjustified extrapolation and selective repetition; reduce reporting bias; and improve the overall quality of reporting. Such a supposition could readily be tested.

Results

The Materials and Methods section shows how you obtained the results, and the Discussion section explores the significance of the results, so clearly the Results section forms the backbone of the scientific report. The Results section is often both the shortest and most important part of your report. It provides the most critical information about your experiment: the data that allow, you to discuss how your hypothesis was or was not supported. But it does not provide anything else, which explains why this section is generally shorter than the others.

The Results section of a paper has two key features: an overall description of the major findings of the study, and the data, presented clearly and concisely. It is not necessary to present every scrap of data that you have collected. There is a great temptation to give all the results, particularly if they were difficult to obtain, but this section should contain only relevant, representative data.

The statistical analysis of the results must be appropriate. While the availability of statistical software packages makes statistical computations much easier, it has not encouraged young research workers to understand the principles involved. The analysis presented must pass what is called the "Mark I Eyeball Test," a visual inspection whose name is derived from the US Military, and to do so the statistics must be explained.

An assessor is only able to estimate the validity of the statistical tests used, so if your analysis is complicated or unusual, expect your paper to undergo appraisal by a statistician. You must strive for clarity in the Results section by avoiding unnecessary repetition of data in the text, figures, and tables. It is worthwhile stating briefly what you did not find, as this may save other workers in this area from undertaking unnecessary studies.

Discussion

In the discussion section, you should present:

- What principles have been established or reinforced;
- What generalizations can be drawn;
- How your findings compare to the findings of others or to expectations based on previous work; and
- Whether there are any theoretical/practical implications of your work.

When addressing these questions, it is crucial that your discussion rests firmly on the evidence presented in the Results section. Refer briefly to your results to support your discussion statements. Do not extend your conclusions beyond those that are directly supported by your results. A brief paragraph of speculation about what your results may mean in a general sense is usually acceptable but should not form the bulk of the discussion. Be sure to address the objectives of the study in the discussion and to discuss the significance of the results. End the discussion with a short summary or conclusion regarding the significance of the work. In simple terms, here you tell your readers what to make of the results you obtained. If you have done the Results part well, your readers should already recognize the trends in the data and have a fairly clear idea of whether your hypothesis was supported. Because the results can seem so self-explanatory, many writers/authors find it difficult to know what material to add in this last section.

Basically, the Discussion section contains several parts, in no particular order, but roughly moving from specific (i.e., related to your experiment only) to general (how your findings fit in the larger scientific community). To reiterate, this section, as a rule, must:

- Explain whether the data supports your hypothesis;
- Acknowledge any anomalous data or deviations from what you expected;
- Derive conclusions, based on your findings, about the process you're studying;
- Relate your findings to earlier work in the same area (if you can); and
- Explore the theoretical and/or practical implications of your findings.

Explain Whether the Data Supports your Hypothesis

Begin the Discussion section with an explanation of whether your hypothesis is supported by the data. You might use this part of the Discussion to explicitly state the relationships or correlations your data indicate between the independent and dependent variables. From there, you can show more clearly why you believe your hypothesis was or was not supported. For example, if you tested efficacy at various temperatures, you could start this section by noting that the rates of efficacy increased as the temperature increased. If your initial hypothesis surmised that temperature change would affect efficacy, you would then say something like, "The hypothesis that temperature change would affect efficacy was supported by the data." Note that the example uses the word "supported," not "proven." Scientists tend to view labs as practical tests of undeniable scientific truths. As a result, you may have the urge to say that the hypothesis was "proved" or "disproved," or that it was "correct" or "incorrect." These terms, however, reflect a degree of certainty that you as a scientist aren't supposed to have. Remember, you're testing a theory with a procedure that lasts only a few hours and relies on only a few trials, which severely compromises your ability to be sure about the "truth" you see. Words like "supported," "indicated," and "suggested" are more acceptable ways to evaluate your hypothesis.

Also, recognize that saying whether the data supported your hypothesis or not involves making a claim to be defended. As such, you need to show the readers that this claim is warranted by the evidence. Make sure that you're very explicit about the relationship between the evidence and the conclusions you draw from it. This process can be difficult for many writers, because we don't often justify conclusions in our regular lives.

Acknowledge any Data that is Anomalous or Deviates from Expectations

You must account for exceptions and divergences from the expected outcome in order to qualify your conclusions sufficiently. For obvious reasons, your readers will doubt your authority if you (deliberately or inadvertently) overlook a key piece of data that doesn't square with your perspective on what occurred. In a more philosophical sense, once you've ignored evidence that contradicts your claims, you've departed from the scientific method. The urge to "tidy up" the experiment is often strong, but if you give in to it you're no longer performing good science.

Sometimes, after you've performed a study or experiment, you realize that some part of the methods you used to test your hypothesis was flawed. In that case, it's acceptable to suggest that, if you had the chance to conduct your test again, you might change the design in a specific way to avoid repeating the problem. The key to making this approach work, though, is to be very precise about the weakness in your experiment, why and how you think that weakness might have affected your data, and how you would alter your protocol to eliminate—or limit the effects of—that weakness.

Often, inexperienced researchers and writers feel the need to account for "wrong" data, even though there is no such creature, and speculate wildly about what might have caused divergences. These speculations include such factors as the unusually hot temperature in the room, or the possibility that their lab partners read the meters wrong, or the potentially defective equipment. Don't indicate that the experiment had a weakness unless you're fairly certain that a) it really occurred and b) you can explain reasonably well how that weakness affected your results.

Derive Conclusions, Based on Your Findings, about the Process you are Studying

With an explanation of if the data supported the hypothesis and acknowledgement of any deviations from what was expected, you can now make more general statements about the process of efficacy. This part of the Discussion section is another place where you need to be careful to avoid overreaching. Again, nothing you've found in one study would remotely allow you to claim that you now "know" something, or that something isn't "true," or that your experiment "confirmed" some principle or other. Use less absolutely conclusive language, including such words as "suggest," "indicate," "correspond," "possibly," "challenge," etc.

Explore the Theoretical and/or Practical Implications of Your Findings

Explaining the implications of your findings is often the best way to end the Discussion (and, for all intents and purposes, the report). In argumentative writing, you want to use your closing words to convey the main point of your writing. This main point can be primarily theoretical ("Now that you understand this information, you're in a better position to understand this larger issue") or primarily practical ("You can use this information to take such and such an action"). In either case, the concluding statements help the reader to comprehend the significance of your project and your decision to write about it.

Since a lab report is argumentative – after all, you are investigating a claim and judging the legitimacy of that claim by generating and collecting evidence – it's often a good idea to end your report with the same technique for establishing your main point. If you want to go the theoretical route, you might talk about the consequences your study has for the field or phenomenon you're investigating. To return to the examples regarding efficacy, you could end by reflecting on what your work on efficacy as a function of temperature tells us (potentially) about efficacy in general. If you want to go the practical route, you could end by speculating about the medical, institutional, or commercial implications of your findings – in other words, answer the question, "What can this study help people to do?" In either case, you're going to make your readers' experience more satisfying by helping them see why they spent their time learning what you had to teach them.

Chapter 4

Writing Effective Issue Papers

An issue paper is the instrument designed to educate Government executives on the alternatives for addressing an issue. The primary purpose of an issue paper is to examine an issue and discuss approaches associated with addressing that issue. Preparation of issue papers follows consideration of white papers and policy papers in the Government's overall decision-making process. Following the evaluation of each alternative, a comparative analysis of the pros and cons is required. The final requirement is to propose the next steps associated with addressing the issue. If your issue paper is longer than 3 pages, you may need to narrow your statement of the issue.

Because issue papers are so pervasive as catalysts to Government decision-making, the private sector often employs this approach in their effort to influence the Governmental decision-making process from the outside. Advocacy groups, the NRA for example, will utilize this type of document to outline an issue, like the right to bear arms. Alternately, issue papers serve as internal catalysts within the Government, as the preferred approach to examine the alternatives bearing on an issue of concern. For instance, an official within the Department of Defense may have concerns regarding the structure associated with purchasing goods and services for the Department, and may utilize such a document to educate management about alternative approaches to the status quo. In an effort to ensure that the policy has been appropriately evaluated, an issue paper clearly articulates the alternatives inclusive of the justification and argument for each.

An effective issue paper provides a brief but expert comparison of alternatives in a concise and accurate manner. It is important for the author to keep his audience in mind. Superfluous words and information can only serve to hinder the author's intent. The audience is comprised of those that can influence policy; the most influential will be career executives whose position includes jurisdiction over the disposition of the issue discussed. Thus, it is critical to understand that the time expended by the executive relying on the issue paper is valuable.

Writing unnecessarily lengthy issue papers is discouraged. Such papers either cause confusion or change the focus of the issue paper with every word that does not add value in examining and comparing relevant alternatives associated with the issue.

The career executive is likely to know the current rationale for the manner in which the program operates (the status quo). However, the executive is not likely to know the breadth or details of viable alternatives. Thus, the document is composed under the assumption that the audience is not sufficiently educated in the topic of interest. In the spirit of preserving the contrasting ideals of brevity and comprehensiveness, it is important to write the paper with a time-tested issue paper format in mind. The following represents the Government's regular format for issue papers:

Statement of the Issue

The audience should not be confused about what the issue is as it would compromise the effectiveness of the document. If the reader does not understand why there is an issue, not only does it threaten accurate conveyance of key considerations and/or information relevant to the issues, but also the audience's perception of the argument's strengths will be diminished.

Issue papers are, at the core, meant to be educational resources to keep executives apprised of viable alternatives with which they have little or no previous experience. Setting the context of the issue up front facilitates comprehension of the new concepts, data, and justification to be examined and presented. Clarity should be a very high priority.

Background

Following a clear statement of the issue, it is critical that a brief, focused background be written. This must provide the relevant facts and context required to understand why the alternatives in the issue paper that have been selected are relevant to the issue. Without this information, the issue statement is not necessarily understood.

The background also educates the reader about why the issue is being vetted in the paper. An example of an issue statement follows: "Is the structure by which goods and services are priced providing the lowest costs and highest quality to the Department?"

An example of the background would state: "The authority to procure goods and services is, etc., the current pricing structure is, etc., changes which impact that structure are, etc., and new authorities who may improve the structure are, etc."

Statement of Alternatives

With a clear understanding of the context in which the issue of concern resides, the reader should be able to digest the range of alternatives presented. Each alternative should be clearly stated. Management should not have to determine where each alternative begins and ends. This should be clear in the statement of alternatives. The list of alternatives should be comprehensive but credible. The status quo alternative should be presented as a baseline.

Analysis of Each Alternative

Once the alternatives are clearly presented, the data, facts, and rationale for the alternatives should be stated. This section acquaints the reader with an explanation of why each proposal is a viable policy alternative. In order to gain credibility, it is important that the analysis is both logical and objective. To accomplish this task, a comprehensive assessment of feasibility (economically, logistically, and politically) should be prepared along with any operational considerations. It is equally important to reference the policy footprint associated with the alternative and any anticipated future impacts. It would also be critical for the career executive to understand how the projected outcomes of the alternative align with the policy goals in other areas of a particular department or the Government as a whole.

Comparison of Alternatives

Following the comprehensive analysis of each proposal, a direct comparison must be made to provide the reader with a clear picture of the pros and cons associated with each alternative. This comparison also provides an un-obstructed view of the relative worth of each action considered. Direct comparison of the individual impacts, good and bad, of each proposal facilitates educated decision-making, and allows the management the means to objectively prioritize various alternatives.

Conclusion

Effective presentation up to this point can provide the reader with a clear view of the field and its competing components. The conclusion should briefly recapture all that has been learned in the preceding analysis. Emphasis should be given to the major or unexpected findings. It may also be appropriate to provide next steps. These next steps may be an effort to uncover information that has not yet been presented or to refine the existing analysis.

Chapter 4: Writing Effective Issue Papers

If properly utilized, issue papers are a very effective instrument to facilitate decision-making. Issue papers can result in wide-scale influence among multiple audiences, particularly the career executives within the Administration. They are also a significant source of general education on a myriad of subjects. Issue papers are vital within the context of American policy making, and serve as a catalyst for the creativity and innovation required to move our country in a positive direction.

Chapter 5

Writing Effective Decision Documents

Federal agencies and program managers are faced with complex decisions on a daily basis. The breadth of these decisions is often vast; it may impact many members of the public, non-governmental organizations (NGOs) or sanctions, private corporations, state-level Government agencies, other federal agencies, or even international interests. Because major decisions tend to carry hefty impacts to the federal budget (both positive and negative), they spark the attention of key members of Congress. As a result, it is necessary to consider viable alternatives, weigh expected impacts, and document all aspects of the logic and reasoning behind major decisions made by the Federal Government. These documents are called "decision documents."

Examples of Public Decision Documents

Each federal agency follows its own protocol for documenting decisions. Across the Government, decision documents come in various formats. Some common types of decision documents are:

- **Record of Decision (ROD):** A signed federal document wherein the deciding official states which alternative path will be pursued and outlines the logic for this decision. A ROD is most commonly associated with the conclusion of an

Environmental Impact Statement (EIS). Some agencies that issue RODs are EPA, the Fish and Wildlife Service, Department of Defense, and the Federal Highway Administration.

- **Finding of No Significant Impact (FONSI):** A public document written by a federal agency under the National Environmental Protection Act (NEPA) that concludes an EIS is not needed because the contemplated project or action will have no significant impact on the environment or community.

- **Categorical Exclusion Form (CEF):** Under some statutes that are broadly written, a mechanism is included to allow federal officials to determine on a case-by-case basis whether or not investigation or regulation is the best use of resources. Following the NEPA example, Superintendents of National Parks are allowed to grant Categorical Exclusions from further investigation under certain aspects of the NEPA. This must be documented by a CEF bearing the signature of the Superintendent.

- **Director's Review Paper:** This is a paper that the OMB Career budget examiner prepares to facilitate decision-making on a Government program, budget, or regulatory issue. These papers explain the political and pragmatic controversy of various finding levels including terminating the program. Issues raised in the process move from the highest career level within OMB to the political level prior to reaching the Director of OMB.

Non-Public, Internal Decision Documents

Decision documents are also used behind agencies' closed doors in a less formal manner. Typically, they begin when a low or mid-level official is faced with a decision that has no direct precedent and, therefore, requires approval from someone at the program director level. These internal documents may be associated with budget matters, regulatory determinations, or policy decisions. For example, imagine that an official at the IRS is reviewing corporate tax returns and notices that the XYZ Corporation has come up with an innovative and unique way to claim a deduction. The official researches the matter and finds no comparable precedent to guide his ruling on the matter. Realizing that his decision will become the de facto regulatory precedent, he chooses to document the facts of the case, recommend a course of action, justify his recommendation, and present it to his division director for a final decision. That IRS official has just written a decision document.

The Timing of a Decision Document

Decision documents provide the transition between pre-decision efforts and post-decision efforts. In general, decision documents must accomplish two goals:

- Provide closure for pre-decision activities; and
- Establish expectations and metrics for the design, implementation, and performance of the preferred response action.[1]

Consider a case where a federal agency is working to clean up a site where the environment has been contaminated or polluted. Pre-decision efforts would include site investigation, response evaluation, and analysis of potential alternative cleanup technologies, to name a few. Post-decision efforts would have to do with designing and implementing a response. The decision document lays out the path for progressing between these two stages.

Proper Content and Clarity of a Decision Document

As mentioned above, the decision document comes at the conclusion of the pre-decision phase. The pre-decision phase has several objectives:

- Identifying problems that warrant federal action;
- Clearly communicating the scope of these problems;
- Defining the objectives of a federal response; and
- Choosing the appropriate responses needed to achieve these objectives.

The decision document should address all of these categories clearly and in a way that is not open to interpretation. Consider the following hypothetical, generic scenario as a method of walking through the content of the decision document.

Identify the problem and explain why federal action is needed:

> *Coffee filters used in break rooms of a Federal Building exceed absorbency standards. This will likely result in a failure to meet Minimum Caffeine Levels (MCLs) for coffee under the Federal Employee Alertness Act (FEAA).*

Define the problem using sufficient detail to support a preferred action alternative. In doing so, however, be sure to note potential uncertainties that could affect a decision:

> *Based upon empirical data from testing, average caffeine content of coffee in the Building was 114 milligrams (mg) per serving - 21 mg under the recommended MCL of 135 mg per serving. This level has remained constant for 14 months. However, caffeine levels are affected by multiple factors including impurities in input water and production variance in coffee beans from the supplier. In the event this level dips below the Productivity Failure Threshold*

---

[1] Preparing Effective Decision Documents, Department of Energy, October, 2000, http://homer.ornl.gov/nuclearsafety/env/guidance/cercla/decdocs.pdf, accessed June 2010

> *under FEAA, a plan is in place to supply supplemental pills to staff members in need.*

Objectives for moving forward cannot be vague:

> *Caffeine levels will be restored to acceptable levels within 90 days.*

This objective might be interpreted any of the following ways:

- All coffee in the United States is subject to FEAA standards.
- All beverages consumed in the building must have a certain level of caffeine under FEAA – even water.
- Old coffee will be stored and injected with additional caffeine to bring it up to standards.

A better way to state the objective is as follows:

> *Achieve MCLs at all coffee brewing stations within the Building within 90 days.*

The decision document should then discuss various alternatives for achieving this goal. In our hypothetical example, these might include evaluating replacement coffee filters, managing input water quality, increasing brewing station pressure to ensure concentrations are high enough, etc.

Making the Decision Achievable

The course of action prescribed in a decision document should, to the extent possible, define goals and objectives while leaving room for engineers (or other agents of implementation) to apply their expertise to achieve the desired endpoint. In other words, more effective decision documents recommend performance based solutions, not those that are technology based.

To this end, technical details should be included to facilitate the actual design and implementation of a solution. The more detail included, the more effectively the implementing engineers can carry out the plan outlined in the decision document.

Chapter 6

Writing Effective Appeal Documents

Government career executives have a responsibility to ensure that political executives do not change Government policy or program direction without a comprehensive education about the impacts of their decisions. The career executive is the institutional interface between political decisions that are made and the consequences of those decisions. Thus, the preparation of appeals is critical to highlighting what the unintended consequences of a decision are. The appeal process results in another, more targeted review of a decision the *institution* believes the administration should reconsider.

Appeal documents must be concise, clear, and conform to the principles of neutral competence discussed earlier. This chapter discusses how to draft them effectively. The most common appeals are policy related, budgetary or regulatory. Appeals should also consider inter- and intra-agency concerns or perspectives.

General Structure of Appeals Documents

Organization is the key to a good appeal document. When drafting an appeal document, it is important to begin with a statement of the issue that articulates the reason the decision is being appealed. The tone should be neutral, factual, and straightforward.

Examples

Subjective

Will failure to enforce the new stringent, expensive air standard make a difference in cancer related deaths?

Neutral

Does the latest scientific study demonstrate that a new toxic air standard should be promulgated?

In the first example the tone is politically charged. In the second, it is focused and to the point. Thus, carefully choosing words that do not trigger a political or immediately negative response is critical to the effectiveness of the appeal document.

The appeal documents should contain a background section which outlines:

- A description of the program, event, or original decision that has been made;
- The reasons why the subsequent decision made should be reconsidered; and
- The potential unintended consequences that should be brought to the attention of the political executive.

The statements here should be stated as factually and objectively as possible and should reflect the earlier executive's exact knowledge. Obviously, *a professional/expert opinion* can be debated while a *subjective or politically charged document* likely will be ignored.

The appeals document should provide three alternatives for the political executive to consider. It should begin with the political executives' option adjusted to minimize as many of the unintended consequences as possible without a material change in the substance of the option. The second option should reflect the institutions' expert opinion and best approach to the issue. Each of these options should be constructed to include components of the political executives' *intent* that either improve or do not negatively impact the institution's option. The third option should showcase the perspective of stakeholder groups (or another federal agency if the appeal involves an interagency disagreement) which is neither supported by the political executive, or the institution. This option is particularly important to the balance of the appeal and integrity of the appeal process.

Budget and Regulatory Appeals Documents

Budget appeal documents focus on the actual impacts to programs or services associated with a decision to increase/decrease funding. Regulatory appeal documents tend to focus on whether and how the initial decision impacts the administrator's ability to effectively discharge statutory intent addressing the regulatory approach being taken. While budget appeal documents are intra-/ inter-agency documents that are not shared with the public, regulatory appeal documents are often publicly available in the docket.

As stated earlier, the budget appeal begins with the definition of the problem (e.g. funding is approved for a shorter period than requested, a program will fail to achieve the desired goal due to the resource constraint). The consequences of the initial decision must be stated clearly so that the gravity of the decision is conveyed to the executives considering the appeal. Thus, an analysis which supports your assertions must be written in the most persuasive manner.

The most effective analysis is a thorough assessment of the major impacts of the decision on the Government's programs. A broad overview of the issues should not be necessary, because the issue was previously considered, and likely will be ineffective. The analysis should be specific to the performance measure, federal purpose, or political argument as the basis for reconsidering the initial decision. The analysis can cite new evidence; if it exists, new information can be crucial to the success of the appeal. This assures the deciding official that the information in the appeal reflects the current information relevant to the issue.

Regulatory appeal documents are more quasi legal in nature. They include more narrative discussing statutory intent as well as costs and benefits which should be taken into account for effective implementation. A strong rebuttal is imperative. Thus, it is critical that the analyses state the facts, data, and chain of logic in the most persuasive manner possible.

Both budgetary and regulatory appeal documents should conclude with a summary of the issues and any requirement which should be undertaken as part of the reconsideration, (e.g. a legislative proposal, a full-time employment adjustment, a changed metric, etc).

Appeals of policy related matters and management related issues follow the same organization and structure as budget and regulatory issues.

Chapter 7

Writing Effective Briefing Memoranda

General Information

The memorandum is an important communication tool that is used primarily to share information between employees within the Federal Government. Memoranda are intended to be short, concise, and to the point. There is no Government-wide standard or format for writing them, although some agencies, such as the Department of Defense, have their own memorandum-writing manual. In other agencies, the memorandum standards vary from office-to-office. There are four general categories of memorandum.

1. Intra-office information – written communication between officials within the same agency, department, or office.
2. Inter-agency discussion – written communication between different Government agencies, for example between the United States Forest Service and the United States Bureau of Reclamation, or between a Government agency and outside consultants hired by them.[1]

---

[1] Inter-agency memoranda are exempt from FIOA disclosure and courts have held that outside personnel hired by an agency to represent that agency's interests are considered the same as a government official in the agency's process of deliberation. See, *Department of Interior v. Klamathwater Users protective Assn.* 532 U.S. 1 (2001).

3. Policy clarification – a document that defines the requirements and responsibilities required from a broader policy statement, as interpreted by a Government agency.

4. Formal guidance – even more specific than a policy clarification memorandum, a guidance document will address a single issue or a small subset of issues and state the agency's position on that issue. For example, in regards to water testing to comply with a discharge permit, the regulation may state that it must be performed "with sufficient regularity" to ensure compliance. The agency may use a guidance memo to clarify that testing must be performed every three months.

Basic Elements

There are five basic elements of a memorandum:

1. Header;
2. Purpose;
3. Summary;
4. Discussion; and
5. Action.

Each element is described below. If there is more information that needs to be passed along than can be covered in a page or two, it's appropriate to create an attachment(s).

Header

The header is used to convey essential information such as who the memorandum is from, who it is to, the subject, and the date drafted. While all of these sections need to be included in every memorandum, there are no Government-wide guidelines that specify the order of these sections. However, agencies may provide guidance to their employees. The most common order of arrangement is the date first (either centered or right justified), followed by the recipient, the sender, and lastly the subject. Another arrangement, used by the Department of Transportation, is the subject and date first, on the same line, followed by the sender and the recipient. The date should always be spelled out, i.e., July 14, 2010. Salutations should never be used when writing a memorandum. When putting in the subject line, use descriptive, precise titles. For example, don't use "Policy Position" but instead "Proposed NRC position on the licensing of new nuclear energy facilities." An example of a proper memorandum header follows.

MEMORANDUM

TO: Regional Administrators

FROM: Lisa P. Jackson, Administrator

RE: EPA's Interpretation of Regulations that Determine Pollutants Covered by Federal Prevention of Significant Deterioration (PSD) Program

---

Purpose

The first few sentences of the purpose should answer the basic questions of: who, what, where, when, why, and how. For example, you would not want to say: "This memo is the first step in NRC's proposed changes to its requirements for some nuclear facilities during licensing." A better, more descriptive statement would be: "NRC solicits comment on proposed changes to the licensing procedures for new nuclear energy facilities licensed after January 1, 2010." The purpose should not be longer than a few sentences or go beyond the scope of the areas previously identified. Any further description that is needed should be included in the 'summary' or 'discussion' sections that follow.

Summary

A good summary allows a large portion of the readership to get the information it needs from reading the summary only. Obviously, the summary must capture the essential information covered in more detail in the memo. It is critical that the most important information be placed at the front of this section. Bulleted lists are perfectly acceptable in order to achieve this end.

Discussion

Memoranda often are prepared to preserve as institutional memory. Thus, all relevant background information must be presented. Begin with the big picture and then, as quickly as possible, narrow the focus down to the specifics of the memo. The memo should logically guide the reader through the various aspects of the discussion topic and then quickly conclude.

Chapter 7: Writing Effective Briefing Memorandum

Action

This section does not apply to all memoranda; however, when there is an action to be taken, it should clearly state who should act and what specific action is required.

Chapter 8

Drafting Effective Testimony and Responses to Questions

The most important written instrument for the career service associated with communicating with the Congress is testimony and responses to Member/Committee questions. Testimony has several objectives. First, it formally conveys the Administration's position on many of the issues that Congress addresses. Second, it provides expert, technical, operational, or other assessment-related information to the Congress. Third, it is responsive to Congressional investigations, inquiries, or oversight of federal programs and policies. Finally, it articulates the details and justification for the Administration's proposed legislative initiative or position on Congressional initiatives.

Testimony integrates the Administration's political, substantive, and institutional considerations on an issue. This is the Administration's only formal record provided to inform the legislative process. The Administration determines the testimony's content based upon the message they believe must be communicated to the Congress prior to consideration of the issues, proposals, budget, etc. and is integral to the Administration's agenda.

Testimony is transmitted in advance to the congressional committee with jurisdiction over the issue to be addressed. The various committees have their own unique rules and standards governing all aspects of the testimony, from preparation through the delivery of testimony before the committee. A general summary of the committee structure, composition, and process is presented below.

A congressional committee is composed of members of Congress representing both the majority party and minority party. Committees are authorized by the main congressional body to address specific areas and issues. The main body also ratifies the committee's jurisdiction.

Committee membership is assigned by the party's leadership and enables members to develop specific knowledge and also expertise of the matters under their jurisdiction. The political make-up of each committee reflects the political make-up of the body as a whole with the majority party chairing the committee and having a greater number of committee members. The committee's lead for the minority is the ranking minority member.

Committees monitor on-going governmental operations, identify issues suitable for legislative review, gather and evaluate information, and recommend courses of action to the main body. Committees also monitor Executive Branch performance and investigate allegations of impropriety.

Congress divides its legislative, oversight, and internal administrative tasks among approximately 200 committees and subcommittees.

There are three main types of committees—standing, select/special, and joint.

Standing committees are permanent panels identified as such by the respective body and pursuant to it rules, e.g. House Rule X, Senate Rule XXV.

Most standing committees recommend funding levels, or authorizations, for Government operations and for new and existing programs. A few have other functions. The *Appropriations Committees* recommend legislation to provide budget authority for federal agencies and programs. The *Budget Committees* establish aggregate authorized levels for total spending and revenue that serve as the guideline to assist authorizing and appropriating panels.

Select/special committees are usually established by a resolution of the House or Senate to conduct investigations and studies to address specific measures. These committees are often established to address emerging issues that overlap standing committee jurisdictions. A select committee may be permanent or temporary; however, all of the existing committees are all considered permanent at this point in history. The Senate is most likely to designate a committee as a "special" committee.

Joint committees are comprised of members from both the House and Senate. These permanent committees conduct studies or are charged with addressing housekeeping responsibilities relevant to both the House and Senate. The chairmanship of joint committees usually alternates between the House and Senate. Conference committees fit under this classification but are temporary and are usually charged with resolving differences between competing House and Senate versions of a measure. Conference committees are joint committees that draft compromises between House and Senate positions to be ratified by the full House and Senate prior to enactment.

Subcommittees are established by the majority of committees to complete work on issues prior to full committee approval. Subcommittees work within guidelines established by the full committee.

There are 21 permanent committees in the House of Representatives, and 20 in the United States Senate. Four joint committees operate with members from both houses on matters of mutual jurisdiction and oversight.

Committees in the House generally have more members, due to its larger size (435 members), as compared to the smaller, 100-member Senate. Senate rules fix the maximum size for many of its committees. However, the House determines the size and makeup of each committee at the beginning of each new Congress.

Although the roster of each committee is officially approved by a full vote of the House or Senate, the party leadership informally decides who will serve as chair and members of each committee and sub-committee are generally decided based on the members seniority. Other considerations in making the assignments include each member's areas of expertise and the interests of their constituents. Political favors also often come into play in committee assignments and sometimes defy the principles discussed above.

Senate Standing Committees and Associated Subcommittees

Agriculture, Nutrition and Forestry
- Commodities, Markets, Trade and Risk Management
- Jobs, Rural Economic Growth and Energy Innovation
- Conservation, Forestry and Natural Resources
- Nutrition, Specialty Corps, Food and Agricultural Research
- Livestock, Daily, Poultry, Marketing and Agriculture Security

Appropriations
- Agriculture, Rural Development, Food and Drug Administration, and Related Agencies
- Commerce, Justice, Science, and Related Agencies
- Defense
- Energy and Water Development
- Financial Services and General Government
- Homeland Security
- Interior, Environment, and Related Agencies
- Labor, Health and Human Services, Education, and Related Agencies
- Legislative Branch
- Military Construction, Veterans Affairs, and Related Agencies
- State, Foreign Operations, and Related Programs
- Transportation, Housing and Urban Development, and Related Agencies

Armed Services
- Airland
- Emerging Threats and Capabilities
- Personnel
- Readiness and Management Support
- SeaPower
- Strategic Forces

Banking, Housing, & Urban Affairs
- Economic Policy
- Financial Institutions
- Housing, Transportation, and Community Development
- Securities, Insurance, and Investment
- Security and International Trade and Finance

Budget
No subcommittees

Commerce, Science & Transportation
- Aviation Operations, Safety, and Security
- Communications and Technology, and the Internet
- Competitiveness, Innovation, and Export Promotion
- Consumer Protection, Product Safety, and Insurance
- Oceans, Atmosphere, Fisheries, and Coast Guard
- Science and Space
- Surface Transportation and Merchant Marine Infrastructure, Safety, and Security

Energy and Natural Resources
- Energy
- National Parks
- Public Lands and Forests
- Water and Power

Environment and Public Works
- Clean Air and Nuclear Safety
- Green Jobs and the New Economy
- Oversight
- Superfund, Toxics and Environmental Health
- Transportation and Infrastructure
- Water and Wildlife

Finance
- Energy, Natural Resources, and Infrastructure
- Health Care
- International Trade, Customs, and Global Competitiveness
- Social Security, Pensions, and Family Policy
- Taxation and IRS Oversight
- Fiscal Responsibility and Economic Growth

Foreign Relations
- African Affairs
- East Asian and Pacific Affairs
- European Affairs
- International Development and Foreign Assistance, Economic Affairs, and International Environmental Protection, and Peace Corps
- International Operations and Organizations, Human Rights, Democracy and Global Women's Issues
- Near Eastern and South and Central Asian Affairs
- Western Hemisphere, and Global Narcotics Affairs

Health, Education, Labor, and Pensions
- Children and Families
- Employment and Workplace Safety
- Primary Health and Aging

Homeland Security and Governmental Affairs
- Capital Markets and Government Sponsored Enterprises
- Financial Institutions and Consumer Credit
- Housing and Insurance
- Monetary Policy and Trade

Judiciary
- Bankruptcy and the Courts
- Antitrust, Competition Policy and Consumer Rights
- The Constitution, Civil Rights, and Human Rights
- Crime and Terrorism
- Immigration, Refugees, and Border Security
- Oversight, Federal Rights and Agency Actions
- Privacy, Technology and the Law

Rules and Administration
- No subcommittees

Small Business and Entrepreneurship
• No subcommittees

Veterans' Affairs
• No subcommittees

House of Representatives Standing Committees and Associated Subcommittees

Agriculture
• Conservation, Energy, and Forestry
• Department Operations, Oversight, and Nutrition
• General Farm Commodities and Risk Management
• Horticulture, Research, Biotechnology, and Foreign Agriculture
• Livestock, Rural Development, and Credit

Appropriations
• Agriculture, Rural Development, Food and Drug Administration, and Related Agencies
• Commerce, Justice, Science, and Related Agencies
• Defense
• Energy and Water Development, and Related Agencies
• Financial Services and General Government
• Homeland Security
• Interior, Environment, and Related Agencies
• Labor, Health and Human Services, Education, and Related Agencies
• Legislative Branch
• Military Construction, Veterans Affairs, and Related Agencies
• State, Foreign Operations, and Related Programs
• Transportation, Housing and Urban Development, and Related Agencies

Armed Services
• Readiness
• Seapower and Projection forces
• Tactical Air and Land Forces
• Oversight and Investigations
• Military Personnel
• Intelligence, Emerging Threats, and Capabilities
• Strategic Forces

Budget
• No subcommittees

Education and Workforce
• Early Childhood, Elementary and Secondary Education
• Healthy Families and Communities
• Health, Employment, Labor, and Pensions
• Higher Education and Workforce Training
• Workforce Protections

Energy and Commerce
- Health
- Energy and Environment
- Commerce, Trade and Consumer Protection
- Communications, Technology and the Internet
- Oversight and Investigations

Financial Services
- Capital Markets and Government Sponsored Enterprises
- Financial Institutions and Consumer Credit
- Housing and Insurance
- Monetary Policy and Trade

Foreign Affairs
- Africa, Global Health, Global Human Rights, and International Organizations
- Asia and the Pacific
- Europe, Eurasia, and Emerging Threats
- International Organizations, Human Rights, and Oversight
- The Middle East and North Africa
- Terrorism, Nonproliferation, and Trade
- Western Hemisphere

Homeland Security
- Boarder and Maritime Security
- Emergency Preparedness, Response, and Communications
- Cybersecurity, Infrastructure Protection, and Security Technologies
- Counterterrorism and Intelligence
- Oversight and Management Efficiency
- Transportation Security

House Administration
- Capitol Security
- Elections

Judiciary
- Constitution and Civil Justice
- Courts, Intellectual Property and the Internet
- Crime, Terrorism, Homeland Security, and Investigations
- Immigration and Border Security
- Regulatory Reform, Commercial and Antitrust Law

Natural Resources
- Energy and Mineral Resources
- Insular Affairs, Oceans and Wildlife
- National Parks, Forests and Public Lands
- Water and Power
- Fisheries, Wildlife, Oceans and Insular Affairs
- Indian and Alaska Native Affairs
- Public Lands and Environmental Regulation

Oversight and Government Reform
- Economic Growth, Job Creation and Regulatory Affairs
- Energy Policy, Health Care and Entitlements
- Federal Workforce, US Postal Service and the Census
- Government Operations
- National Security

Rules
- Legislative and Budget Process
- Rules and the Organization of the House

Science, Space, and Technology
- Energy
- Space
- Research and Technology
- Oversight
- Environment

Small Business
- Agriculture, Energy, and Trade
- Health and Technology
- Economic Growth, Tax and Capital Access
- Investigations, Oversight and Regulations
- Contracting and Workforce

Standards of Official Conduct
- No subcommittees

Transportation and Infrastructure
- Aviation
- Coast Guard and Maritime Transportation
- Economic Development, Public Buildings and Emergency Management
- Highways and Transit
- Railroads, Pipelines, and Hazardous Materials
- Water Resources and Environment

Veterans' Affairs
- Disability Assistance and Memorial Affairs
- Economic Opportunity
- Health
- Oversight and Investigations

Ways and Means
- Health
- Social Security
- Human Resources
- Trade
- Oversight
- Select Revenue Measures

A congressional hearing is a committee meeting or session of a Senate, House, joint, or special committee of Congress usually open to the public. Its purpose is to obtain information and opinions on proposed legislation, conduct an investigation, or evaluate/ oversee the activities of a Government department or the implementation of a Federal statute of interest. In addition, hearings may also be solely exploratory in nature and provide varying positions and data about topics of interest. Most congressional hearings are published shortly after they are held. The information is utilized as the substantive record guiding congressional deliberations.

Congress has the authority to subpoena or simply request a witness to appear before a Congressional Committee to give testimony while under oath.

The purpose of this chapter is to discuss the most effective approaches for preparing congressional testimony and responding to questions raised by committee members.

A briefing book includes staff generated materials that address the range of issues which are anticipated to be raised and summarizes previous related testimony that is prepared and made available to the witness who is going to testify.

Briefing materials, anticipated questions and the associated responses, as well as any other information relevant to a hearing are coordinated by the agency's congressional affairs office (lead), the budget office, the general counsel, the policy office, and the appropriate program office. In cases involving other federal agencies, these materials are coordinated with potentially impacted agencies. This material is integral to the preparation of the witness' formal testimony.

The Agency's Office of Congressional Affairs (OCA) is generally responsible for:

- Staffing and material development for congressional hearings inclusive of briefing books, written testimony, and supplemental material.
- Concurrent internal clearance of written testimony within the Agency involving appropriate senior officials.
- Clearance of hearing materials with other interested agencies and OMB.
- Preparation of witnesses including coordinating and scheduling policy and subject-focused "murder boards" as necessary prior to the hearing date. Murder boards simulate congressional hearings and include the full array

of questions anticipated inclusive of the anticipated behavior exhibited by individual members during the hearing.

- Coordinating and managing a final briefing 24-48 hours in advance of the hearing. The final briefing provides the best intelligence available associated with the political landscape, possible questions and recommended answers, information on other witnesses scheduled to testify, as well as other last minute insight from the agency's congressional team.
- Provision of escorts for witnesses and management of logistical details and delieverables resulting from committee hearings.

The simple guidance for political or career executives responsible for delivering testimony before a committee follows:

- Carefully review the content included in all briefing books to facilitate their understanding of the issues and ensure their comfort as a witness at a committee hearing before testimony is drafted.
- Participate in the drafting of the testimony to ensure that the tone, wording, and position articulated are consistent with the witness' style, views, and comfort level.

1. Congressional testimony always begins with a heading that includes:

   o Testimony of <u>Your Name</u>;
   o Title of <u>Name of your Stakeholder Organization or Agency</u>;
   o Before the <u>House or Senate</u> and the <u>Name of Committee</u>; and
   o <u>The Date.</u>

Example:

TESTIMONY OF
LISA P. JACKSON
ADMINISTRATOR
U.S. ENVIRONMENTAL PROTECTION AGENCY
BEFORE THE
SUBCOMMITTEE ON ENERGY AND ENVIRONMENT
COMMITTEE ON ENERGY AND COMMERCE
UNITED STATES HOUSE OF REPRESENTATIVES
May 27, 2010

2. After the heading, a one or two paragraph introduction is appropriate. This section should introduce the witness. It should also state the witness' position on the bill or issue being addressed. It is also advisable to clearly state the witness' recommendation to the committee on the bill or issue being discussed.

Example:

Madam Chairman and Members of the Subcommittee: I am Mike Daulton, Director of Conservation Policy for the National Audubon Society. Thank you for the opportunity to testify regarding the impacts of wind turbines on birds and bats. I commend you for holding this important hearing today. As the threats of global warming loom ever larger, alternative energy sources like wind power are essential. Many new wind power projects will need to be constructed across the country as part of any serious nationwide effort to address global warming. (Benefits of Wind Power Congressional Testimony, Mike Daulton, 5-1-07)

3. Following the introduction, provide the background information deemed necessary to establish the basis for the position the witness is taking. It should also place the analysis on the issue in context. The background should be well documented and factual with appropriate citations.

Example:

The proposed Clean Energy Deployment Administration (CEDA) builds upon and greatly strengthens the current DOE Loan Guarantee Program Office without the need to establish a new, wholly independent entity such as a Government corporation. Placing the CEDA within the Department will enable the new organization to achieve operational status more quickly, while establishing its independence in the areas of personnel management, legal support, procurement, and administrative services. This organizational placement will also foster better integration of CEDA activities with the proposed Energy Technology Deployment goals established by the Secretary of Energy. The draft bill provides that, upon transfer of Title XVII functions to CEDA, an additional $10 billion in direct funding will be provided to CEDA from the treasury. Assuming that the CEDA manages its portfolio with a loan loss target rate of 10 percent or less, the funding should be sufficient to support over $100 billion in loans, loan guarantees and other forms of credit enhancement. (21st Century Energy Technology Deployment Act Congressional Testimony, Joe Hezir, 4-28-09)

4. Following the background, the most significant section of the bill/program should be analytically and systematically addressed. It is appropriate to quote sections of the bill or specific issues in the program so that the witness' audience can easily follow the analysis, assertions, and arguments being made. This portion of the witness' testimony is the most critical statement of the case being made or opposed in the statement.

Example:

The Institute for Energy Research has found that the Waxman-Markey bill will result in a $14 billion redistribution of resources from the poor to the rich. This is primarily because shareholders and those involved in trading allowances will be in a position to make money, while those with lower incomes will be paying for the increased taxes and costs.6 Increased burdens on lower class families will also come in the form of new regulations on home sales. The Waxman-Markey bill contains 397 new regulations, one of which requires almost all homes to undergo environmental inspections prior to sale. These inspections will increase home prices, as additional inspections and repairs increase base prices. This cost increase is passed on to the buyers making home ownership more difficult. This will also eliminate the "fixer-upper" type homes upon which many low income buyers depend. Many low income families buy less-than-perfect homes because they are cheaper and they can perform needed repairs and improvements themselves. If the home has to pass an inspection prior to sale, the seller will have to make all of the necessary improvements before selling the home. The cap and trade proposal considered today will make home ownership nearly impossible for millions of Americans. (Cap and Trade Congressional Testimony, Grover Norquist, 10-27-2009)

5. The witness' statement and evidence (e.g., studies, surveys, news articles, and scholarly articles) must be compelling. Remember these are the witness' only opportunity to develop and present uncontested arguments on the formal committee record.

Example:

The double-hulled tanker "TINTOMARA," loaded with styrene and biodiesel and outbound for Europe, had only minor damage and did not spill any material. This spill was approximately five times larger than the 53,000 gallons of fuel oil spilled in November 2007, from the COSCO BUSAN in San Francisco Bay. The U.S. Coast Guard (USCG) has the primary responsibility for managing oil spill clean-up activities. NOAA provides Scientific Support Coordinators (SSCs) to assist the USCG in its role as federal On-Scene Coordinator. SSCs lead a team of scientists who provide scientific information that enables better decisions to be made during the response and clean-up. NOAA's response to each incident is dependent on that spill's characteristics and scientific coordination is critical. Through experience, expertise, and state-of-the-art technology, NOAA forecasts the movement and behavior of spilled oil, evaluates the risk to resources, and recommends protection priorities and appropriate clean-up actions. The OR&R team was notified shortly after the collision and we provided our first spill forecast predictions to the Unified Command within two and a half hours of the event. Over the following month, we provided 24/7 scientific support, both on-scene and in our Seattle Operation Center. This included daily or twice daily trajectories of the spilled oil, information management, overflight observations, weather and river flow forecasts, and shoreline assessment. (Oil Spill in New Orleans in July 2008 Congressional Testimony, Dave Westerholm, 9-16-2008)

6. The conclusion must clearly state the witness' desired outcome. Further, any summary of the most relevant rationale is also appropriate in the conclusion.

Example:

In conclusion, it's not surprising that support for Waxman-Markey is heaviest in those parts of the country, the urban centers in the West Coast and Northeast, that are least harmed by it. Even there, the economic damage would be bad enough, but the citizens in the rest of the country and their representatives should really be asking many tough questions about the economic impact of cap and trade. Thank you. (Economic Impact of Cap and Trade Bill Congressional Testimony, Ben Lieberman, 6-22-09)

It is important and proper protocol to thank the committee for considering the witness' testimony as a part of the committee's deliberations.

Many departments and agencies have developed a key or shorthand which delineates the tracking and departmental official signing off or managing the document as testimony is being written.

Key:

CC	Correspondence Clerk
Code B	Office of the Comptroller
Code L	Office of Legislative Affairs
Code LB	Office of Legislative Affairs/Liaison Division
Code LD	Office of Legislative Affairs/Inquiry Division
DMS	Document Management System
HATS	Headquarters Action Tracking System
LAS	Legislative Affairs Specialist, a position within Code L
OMB	Office of Management and Budget

The following are the steps an agency engages in when preparing for congressional testimony:

- Agencies are formally requested to testify before congressional committees by letter. The letter of invitation is typically preceded by a phone call notifying the agency contact within the office of congressional affairs of the proposed date, subject, and committee's preferred witness for the hearing.
- The testimony preparation process commences following the committees informal notification of the office of congressional affairs and the agency's hearing team is designated.
- The key messages to be highlighted at the congressional hearing are articulated. It is important that the agency's political strategy is discussed prior to finalizing the key messages. It is also important to respectfully articulate and

acknowledge the committee's historic differences with the Administration's key messages.

- Deadlines are established for various drafts of all materials relevant to the committee hearing including the draft testimony itself. The agency's tracking system should be utilized and reinforced to ensure compliance with the schedule established.
- Draft testimony should be distributed to everyone on the established clearance list without exception.
- All comments on the draft testimony should be redlined for the succeeding draft for review at the agency level. All comments are relevant at this stage.
- The witness and key senior executives on the hearing team should eliminate comments which are deemed unnecessary to clearly articulate and advocate the key messages in the testimony.
- Following clearance by the agency's witness, the agency's office of congressional affairs submits the testimony to OMB and other impacted agencies for review. Agency officials must hold OMB and other impacted agencies to clearance deadlines. In the event that OMB career officials object to the imposition of clearance deadlines, agency political officials and OMB must communicate to resolve the issue. In the event the deadline will cause the testimony to be submitted to the committee later than their deadline, the committee should be notified by the agency's lead coordinating official.
- OMB's comments are reviewed and a redline copy of the testimony is included unless there are policy issues that require an appeal of OMB comments. If there are policy disagreements, follow the normal appeal process with OMB until the issues are resolved. In the event political executives must become involved, the normal political appeal process should be triggered.
- Final OMB comments following resolution of any remaining issue should be inserted into the testimony and cleared for transmittal to the congressional committee.
- At this point, the testimony should be printed final and the appropriate number of copies should be provided to the distribution list.
- The testimony logistics process should be followed from this point on.
- The agency should take the opportunity to review the record and make corrections where errors have been found.

Question and Answer Session

Members of Congress have three specific objectives which motivate their questions:

1. To gather information they don't currently have and feel is relevant to their member-related responsibilities.

Example:

Asked if there are any other "bombshells" still to come:
Mr. Lentz: "God, I hope there aren't anymore."

Phil Gingrey (R-GA): "Is there a hardware or a software problem?"
Mr. Lentz: "I don't think it's either." (Toyota Safety Congressional Testimony, James Lentz, 5-20-10)

2. To build a record that is the Member's position regardless of whether the Administration agrees or disagrees.

Example:

John Dingell, Democrat for the car-making state of Michigan, is giving Lentz a very hard time with scattergun questioning.
Dingell: "Mr Lentz, what date did Toyota first hear about sudden unintended acceleration?"
Lentz: "I don't know the answer to that".
Dingell: "What date did you commence your first recall?"
Lentz: "If I didn't know the answer to the first, I don't know the answer to that either."
Dingell: "Please submit that to the record." (Toyota Safety Congressional Testimony, James Lentz, 5-20-10)

3. To show support for or to oppose a program or initiative and to build a record that is consistent with their position.

Example:

Henry Waxman (D-CA): "Do you believe the recall (of the floormats and sticky pedals) will solve the problem of sudden unintended acceleration?"
Lentz: "Not totally".
Waxman: "What do you need to do?"
Lentz: "We need to continue to be vigilant and continue to investigate all of the complaints we get from consumers that we've done a relatively poor job of in the past." (Toyota Safety Congressional Testimony, James Lentz, 5-20-10)

Congressional Hearing Transcripts and Testimony

LexisNexis (LN) receives committee hearing transcripts from Federal News Service (FNS), and Federal Document Clearing House (FDCH). Coverage between the services may overlap. LN also receives the full text of officially submitted testimony given at committee hearings from FNS and FDCH.[1]

---

[1] FNS and FDCH also provide coverage of White House and Agency briefings, press conferences held by major political leaders, and public statements by and interviews with the President and other political leaders.

Committee Coverage

LN's committee coverage varies from day-to-day. Both FNS and FDCH provide LN with transcripts of the most newsworthy hearings taking place each day. As a result, the coverage will vary depending on the hot topics of the day.

FDCH covers around 200-250 additional congressional hearings per year. These are delivered to LexisNexis within 2-3 days of the event. Each of these committee hearings is covered gavel-to-gavel.

Committee Hearing Transcript Vs. Committee Testimony

A committee hearing transcript is verbatim text of what was spoken at a committee hearing. This will usually include the Question & Answer (Q&A) part of a committee hearing, although not always. Committee testimony is the official, *written* statement presented by a witness at the hearing. Although the testimony may be spoken during the hearing and consequently also part of the verbatim transcript, it is also written and submitted to the committee. Both FNS and FDCH provide *all* the written testimony that is submitted to each committee holding a hearing on a given day.

Certain very high profile witnesses, such as Hillary Rodham Clinton, rarely provide a written statement to a committee. In these cases, FNS and FDCH will not provide this data to LexisNexis – unless, of course, they cover the entire hearing gavel to gavel, in which case the transcript will be available.

Transcripts

FNS provides the transcripts of the most "newsworthy" hearings on a same day basis. Other hearings covered by FNS are updated within 24-48 hours.

FDCH provides the transcripts of "newsworthy" hearings to LexisNexis within 48 hours of the hearing taking place. Other hearings are provided within 2-5 days after the hearing takes place.

Chapter 9

Drafting Authorizing Legislation and Committee Directives

Authorizing Legislation

In order to establish federal agencies or programs, Congress should enact legislation to authorize the agency to conduct activities and to seek appropriations to carry them out. The official vehicle is authorizing legislation. It establishes, continues, or modifies agencies' programs and establishes the baseline for funding. House and Senate rules mandate these actions. Without this legislation in place, members may utilize parliamentary procedure and points of authorizing order to stop appropriations or terminate the proposed program, project, or activity.

A properly drafted piece of authorizing legislation consists of five components:

1. **Purpose:** The purpose must state the mission and action the designated federal agency or program is to carry out. It should be drafted as simply as possible when describing those functions.
2. **Administration:** The administrative component should describe who is responsible for the administration of the federal agency or program. This section must list all the offices with administrative control over the federal program or agency.

3. **Duties and Functions:** The third component to be drafted is a section that identifies and justifies the positions required to staff the federal agency and effectively implement programs. The responsibilities for each position must also be defined.

4. **Responsibilities:** This section that sets out what the duties of the program or agency are, as well as what function the program or agency will serve. It is important that the various functions of either the federal agency or program are clear in the proposed authorizing legislation. This ensures that a complete description of the federal agency or program is included.

5. **Authorization of Appropriations:** This section should state the levels of funding required both for each specific program/project authorized and in total what may be appropriated for the agency or program. Additionally, this component must also state the number of fiscal years associated with implementation of the programs.

These five components are drafted in bill format and designate what federal agency or program is authorized. See Figure 9.1 as an example of properly drafted authorizing legislation.

Figure 9.1[1,2,3,4,5]

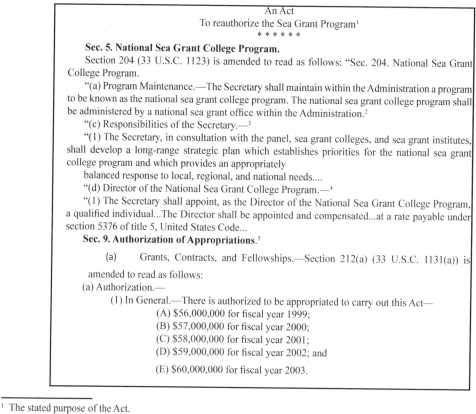

An Act

To reauthorize the Sea Grant Program[1]

* * * * * *

Sec. 5. National Sea Grant College Program.

Section 204 (33 U.S.C. 1123) is amended to read as follows: "Sec. 204. National Sea Grant College Program.

"(a) Program Maintenance.—The Secretary shall maintain within the Administration a program to be known as the national sea grant college program. The national sea grant college program shall be administered by a national sea grant office within the Administration.[2]

"(c) Responsibilities of the Secretary.—[3]

"(1) The Secretary, in consultation with the panel, sea grant colleges, and sea grant institutes, shall develop a long-range strategic plan which establishes priorities for the national sea grant college program and which provides an appropriately

balanced response to local, regional, and national needs....

"(d) Director of the National Sea Grant College Program.—[4]

"(1) The Secretary shall appoint, as the Director of the National Sea Grant College Program, a qualified individual...The Director shall be appointed and compensated...at a rate payable under section 5376 of title 5, United States Code...

Sec. 9. Authorization of Appropriations.[5]

(a)   Grants, Contracts, and Fellowships.—Section 212(a) (33 U.S.C. 1131(a)) is amended to read as follows:

(a) Authorization.—

(1) In General.—There is authorized to be appropriated to carry out this Act—

(A) $56,000,000 for fiscal year 1999;

(B) $57,000,000 for fiscal year 2000;

(C) $58,000,000 for fiscal year 2001;

(D) $59,000,000 for fiscal year 2002; and

(E) $60,000,000 for fiscal year 2003.

---

[1] The stated purpose of the Act.
[2] The administrative section of the Act.
[3] The responsibilities component.
[4] The listed duties and functions.
[5] The authorization of appropriations.

Chapter 9: Drafting Authorizing Legislation and Committee Directives

There are two types of authorizing legislation – permanent authorization and temporary authorization. If the authorizing legislation does not limit the duration of the appropriation, the authorizing legislation is a permanent authorization. If the authorizing legislation is specific concerning the number of fiscal years the authorization is valid, it is temporary.

A temporary authorization gives Congress frequent opportunities to review an agency's or program's activities and make such changes in the law that it deems appropriate. A temporary authorization must also specify the amount to be appropriated. A permanent authorization states the overall level of funding authorized for appropriation in order to carry out the purpose of the authorizing legislation without further detail.

Committee Directives

Committee directives are utilized by Congressional committees to direct a department or agency to conduct an activity, program or operation. It is most commonly used by appropriation committees. In some cases, committee directives are included as a part of the appropriation language, which is legally enforceable. More commonly, committee directives are included as part of committee reports. For most departments and agencies, the committee's career staff and the Executive Branch's career executives have agreed to treat the committee directives as law. This consensus keeps a number of annual committee requirements from being a part of the law. It is important because if either the committee or department/agency has a desire to change or eliminate the directive, it can only be done by an Act of Congress. If the directive is simply included in the report it can be addressed by verbal or written agreement between the committee and the department or agency.

An example of a committee directive follows:

No funds shall be used to fund the hunting of ducks on the National Mall between 1st Street and 26th Streets, NW.

The committee directives are typically drafted by either departmental budget or congressional appropriation's staff and concurred on in by both parties prior to inclusion.

Chapter 10

Drafting Effective Legal Document

In the Government, both lawyers and non-lawyers draft legal documents. Examples include regulations, contracts, compliance related materials, etc. Thus, it is not surprising that this chapter will emphasize attention to detail, clarity, and accuracy.

There are several reasons for a legal drafter to focus on clarity:

- Legal documents often communicate complex subject matter to individuals without legal training.
- Legal documents are often written utilizing specialized and uncommon vocabulary and terms.
- Poorly drafted legal documents could result in severe consequences. Examples include unnecessary fines, lawsuits, and imprisonment.

Concentrating on accurate, concise, and plain language improves clarity. This approach should be executed in a serious tone.[1] Accurate writing expresses a single determinable outcome. Legal writing should lead a reader to a single conclusion. Concise writing is using the fewest words possible. There is a purpose to every document. Every word

---

[1] Haggard, Thomas R., Legal Drafting, In a Nutshell series.

used should serve the purpose of the document. Extra words muddle communication and detract from the purpose. Writing plainly – avoiding complicated or antiquated words and legalese[2] – improves a document's accessibility. In standard writing, slang is problematic. In legal writing slang is rarely attempted, but legal drafters often use terms and phrases not understood by the general public.[3] Short words with direct meaning are best. When a complex term is necessary, the author needs to define the term plainly.

Legal drafters may violate the above principles to improve the gravity of a document. If so, this is a destructive tendency. The gravity of a legal document is a matter of the law, not ambiguous, verbose, or complicated language. In fact, a clear document is more difficult to dispute and thus carries greater authority.

The primary reference for legal drafting in the Government is the *U.S. Government Printing Office Style Manual*.[4] The following is a brief overview of general drafting rules most applicable in a legal drafting context as opposed to the more detailed summary chart later in the book:

TYPE	Error	Solution	Example: Error	Example: Solution
Clarity	Passive Voice	Active Voice	The law will be modified by a majority.	A majority will modify the law.
	Excess Nouns	Use Verbs	A slight *increase* occurs in case load.	Case load *increases* slightly.
	Confusing Lists	Parallel Lists	The issues are complicated, *need* to be addressed, *investigated* annually, and *available* for review by the general public when they are resolved.	Complicated issues must be *investigated* annually, *addressed*, and *published* when resolved.
	Confusing Qualifiers	Keep Verb and Subject Close; Keep Verb and Direct Object Close	The *reason* the rule on loan guarantees, published for notice and comment in March of 2004 and amended in February of 2005, *was* changed…; The DOE *announced*, among other things, but did not provide the exact dates and locations for upcoming *public comment meetings*.	The rule was published for notice and comment in March of 2004 and amended in February of 2005. The *reason* the rule *was* changed for loan guarantees…; The DOE *announced public comment meetings*, but did not provide meeting dates or locations.

---

[2]   Available at: http://www.law.ucla.edu/volokh/legalese.htm;http://www.lawpundit.com/blog/2004_12_01_ lawpunditarchive.htm (Volokh's Legalese and Gender Linguistics).

[3] "Legalese", www.dictionary.com: language containing an excessive amount of legal terminology or of legal jargon; Modern Language Association (MLA): "legalese." *The American Heritage® Dictionary of the English Language, Fourth Edition*. Houghton Mifflin Company, 2004. 04 Jun. 2007. Dictionary.com http://dictionary.reference.com/browse/legalese.: The specialized vocabulary of the legal profession, especially when considered to be complex or abstruse.

[4] *U. S. Government Printing Office Style Manual: An Official Guide to the Form and Style of Federal Government Printing*, 2008, available at: http://www.gpoaccess.gov/stylemanual/browse.html, accessed July 2010.

Concision	Excess Words	Omit Unnecessary Words	~~The~~ DOE proposed a rule and hopes ~~that~~ compliance will result ~~from the rule~~.	
		Eliminate *To Be* Verb Construction	If there is an error in an application, it will have *to be* corrected and resubmitted.	Correct and resubmit an application if it has an error.
		Eliminate Redundant Couplets and Triplets	Each and every…; Cease and desist…; Final and conclusive…; Dispute, controversy, or claim…	Each (or every); Stop; Settled; Dispute
		Active Voice	(see *Clarity*)	
Writing Plainly (Simplicity)	Poor Organization	Outline		
	Difficult to Identify Document Parts and Flow	Descriptive Headings	Large block paragraphs; long in-sentence lists.	Sub-headings identifying short paragraphs; itemized, numbered lists.
	Legalese (including terms of art)	Replace (or define)	Notwithstanding…; In accordance with…; Last antecedent rule…	Subject to; Conforming to; Last antecedent rule is a default rule and means the doctrine of statutory interpretation that qualifying words and phrases refer to their immediately preceding words and phrases.
Tone	Clear, Concise, Plain Language Loses Authority	Active Direct Statements	(see *Clarity*)	
		Eliminate Contractions	It's	It is
		Replace Idioms	Came by… honestly; Crack down on…	Acquired; Enforce

The aforementioned general rules of legal drafting apply to the Government. It is important to note the differences, however, between drafting legal documents in the Government versus the private sector. The most significant differences include:

- The subject and type of documents produced; for example, producing and promulgating regulations is a federal responsibility, not private;
- The audience for the documents;
- The authority requiring publicly produced legal documents; for example, private parties use demand letters to collect funds owed them, but pre-claim collection assistance letters available from Housing and Urban Development (HUD) are not produced in the private sector; and

- This authority is manifest in the specific language used; another example is how a command from the Government is preceded by *shall*, which replaces the *will* in private agreements.

The following sections each explore various types of legal documents: (1) Letters; (2) Contracts; (3) Regulations; and (4) Consent decrees. Each is described generally, then more specifically. Each specific description (and example) of these documents uses the hypothetical of Department of Energy (DOE) loan guarantees.

Government Letters

The Government prepares and transmits many different types of letters. This section concentrates on letters of legal consequence. The examples used in this chapter are all from federal loan guarantee programs.

A loan guarantee program functions as follows: An agency approves and ensures all or a portion of a loan by bringing the full faith and credit guarantee of the U.S. Government to bear. The guarantee limits lender risk and cures market imperfections such as insufficient information and imperfect competition. The loan guarantee instrument aids, among other things, the development of new technologies beneficial to society. There are two basic approaches to loan guarantees. HUD mechanism, for example, uses loan-default insurance, provided on a lender-to-lender basis. The second approach is the recently authorized DOE program. The DOE program will promote investment in technology and is provided on a loan-to-loan basis.

The size of the loan is often the determining factor associated with whether an agency independently reviews the loan. General practice is to monitor approved lenders based on their reviews on a loan-by-loan basis.

Examples of the types of letters for which guidance is provided include:

- Pre-claim collection assistance letters, which are sent before an insurance claim is made because collection efforts by the lender are exhausted;
- Approval letters;
- Disapproval letters; and
- Letters of withdrawal.

The principle criteria common to all of the aforementioned letters is communicating the presence and authority of the federal agency. Close adherence to the first principle of legal drafting—clarity—serves the agency's purpose and benefits the loaning party.

> **Pre-claim collection assistance letters**, like business letters, contain basic elements such as a return address, date, inside address, attention line, reference line, and salutation. The body of the letter includes: (1) a statement of applicable law; (2) a description of actions required of the borrower; (3) a description of

consequences if the required actions are not taken; and (4) contact information for the borrower to obtain further information.

Approval letters include: (1) a notification of approval; (2) a description of actions required of the lender or borrower; (3) a reference to rules and regulations the lender or borrower must follow; (4) a list highlighting rules and regulations especially significant to the particular lender or borrower; and (5) contact information for the lender or borrower to obtain further information.

Disapproval or withdrawal letters include: (1) a statement of the lender or borrower's status; (2) a description of reasons for the lender or borrower's disapproval or withdrawal with specific cites to applicable law; and (3) contact information and guidance on the availability of appeal or reapplication.

[DEPARTMENT LETTERHEAD]

November 1, 2013

Mr. Bob Smith
Executive Director
DOE Office of Loan Gurantees
Government Individual
Title of position

Mr. Government individual
President and Chief Executive Officer
XYZ Energy, Inc.
1234 Main Street, NW
Washington, DC 20585

Re: Application for a Loan Guarantee Under the Energy Policy Act of 2005

Dear Mr. Smith:

This letter refers to the application of XYZ Energy, Inc. (Applicant) dated June 7, 2012, as supplemented (Application), for a Federal loan guarantee under the Energy Policy Act, Pub. L. No. 111-22, 333 Stat. 444 (Act) and its promulgated regulations, 55 CFR Part 6666 (Regulations). The Applicant's loan guarantee request is approved according to the following:

To facilitate the acquisition of a loan for the Applicant-proposed Bio-Fuel Program (Project) (see attached proposal), DOE guarantees funds loaned to Applicant and not exceeding $1 billion, 80% of the total cost of Project, or 90% of the total funds borrowed for Project.

Determined solely by DOE, approval is subject to the Applicant's satisfaction of all conditions in the Act, Regulations, and the following:

- Applicant conclusion of all legally binding agreements regarding concessions and initiatives, described in the revised business plan.
- Applicant resolution of all specific collateral issues.
- DOE negotiation and approval of all final loan documents, including related collateral security documents and filings, affiliate guarantees, certifications, the warrant and registration rights agreement, and appropriate opinions of counsel.

If any material, adverse change occurs in the condition (financial or otherwise), business, property, operations, prospects, assets or liabilities of the Applicant, Applicant's ability to repay the loan, or in the value of the collateral between the date of this letter and the date the guarantee is issued, the guarantee may be revoked at DOE's discretion. If DOE discovers any materially negative information concerning the Applicant, DOE may decline to issue its guarantee.

DOE looks forward to working with you toward the successful completion of this transaction and are prepared to devote all the resources necessary to accomplish this end.

Sincerely,
Bob Smith

cc: Edward X. Fisher

Government Contracts

Whenever an agency engages the private sector in a transaction, a contract is drafted. "Standard contract terms" is a part of popular nomenclature. Even though a contract may be extremely complex, they are the most flexible legal document and thus the least standardized. Contracts must primarily be drafted to be clear.

Drafting a contract requires great care and attention to detail. While contract drafting should not be constricted to a formulaic approach, there are several tools available which make drafting a clear and effective contract simpler.

These tools are described by example:

1. structural options and components;
2. general clauses; and

3. specific clauses.

Our intent is to provide a sense of the nuance and variety available to a contract drafter.

> *Comments and explanations are in italics and not a part of the example clauses. Brackets serve as placeholders for contract-specific information.*

Structural Component

Title: Master Guarantee Agreement[5]

The title, headings, and order of the clauses in this contract are structural components.

Structural Component and General Clause

Parties Clause: [borrower name] (Borrower), [address], and the United States of America acting through the Department of Energy (Government), enter this loan guarantee agreement. Borrower will build, and Government will guarantee the loan for, [title, brief explanation of clean air technology project] (Project), according to [citation of statute setting forth the loan guarantee program]. The parties mutually agree as follows:

The headings system used throughout the rest of a contract is not used on the parties clause. This clause only sets forth the basic agreement. It should read to satisfy the basic elements of a contract—multiple parties, consent, and consideration. Additionally, one may reference the date of agreement and any applicable law.

General Clauses

SECTION 1: Definitions and principles of construction.

A definitions section is always advisable and rarely unnecessary.

    1.01. Defined Terms
        "Agreement" means this Master Guarantee Agreement, including any Annex, Exhibit, or other attachment, as amended or otherwise modified.

This is an example of a common word defined because of its special meaning in the agreement.

---

5 "EX-IM BACK STANDARD FORM MGA-M (03/01)" is used with direct, modified, and substituted language.

"Interest Payment Date" means each date interest is due as specified by a DOE Approval Letter.

This is an example of a definition of an uncommon phrase; a phrase specific to a certain industry and activity. It is also an example of an external reference. A contract drafter may use external references—to documents other than the agreement—or internal references—to parts of the agreement itself. In either instance, the drafter should limit the volume of references, especially reference chains. A high-volume of references and references leading to further references create unnecessary complexity.

"U.S." means the United States of America.

This is an example of an abbreviation definition. Alternatively, abbreviations may be defined in-line, as in the United States of America (U.S.).

1.02. Principles of Construction

The following principles of construction apply to this Agreement:

Principles of construction are not always necessary. Case law has established many default principles of construction. Principles of construction should be included in contracts where:

- the parties want to opt out of or create a default construction,
- the default is not settled in all jurisdictions the contract may be performed in, or
- there is possible ambiguity and custom has created a default practice.

   o The meanings set forth for defined terms in Section 1.01 or elsewhere in this Agreement are equally applicable to both singular and plural forms of the defined terms.

This is an example of a potentially unnecessary clause which should be included in Government documents to avoid all possible ambiguity. It is a clause included so often in Government documents that its absence could cause a contrary interpretation.

   o Any provision of this Agreement obligating the Lender to "require" a Borrower to do a specified act means the Lender is obligated to cause a duly authorized officer of the relevant Borrower to agree in writing the Borrower will do the act.

This is an example of creating a default construction.

   o Headings used in this Agreement are for convenience only and do not affect the meaning or construction of the Agreement.

This is an example of clarifying possible ambiguity, depending on jurisdiction.

o   The use of the word "including" in this Agreement denotes examples and is not limiting.

It is also an example of opting out of a default construction. This clause accomplishes the same end as the phrase: "but not limited to."

SECTION 2: Obligations.

This section sets forth what each party will do to satisfy contractual obligations.

2.01. Government

Specific Clauses

Government will:

The following is a short list of typical obligations under a loan guarantee program.

- provide the Borrower with an Approval Letter certifying the U.S. Government's full faith and credit guarantee of a loan to the Borrower;
- guarantee a loan amount up to [amount] dollars;
- guarantee a maximum of 80% of the Borrower's underlying loan obligation; and
- monitor Borrower's status, including a review of an annual independent audit.

2.02. Borrower

Borrower will:

- comply with regulations and auditing requirements set forth in Schedule A;
- provide a detailed description of the Project, including a business plan, that meets the requirements set forth in Appendix A;
- use the loan for the purpose of completing [project title]; and
- make all loan payments in accordance with Borrower's loan contract.

The preceding is a simplified list of obligations for the contracting parties. Lists, especially for party obligations, are useful for producing a clear contract. A principle requirement of a list is parallel construction. Here, each obligation begins with a verb.

Schedule 'A' is incorporated into the contract by reference. This is done to maintain a readable contract while including detailed and technical terms into the contract. Another reason to incorporate external documents is to maintain an up-to-date contract. If a transactions log was a contract requirement, that log should be incorporated by reference. Using this technique avoids having to continually update or re-negotiate a contract and creates a clear duty. Additionally, if a dispute arises later, the contract interpreter knows precisely where to turn for evidence of contract compliance.

SECTION 3: Claim Procedures.

3.01. Failure to Pay

If for any reason Borrower fails to meet its payment obligations for a more than thirty calendar days and more than fifteen days have passed since written demand for payment was made, the loaning party may make demand for payment on the Government.

3.02. Demand for payment shall be made according to DOE rules at the time of demand.

General Clauses

SECTION 4: Conditions Precedent.

This section would contain any actions by either party which must occur before the contract takes effect. In other words, a party is not bound to the contract (and not in default for failure to comply with the contract) unless the conditions precedent are met.

SECTION 5: Miscellaneous.

5.01. Governing Law

New York State law governs this Agreement.

5.02. Modification

Before the Borrower enters into a loan contract, this Agreement cannot be modified except in writing, signed by both parties. After Borrower enters into a loan contract, this Agreement cannot be modified except in writing, signed by both parties with notice provided to the lender.

5.03. Severability

Unenforceability of any provision of this Agreement does not affect the enforceability of any other provision.

The preceding example and explanations include the most common elements and organization of a Government contract. There are additional common contract elements not specific to Government contracts such as a termination clause, indemnification clause, breach clause, and delivery terms.

There are also contract elements unique, or nearly unique, to Government contracts such as statements, notice clauses, and formalities. The following examples are statements taken from a Bureau of Indian Affairs (BIA) loan guaranty agreement:

1) **Paperwork Reduction Act Statement:** *This form is covered by the Paperwork Reduction Act. It is used to calculate and request subsidy payments from the Federal Government. The information is provided by respondents to obtain or retain a benefit. In compliance with the Paperwork Reduction Act of 1995, as amended, the collection has been reviewed by the Office of Management and Budget and assigned a number and an expiration date. The number and expiration date are at the top right corner of the form. An agency may not sponsor or conduct, and a person is not required to respond to, a request for information collection unless it displays a currently valid OMB Control Number.*

2) **Burden Estimate:** *The public reporting burden is estimated to average 2 hours per respondent. This includes the time needed to understand the requirements, gather the information, complete the form, and submit it to BIA. Comments regarding the burden or other aspects of the form may be directed to the Information Collection Control Officer, Bureau of Indian Affairs, 1849 C Street NW, MS - 4603 MIB, Washington, DC 20240.*

3) **Note:** *comments, names and addresses of commentators are available for public review during regular business hours. If you wish us to withhold this information, you must state that prominently at the beginning of your comment. We will honor your request to the extent allowable by law. Privacy Act Statement (5 U.S.C. 552(a)): The authority for collecting this information is 25 U.S.C. 1511. The information will be used to administer the interest subsidy provisions relating to the Loan Guaranty and Insurance Program, 25 U.S.C. 1481 et seq. Disclosures of this information may be made to consumer reporting agencies; Federal, State, or local Governments; law enforcement personnel responsible for investigating or prosecuting violations of, or for enforcing or implementing, statutes, rules, regulations, orders, or licenses; the U.S. Department of Justice; courts of law or adjudicative bodies; Members of Congress; the U.S. Department of the Treasury; and other Federal agencies responsible for collecting debts or detecting and eliminating fraud.*

In the "Paperwork Reduction Act Statement," reference is made to the formality of displaying a valid OMB Control Number in the upper right-hard corner. Notice clauses explain who must provide who notice, for what, under what conditions, and in what manner. For example: "The *Lender* is required to *promptly* notify *DOE* if it becomes aware of *any problems or irregularities concerning the project or the ability of the*

Borrower to make payment on the loan or other debt obligation."[6] An actual notice clause would also include whether notice could be by telephone, letter, electronic mail, etc.

Consent Decrees

Consent decrees and contracts share many elements. A consent decree expresses an agreement between parties. Unlike a contract, however, a consent decree is a judicial document. Thus, while the parties to the contract—private and public—may propose the conditions of the decree, the document's composition and authority are judicial.

In a typical consent decree, a private party consents to quit an action without admitting guilt to alleged illegal activity. In return, the charges against the party are dropped. From that point forward, the court is the reviewing party, answering whether or not the parties' have complied with their respective duties under the decree.

In the loan guarantee context, a consent decree is a tool for an agency to exercise its authority. This tool is appropriate and useful for the following reasons:

- The borrower or lender would prefer to maintain their good standing versus losing agency support.
- The alleged actions, though inappropriate, do not reflect an outright attempt to commit fraud or abuse Government assistance.
- The borrower or lender has produced positive results concomitant with the alleged inappropriate actions.
- The value of resuming the activities fostered by loan guarantees with new or clarified boundaries exceeds the value of stopping those activities. This decision must factor in the potential cost of litigation to stop the alleged inappropriate actions.

The following example is based on a consent decree between the U.S. and Albank, FSB, and Albank Financial Corporation.[7] The original document is modified for clarity, according to the rules of legal drafting.

Comments and explanations are in italics and not a part of the example.
Brackets serve as placeholders for situation-specific information.

---

6 Federal Register / Vol. 71 No. 156 / Monday, August 14, 2006, 2006 / Notices, DOE, Loan Guarantees for Projects That Employ Innovative Technologies; Guidelines for Proposals Submitted in Response to the First Solicitation, available at http://www.lgprogram.energy.gov/FinalGuidelines.pdf.
7 *United States v. Albank FSB and Albank Fin. Corp.*, C.A. No. 97-CV-1206, P-H Fair Housing-Fair Lending Rptr. 19,401 (N.D.N.Y. Aug. 13, 1997).

UNITED STATES DISTRICT COURT
NORTHERN DISTRICT OF NEW YORK
UNITED STATES OF AMERICA
    Plaintiff,

v.

Case No. 97-CV-1206
ALBANK, FSB, and
ALBANK FINANCIAL CORPORATION,
    Defendants.

CONSENT DECREE

  I.   DEFINITIONS

       [The definitions section in a consent decree is written using the same standards as in contract drafting.]

       The introduction and summary section provides the reader with a background and overview of the document. It will not be used directly for interpreting the document, but should clearly state what the document covers. This section should be drafted for readability by focusing on telling the story of the parties versus detailing legal obligations.

  II.   INTRODUCTION AND SUMMARY

       The United States (U.S.) has entered into this consent decree with Albank, FSB and its parent corporation Albank Financial Corporation (together, Albank), simultaneously with the United States' filing its Complaint alleging Albank has violated the Fair Housing Act (42 U.S.C. §§ 3601-3619) and the Equal Credit Opportunity Act (15 U.S.C. §§ 1691-1691f) ("ECOA").

       Albank is a federally chartered savings bank with $3.5 billion in assets headquartered in Albany, New York. Albank makes slightly more than half its home mortgage loans through mortgage bankers or brokers (Correspondents).[8] Since the late 1980's, Albank has made mortgage loans in Connecticut and Westchester County, New York, entirely through Correspondents.

       The U.S. Complaint alleges Albank gave its Correspondents oral and written instruction it would not fund loans from Westchester County (below Interstate 287) and certain cities and areas in the State of Connecticut, each containing communities identifiable as African American or Hispanic.[9]

       In Connecticut, Albank explicitly stated it would not fund loans secured by residential properties located within Hartford, New Haven, Bridgeport, New

---

[8] United States of America v. Albank FSB, and Albank Financial Corporation. Case No. 97-CV-1206. Filled 8/13/97.
[9] Ibid.

Britain, and Waterbury. In three of these cities, African Americans and Hispanics approach or exceed a majority of the population (Hartford, New Haven, and Bridgeport); in two of these cities, African Americans and Hispanics constitute approximately 25 percent of the population (New Britain and Waterbury). Albank would also not fund loans secured by residential properties located in the corridor along Interstate 95 and Long Island Sound. This area includes the cities of Stamford and Norwalk, Connecticut, where African Americans and Hispanics constitute approximately 25 percent of the population. In Westchester County, New York, Albank excluded the part of the county south of Interstate 287, where more than 75 percent of the county's African American residents live and more than 66 percent of the county's Hispanic residents live. The exceptions made to these policies were predominately for white borrowers.

The U.S. contends Albanks' refusal to fund loans secured by residential properties in the identifiably African American and Hispanic geographic areas has no sound business justification and departs from accepted mortgage banking and loan purchase practices. For example, the restrictions established non-contiguous enclaves within the geographic area where the bank otherwise funded loans. Persons residing in these enclaves were not eligible to obtain Albank residential mortgage loans, without regard to their qualifications for credit or the value of their homes. The U.S. contends the redlining policies and exceptions to those policies were implemented with the purpose of discriminating on the basis of race and national origin.

Albank denies all alleged acts and omissions in the Government's complaint and this consent decree. Albank denies all acts and omissions violating federal law. Albank denies its acts were motivated or influenced by discriminatory intent, consideration of race, or national origin, including, but not limited to, racial or ethnic bias. Albank agrees to the undertakings in this consent decree to settle the Government's claims against it for the following reasons:

- the affirmative mortgage activities and practices described will better serve the communities where Albank funds mortgages, and
- the actions and practices are consistent with Albank's practices in the areas where it is physical present and actually located.

There is no factual finding or adjudication with respect to any matter alleged in the Complaint. The parties enter into this consent decree voluntarily to resolve the claims in this suit and to avoid litigation. The parties agree the terms of this decree provide a reasonable means of addressing United States and Albank concerns. The entry of this consent decree shall not be considered an admission or finding of any violation of law by Albank.

Through this Consent Decree, Albank commits to:[10]

---

[10] Ibid.

- make business decisions without regard to race, color, or national origin;
- serve all communities in the areas where it does business, regardless of the race, color, or national origin of the residents in those areas;
- provide increased access to credit opportunities for individuals in the previously excluded areas by a remedial special mortgage lending program which includes homebuyer counseling and marketing tailored to the communities previously excluded;
- implement a program to underwrite approximately $55 million in residential mortgage financing in the previously excluded communities;
- offer that financing at below-market interest rates; and
- initiate the bank-wide Fair Lending Action Plan incorporated in this decree.

The United States agrees Albank's approximately $8.2 million subsidy for the special lending program together with Albank's plan for providing mortgage loan products to the previously excluded communities, constitutes an appropriate remedy for the violation alleged in the complaint.

Now, therefore, on the basis of the foregoing representations of the United States and Albank, it is hereby.

ORDERED, ADJUDGED, AND DECREED, as follows:[11]

The following sections are direct orders of the court. Stylistically, they mirror regular contract terms. They are, however, interpreted more loosely. In other words, judicial interpretation will focus more on the spirit or intent of the document versus the strict, literal meaning. The drafter should take this into account when composing the decree.

III.   GENERAL INJUNCTIVE RELIEF

1.   Albank and its officials, employees, agents and successors, including newly formed affiliate entities such as Albank Commercial, are permanently enjoined from engaging in activities that discriminate on the basis of race, color, or national origin when involving residential real estate-related transactions, in violation of the Fair Housing Act, 42 U.S.C. §§ 3601-3619, or involving credit transactions, in violation of the Equal Credit Opportunity Act, 15 U.S.C. §§ 1691-1691f. This injunction includes, but is not limited to, using race, color, or national origin to define a market area or determine acceptable geographic areas for potential loan applicants.

2.   Albank shall permanently remove all geographic limitations on the scope of its mortgage lending activities in Connecticut and Westchester

---

[11] Ibid.

County. Albank shall select and define its markets in a manner that does not discriminate on the basis of race, color, or national origin when expanding its lending business.

IV. SPECIAL MORTGAGE LENDING PROGRAM FOR PREVIOUSLY EXCLUDED AREAS

    1. To provide increased access to credit opportunities for individuals in the previously excluded areas, Albank will implement a special mortgage lending program which includes:

        a. outreach to the excluded minority areas;
        b. homebuyer education and counseling services; and
        c. a commitment of $55 million of below-market loans in these areas.

    2. To implement the special mortgage lending program, Albank will institute a targeted marketing program in designated census tracts of the cities of Hartford, New Britain, Stamford, Norwalk, New Haven, Bridgeport, and Waterbury in Connecticut and in southern Westchester County, New York.

    3. The targeted marketing program in the designated Census tracts will include the following:

        [a-x] [Acts required of Albank to accomplish 3.]

    4. Albank will implement a homebuyer education and counseling program designed to assist residents of the listed Census tracts obtain mortgage loans. As described below, Albank has agreed to contribute $350,000 for homebuyer counseling to assist prospective loan applicants in the targeted Census tracts in Connecticut and Westchester County. Albank has also agreed to expend internally, principally in the form of services, and will contribute at least $350,000 to implement its own homebuyer education programs in the aforementioned areas.

    [5-10] [Continued description of the acts and programs required of Albank.]

    11. Albank will retain discretion to implement additional actions it believes are appropriate to achieve the remedial goal without prior approval of the U.S. or this Court, except as otherwise provided in this decree.

The following section follows the overall pattern of the document thus far—general to specific. The previous and following deleted sections are very specific to the example case. The amount of detail in other consent decrees will vary greatly depending on the circumstances of the case.

V.   ALBANK'S FAIR LENDING ACTION PLAN

As demonstrated by its Fair Lending Action Plan, Albank is committed to fair lending throughout its institution. In conjunction with the fair lending and community reinvestment programs already undertaken by Albank, as described in Attachment D, Albank will implement the Fair Lending Action Plan its Board of Directors approved and proposed to the Office of Thrift Supervision in early 1997. The Fair Lending Action Plan includes the following components:

[1-x] [Specific components of the Fair Lending Action Plan.]

Notification clauses are common to consent decrees. The example below is more complex than most. However, because this case involves several parties in addition to the two disputing parties.

VI.   NOTIFICATION AND EDUCATION OF CORRESPONDENTS[12]

1.   Within 30 days of the entry of this decree, Albank shall inform its Correspondents of its commitment to fair lending. All Albank's contracts with its Correspondents will be amended:
   a.   to reference the parties' respective obligations under fair lending laws,
   b.   to reiterate Albank's commitment to fair lending practices, and
   c.   to express Albank's expectation of a similar commitment from the Correspondents.

To further ensure Albank's Correspondents' awareness of Albank policies, Albank's fair lending policy statement shall be provided, in writing, prior to entering a business relationship. Existing Correspondents shall be provided with a copy of the same policy statement. To aid in self-assessment, Albank shall make data available to its Correspondents regarding its own lending activity, as per the Home Mortgage Disclosure Act.

2.   Albank will make fair lending training and informational materials, obtained from organizations such as the Mortgage Bankers Association, available to its Correspondents and encourage them to utilize these materials. Examples of these materials are manuals, videos, and regulatory information.

---

[12] Ibid.

3.   All existing Correspondents in Connecticut and Westchester County, New York, have been informed no geographic restrictions are in effect. Albank mortgage origination staff will use best efforts to meet with mortgage brokers and mortgage bankers providing loans in the designated census tracts four times per year. Albank staff will use these meetings to reiterate Albank's commitment to fair lending, provide appropriate training and information on the special lending program, and assess existing efforts to implement the program and meet the program goals.

Unlike contracts, a recordkeeping and reporting clause is common in consent decrees. This is because of judicial involvement. Contracting parties may or may not wish to maintain elaborate records; they may or may not perceive much risk of having a dispute. Parties to a consent decree, however, have already had a dispute and courts want to monitor the dispute resolution and have strong evidence if a future dispute arises.

VII.   <u>RECORDKEEPING AND REPORTING</u>

1.   During the term of this consent decree and for two additional years, Albank shall retain all records relating to its obligations and compliance with this decree, including, but not limited to:

        a.   data on lending in affected areas;
        b.   employee and correspondent notices;
        c.   information on marketing, advertising, and training; and
        d.   itemized accounts of all expenditures made pursuant to this decree, including, but not limited to, the $700,000 required homeownership counseling program expenditure.

The United States shall have the right to review and copy such records upon request.

[2-3] [Albank reporting requirements, e.g., providing U.S. with Home Mortgage Disclosure Act data.]

2.   All documents required under this consent decree, including, but not limited to notices and reports, will be mailed to:
Chief, Housing and Civil Enforcement Section
U.S. Department of Justice
P.O. Box 65998
Washington, DC 20530-5998
(202) 514-4713
FAX: (202) 514-1116
[Albank contact information.]

The two principle elements of the following section are jurisdiction and termination. A jurisdictional statement is universal to consent decrees. A consent decree may set a definite termination, as in this example, or the court may designate perpetual jurisdiction, conditional on the court's rescission of jurisdiction. In the latter case, the court should set forth the circumstances under which it will rescind jurisdiction. The remaining terms in the section below are optional, to be applied on a case-by-case basis.

VIII.   ADMINISTRATION OF CONSENT DECREE[13]

1.   The Court shall retain jurisdiction for the purpose of enforcing the terms of the decree for a period of six years from the date this consent decree is entered by the Court, or until the final disbursement of funds pursuant to paragraph III.10, whichever is later. The consent decree shall bind Albank and its employees, agents, representatives, officers, heirs, assigns, subsidiaries, and successors in interest. All provisions of this decree except Section III apply to every geographic region where Albank does business, directly or through correspondents.

2.   The parties to this consent decree shall endeavor in good faith to resolve differences regarding interpretation of and compliance with this consent decree informally before bringing disputes to the Court for resolution. This consent decree may be modified by written agreement of Albank and the U.S. Department of Justice. A modification must be submitted to the Court for approval promptly and shall be effective upon execution by the parties until such time, if any, the Court indicates its disapproval.

3.   Within sixty (60) days after U.S. counsel receives Albank's final report—submitted pursuant to Section VI—the U.S. may file a motion with the Court to extend this Decree. If no motion is filed or if the U.S. files a motion but fails to demonstrate why the Decree should be extended, the Decree shall terminate and the case shall be dismissed with prejudice.

4.   Each party to this litigation will bear its own costs.

It is so ORDERED this ___ day of _____, 1997.

_____
United States District Judge
JANET RENO
Attorney General

_____

[13] Ibid.

Chapter 10: Drafting Effective Legal Documents

ISABELLE KATZ PINZLER
Acting Assistant Attorney General

JOAN A. MAGAGNA
Acting Chief, Housing and Civil Enforcement Section

ALEXANDER C. ROSS
VALERIE R. O'BRIAN
STEVEN J. MULROY
ANTHONY H. GRUMBACH
Attorneys, Housing and Civil Enforcement Section
Civil Rights Division
U.S. Department of Justice
P.O. Box 65998
Washington, D.C. 20035-5998
(202) 514-9821

[Albank Representative]; [Referenced attachments]; [Endnotes]

Chapter 11

Drafting and Commenting on Regulations

Government regulations are applicable to every area of life in American society. The Executive Branch interprets and implements public law, as passed by Congress, through the promulgation of regulations and issuance of associated program guidance documents. The purpose of regulation is to control behavior in order to produce desired outcomes as is shown in many areas, from the tax code to requirements imposed on industry. Many argue that without some level of regulation, Government operations would be less efficient and subjective. The result would be adverse to the economy. Others argue that the opposite is true-regulations are burdensome, unfunded mandates that thwart economic growth, exceed Congressional intent, and result in unnecessary Government oversight imposed on state/local Governments and industry.

All Government employees either develop regulatory strategy or interpret statutory imperatives by writing regulations, associated guidance, or preparing evaluations of stakeholder's compliance with applicable requirements. This chapter discusses the keys to effective regulatory writing in the Government.

The History of Writing Regulations using Plain Language

Prior to 1970, many argued that Government regulations were written in a manner that was difficult, if not impossible, for stakeholders to read and comprehend. A mandate for more transparency in Government documents became a hot topic after World War II. Federal officials such as John Minor began to advocate writing regulations in plain and simple language. John O'Hayre, an official of the Bureau of Land Management, created controversy associated with how regulations were written by publishing *Gobbledygook Has Gotta Go.*[1]

His message, as well as that of other advocates of writing plain and simple regulations, was to insist that regulations be less bureaucratic. President Nixon stated that the Federal Register (the database for all regulations) should be written in "layman's terms."[2]

The Federal Communications Commission (FCC) was the first to respond to this requirement in 1977.[3] The FCC issued rules for Citizens Band Radios that were written as a series of short questions and answers, using personal pronouns, writing sentences in active voice, and providing clear and concise instructions. In 1978, President Carter issued Executive Orders that were intended to make Government regulations "cost-effective and easy to understand by those who were required to comply with them."[4]

In the 1980's, President Reagan rescinded President Carter's Executive Orders (EOs)regarding plain-language.[5] The impact of this action was to give each agency the discretion to write in any manner they saw fit. Some agencies, such as the Social Security Administration, decided to make it a priority to communicate more clearly with the public and revised many of their notices into plain-language. Others did not.

In 1998, President Clinton revived plain-language as a major Government initiative. Clinton issued a Presidential Memorandum that formalized the requirement for federal employees to write in plain-language.[6] He made it mandatory that all new regulations were to be written clearly by January 1, 1999. Clinton summed it up by saying, "By using plain-language, we send a clear message about what the Government is doing, what it requires, and what services it offers… Plain-language documents have logical organization; common, everyday words, except for necessary technical terms; 'you' and other pronouns; the active voice; and short sentences."[7] Bill Clinton directed this message mainly to regulation writers and Government attorneys. Vice President Al Gore was a big advocate of plain-language, saying, "Plain-language is a civil right."[8]

---

[1] O'Hayre, John. *Gobbledygook Has Gotta Go.* Washington, D.C.: Bureau of Land Management (1966).
[2] Available at: http://www.plainlanguage.com accessed July, 2010.
[3] Ibid.
[4] Ibid.
[5] Ibid.
[6] Ibid.
[7] President William Clinton, Plain Language in Government Writting Memordandum, June 1, 1998.
[8] Ibid.

Regulatory Writing

Regulations are the Federal Government's universal written communication. The majority of regulations can be categorized as statutory interpretation/implementation guidance. Regulations, except those that are purely administrative, fall into this category since the Executive Branch does not have the authority to enact statutes. However, due to variances in statutory language, the Executive Branch is often accused of altering statutory intent when they promulgate regulations. While Congress can be explicit when enacting a statute, compromises on the controversial issues often result in unclear or vague statutory requirements. Vague statutory language provides the Administration a great deal of discretion when interpreting the written law, resulting in written objections from stakeholders and the assertion that the Executive Branch has effectively rewritten the statute.

When regulations are written to protect the public's interests, federal organizations need to exercise diligence in ensuring all responsible and affected groups and stakeholders, both public and private, have a voice in the development and implementation of regulations. The substance of the regulatory writing must address the following:

- The intent of lawmakers writing the legislation;
- The goals and policies currently in place at the federal entity;
- The current goals and policies of the administration;
- The law's effect and potential conflict with other existing legislation;
- The law's budgetary effect depending on how it is implemented;
- The law's economic effect depending on final rule-making results;
- The human and infrastructure resource effects of various implementations;
- The law's constitutional aspects and "fit" with other passed legislation; and
- Coordination with affected organizations in the implementation of rules.

The Rulemaking Process

Congress created the framework under which rulemaking is conducted in 1946 when it enacted the Administrative Procedure Act (APA). The APA, though affected by statutes and EOs throughout the past 60 years, remains the basic legislative standard. Of those EOs, perhaps the most influential is EO 12866, which mandates presidential review of significant rules through the Office of Information and Regulatory Affairs (OIRA) at the Office of Management and Budget (OMB). The elements of the rulemaking process are as follows.

Pre-Rule Phase

Some agencies, such as the Federal Communications Commission, begin with a Notice of Inquiry for the purpose of gathering information on a subject or generating new ideas.

Following the NOI, if employed, the agency prepares publication of an Advance Notice of Proposed Rulemaking (ANPRM), or Pre-rule, in which an agency publicly announces plans to propose certain requirements. According to the APA, the ANPRM must contain:

- A statement of the time, place, and nature of public rulemaking proceedings;
- A reference to the legal authority under which the rule is proposed; and
- Either the terms or substance of the proposed rule or a description of the subjects and issues involved.[9]

Proposed Rule Phase

Following the ANPRM, the agency will issue the proposed rule. Interested parties must then be given an opportunity to comment. The APA does not specify the length of this comment period, but agencies commonly allow at least 30 days. The rule will remain in this phase until a Final Rule is published in the Federal Register, which can sometimes be months or even years after publication of the NPRM.[10] The format and required sections of a proposed rule include:

- **Preamble**: Background and intent are described.
- **Proposed Rule**: Specific proposed requirements are spelled out in similar detail to how it would be published in the final rule.
- **Listing of Acts and Regulations Affected**: All acts and regulations to be modified are listed.
- **Proposed Timetable**: Specific timetable for comment period and for proposed implementation is provided.

Final Rule Phase

After considering the public comments, the agency may then publish the final rule in the *Federal Register*. In general, according to the APA, a final rule cannot become effective until at least 30 days after its publication.[11]

The format of a final rule includes the following:

- **Preamble**: Background and intent are described.
- **Response to Comments**: All comments on the proposed rule are addressed and responded to.
- **Final Rule**: Specific requirements are spelled out in detail in CFR format and as they would appear in the final regulation published in the CFR.
- **Listing of Acts and Regulations Affected**: All acts and regulations to be modified are listed along with how they are modified.

---

[9] *Federal Rulemaking: Procedural and Analytical Requiremetns at Osha and Other Agencies,* GAO-01-852T, June, 2001 http://www.gao.gov/new.tems/d01852t.pdf accessed June, 2010.
[10] Ibid.
[11] Ibid.

- **Implementation Timetable**: Specific timetable with effective date.[12]

Orientation and Language Style

For regulations to be understood, they must be written clearly and concisely, and use appropriate language and terminology. Directive terminology (i.e. shall/will) is used to describe required actions. The word "should" is used for recommendations or suggested actions.

Regulations follow the general writing structure outlined below:

- **Chapters**: Internal divisions of *titles* numbered in Roman numerals (i.e. I, II), often assigned to an individual agency;
- **Subchapters**: Internal divisions of *chapters* (where need be). Given capital letters (i.e. A, B);
- **Parts**: Internal divisions of *chapters*. Given Arabic numbers (i.e. 1, 2), consist of a unified body of regulations applying to a single function;
- **Sections**: Internal divisions of *parts*. Cited using the number of the part, set off by a decimal point and preceded by the symbol § (i.e. a section under part 25 would be designated §25.3);
- **Paragraphs**: Internal divisions of *sections*. Designated by small letters set in parentheses [i.e. (a), (b)]; and
- **Subparagraph**: Internal divisions of *paragraphs*. Designated by numbers in parentheses [i.e. (1), (2)].[13]

Engage Your Reader

The keys to engaging your reader are:

- Identify your audience:

  o Understand for whom the regulations are intended. Know the expertise and concerns of your typical stakeholder. Be sure to tailor your writing to that stakeholder.

- Organize to serve your reader:

  o Put the most important information first and exceptions last.
  o Organize your material chronologically.

---

[12] U.S. Government Printing Office, http://wwww.access.gpo.gov/nara/cfr/waisidx_06/14cfr11_06.html accessed July, 2010.
[13] Schmidt, Ronald H., Archer, Doglas L. and Olexa, Michael T., *Federal Regulation of the Food Industry: Part 1, The Regulatory Process*, University of Florida, http://edis.ifas.ufl.edu/FS118, accessed June 2010.

- Use questions and answers:

  o This style of writing will keep the reader interested as they attempt to formulate the answer prior to reading it and then validate their thoughts once the answer is read.
- Use "you":

  o Using pronouns makes the regulations more personable and meaningful to the reader. Use "you" for the reader ("I" when writing question headings from the reader's viewpoint) and "we" for your agency.
  o Write regulations as if YOU are speaking to the reader.

- Use active voice:

  o Using active voice clarifies who is doing what. Active voice is generally shorter and more clear than passive. Active sentences are structured with the actor first (as the subject), followed by the verb, and ending with the object of the action.

- Use examples and illustrations:

  o Providing examples makes the regulation easier to comprehend and illustrations provide visual convenience.

Things to Remember When Writing Regulations

- Good regulatory writing:

  o Contains specific information which is relevant to the reader;
  o Keeps to plain-language principles; and
  o Is logically arranged and simple to follow.

- Do not reinvent the English language through regulation.
- Always write with good grammar.
- Choose your words carefully.

Make Main Points Accessible

Keys to Accessibility:

- Use headings:

  o That are logically arranged and simple to follow.
  o To help readers find their way through the regulations. Headings should

capture the essence of all the material under the heading.

- o To transition between subjects there should be one or more headings per page.

- Use short sections:

  - o Regulations should never be more than three layers; if you need more layers it is time to start a new section.

- Use less layers:

  - o Include one issue in each paragraph.
  - o Having fewer layers makes regulations less confusing and more visually appealing.

- Use vertical lists:

  - o The use of lists when writing regulations helps to highlight important information and creates focus.
  - o Use vertical lists if the sentence contains multiple conditions or exceptions.

Figure 11.1

Example of a Vertical List
The following contaminants will be regulated by this Act:
1. Arsenic
2. Barium
3. Cadmium
4. Chromium
5. Lead
6. Mercury

Use Natural Expression

Keys to Natural Expression:

- Use short and simple sentences that are easily understood by the average reader.
- Cut redundant words or phrases to shorten and clarify sentences.
- Be specific rather than general to avoid confusion.
- Use present tense as opposed to past tense.
- Avoid ambiguity so your readers can be certain as to the intent of the regulation.
- Use if/then tables to simplify regulations.

Chapter 11: Drafting and Commenting on Regulations
Table of Contents

The table of contents is perhaps the most important part of a regulation. Regulations can be of significant length and an accurate and informative table of contents will allow the reader to easily find the information they seeks. The table of contents should:

- List key topics, this will help readers focus on the content.
- Group related topics, typical groupings include functions, organizations, and process stages.
- Follow a logical order such as the chronological order that the regulation should follow.

Example of an If-Then Table

§ 163.25 Will BIA withhold any forest management deductions?

We will withhold a forest management deduction if the contract for the sale of forest products has a value of over $5,000. The deduction will be a percentage of the price we get from the buyer. The following table shows how we determine the amount of the deduction.

If ...	and ...	then the percentage of the deduction is ...
a tribe requests an increase in the deduction through a tribal resolution	they send us a written request	the percentage requested by the tribe
an authorized tribal representative requests a decrease in the deduction	we approve the decrease	the percentage requested, with a one percent minimum
an authorized tribal representative requests a waiver of the deduction	we approve the waiver	waived
none of the above conditions apply		the percentage in effect on November 28, 1990, or 10 percent, whichever is less

Use Questions and Other Informative Headings

- Questions, with their subjects and predicates, make the headings informative to the reader; and
- Informative headings make it easy for the reader to find the section of a regulation that interests them.

Use Tables and Illustrations

- Tables lay out material in a visual manner that can help the reader understand relationship better than dense text;

- Using if-then tables simplifies complex relationships (see the example of an if-then table in figure 7.2); and
- Tables help writers and readers sort out multiple options, steps, and conditions.

Figure 11.2[14]

Use "You" for Whoever Must Comply With a Regulation

This direct approach turns vague, passive statements of fact into pointed directions. Write as if you are talking directly to one reader. Although the regulations are intended for thousands of people, only one person reads your writing at any one time.

Organize So Your Reader Can Easily Comprehend

- Explain how you've organized the document and how to use it;
- Summarize complicated topics before you describe all the details;
- Place the items of most interest to your reader at the beginning;
- Start by answering general questions and then move on to specific questions; organize so your reader can easily comprehend;
- Describe the process in chronological order;
- Only include information that is relevant to your reader; and
- Keep sentences short with each sentence averaging around 15 words and never longer than 40 words.

Use Active Verbs, Not Passive

- Try to limit passive verbs. Using passive verbs is ineffective because they rarely say who or what does the verb's action.
- A passive verb has two components:

  o Any form of "to be" (am, are, is, were, was, been, being, be),
  o The past participle of a main verb (the majority end in –ed), e.g. "the discharge rate is to be monitored." This sentence fails to tell who will be responsible for the monitoring.

---

[14] This example was drawn from Use Tables to Make Complex Material Easier to Understand, http://www.plainlanguage. gov/howto/guidelines/bigdoc/writeTables.cfm accessed June, 2010.

Chapter 12

Drafting Effective Budget Justifications

Government programs depend on obtaining funding through the budget process. Consequently, among the most important written materials produced by Government employees are those associated with the budget. These include the justification materials relied on during the formulation, presentation, and execution phases of the annual budget process.

Budget Guidance

Government officials with responsibility for preparing budget justifications – whether to the agency, to OMB, or to the Congress – must understand the budget planning and formulation processes.

Knowledge of the target audience is vital. In preparing the materials, it should be assumed that the budget officers within the department, at OMB, and at the White House, as well as the Members and staff in Congress, are not fully informed about all the facets of a proposed program. It is important, therefore, to provide the readers with all the information they need to make an informed decision.

Chapter 12: Drafting Effective Budget Justifications

Justification materials must discuss: how the program is priced; what performance criteria are to be met within that pricing; and the timeline associated with obtaining the performance objectives. It behooves those who prepare budget material to comply with the most sophisticated requirements for those materials from the initial stages. Thus, whether you are a program, branch, division, office, agency, or departmental official, strict attention to the standards will be beneficial during budget deliberations.

Budget proposals must be prepared as prescribed in OMB guidance documents and circulars during the Executive Branch process. According to OMB Circular A-11, budget justification materials must include performance information as well as detailed descriptions of agencies' activities and proposals at the program, project, and activity level. The performance budget should include the following:

- A description of what the plan to accomplish organized by strategic goal;
- Background on what has been accomplished;
- Performance targets for current budget years and how the department expects to achieve those targets; and
- What resources the department is requesting to achieve the targets.

Before it is submitted to Congress, the performance budget may need to be revised to reflect the decisions made in the Administration's budget process. The resulting performance budget is to be used as the basis for justifying the budget before Congress.

It is important to prepare budget-related materials for Congress to the specifications of the appropriations subcommittee clerk with jurisdiction for the program.

All departments and agencies are required to submit any budget related materials bound for Congress to OMB for clearance before transmittal. These materials include:

- Budget justifications and budget-related oversight materials;
- Testimony;
- Correspondence with congressional committees;
- Written responses to congressional inquiries or other materials for the record;
- Materials responding to committee and subcommittee reporting requirements;
- Capability statements;
- Appeal letters;
- Reprogramming requests;
- Financial management documents addressing budget and policy issues (e.g., accountability reports or transmittal documents for audited financial statements); and
- Proposed press releases relating to the President's Budget.[1]

---

[1] OMB Circular A-11, http://www.whitehouse.gov/omb/circulars_a11_current_year_a11_toc/ accessed June, 2010.

All requested funding levels for education, training of workforce, and energy conservation measures should also be identified. Further information on these criteria can be found in 41 U.S.C. 433(h)[2] and 42 U.S.C. 8255.[3]

The Writing Process

In writing budget justification, three things are critical – style, substance, and spin. Following some common sense rules should help in achieving all three.

Style means making the justification easy for the reader to understand.

- **Short declaratory sentences:** Sentences should be clear to make certain the reader understands the point being made. Sentences should be limited to no more than three lines. Any sentence longer than that increases the chances of misinterpretation and confusion about the point being made.
- **Limit use of technical terms and jargon:** While such terms can have meaning to professionals working in the subject matter under consideration, many, if not most, of the readers who need to be reached and influenced often lack that professional knowledge. Too much use of technical language can irritate the reader as well as add confusion to the issue. Almost all issues can be explained with common words, and reducing them to such may actually improve understanding of the project under consideration.
- **Avoid meaningless words:** Adverbs and adjectives should be used sparingly. Although there may be a temptation to describe expected results as a "great" improvement or "very" good, or "World Class," such words lack meaning. Unless a scale is provided to explain how much improvement is "great" compared to "outstanding" or "good," the word is meaningless and tends to make the reader think it was used to inflate the value of the project.

Substance refers to the point being made.

- **Precision:** State precisely what will be done. There should be no confusion over what is being proposed.
- **Problem to be solved:** The strongest case can be made by stating the problem or opportunity, the magnitude of the problem or opportunity, and how the proposal will help resolve the issue. This is best done in terms of a measurable outcome. Expected performance levels are useful.
- **How the U.S. will be better:** Show how the program will benefit national objectives. This can include meeting the objective faster, more efficiently, or at a higher level of achievement.
- **Uniqueness:** State how the program will make or is making a unique contribution to solving a problem that would not be achieved otherwise.

---

[2] U.S.C. 433(h), http://www.law.cornell.edu/uscode/uscode41/usc_sec_41_00000433----000-.html accessed June, 2010.
[3] 42 U.S.C. 8255, http://www.law.cornell.edu/uscode/42/usc_sec_42_00008255----000-.html accessed June, 2010.

- **Duration:** The duration of a new program or increased level of effort should be made clear. This would include stating whether the increased funding is for a one- time effort or a continuing program. If a new program, then some indication of future costs would be useful. Projected progress (by year) toward obtaining the desired outcome should be included.
- **Stewardship:** If supporting an existing program, it would be helpful to show that the program is being managed well by stating the results of the evaluations.
- **Information needs:** Provide to Congress the type of information it desires. Department and agency legislative affairs and budget staffs know the congressional staff and the types of information they want and expect to see. Program managers should be alerted to the needs of the congressional staff and meet their information requirements.
- **Program risk:** Be up-front about program risks. If the program obtains funding and then falters, OMB and Congress will lose confidence in the department with potentially negative effects on other departmental initiatives unless the risk was stated at the start of the program.
- **Funding sources:** If user fees are proposed to offset all or a portion of the program costs, that should be made clear.
- **Legal basis:** The justification should emphasize the legal basis for the program. This would include a treaty obligation or legislation directing a program for a specific purpose.
- **Other participants:** If the program depends on participation by state, local, or other nation's Governments, make clear the role of those parties.

Spin is the way the proposal is presented to convince the decision-makers and others as to why they should want to support and push the program:

- **Priorities:** Tie the program to Presidential and departmental priorities. A program manager has to get the program through the departmental budget process before it goes to OMB and then to Congress. The connection to departmental priorities is essential to get through the first step of the process. A successful proposal will be very clear about the connection and why the departmental secretary or agency director would want to approve and support the proposal. For OMB approval, the connection to Presidential priorities is essential. In the current environment, for example, showing a direct connection to improving homeland security or energy independence would be helpful.
- **Descriptors:** Since the people who make or influence the key decisions are often busy, the proposal has to be stated in a simple, concise manner. "Buzzwords" or shorthand ways to describe the program can be useful if the program is a major initiative and likely to receive media coverage. An example is using the term "Superfund" to refer to the Comprehensive Environmental Response Compensation and Liability Act. If the proponents do not develop appropriate "buzzwords," program opponents will develop ones to disparage the program.
- **Factual basis:** In presenting a proposal to Congress, the Administration's justification should state the considerations that led the President to include

the proposal in the budget. This should be supported by facts and quantifiable information. This will help counter partisan objections that claim the proposal is based on political factors rather than an objective analysis of the situation.

- **Stakeholders:** The likely views of stakeholders should be understood. Such stakeholders include the program beneficiaries, the service providers, and the bill payers (taxpayers). Formulation of the President's Budget will be focused on the Administration's program priorities. Congressional review, however, will give weight to stakeholder considerations. While stakeholder views should not drive Administration recommendations, agency and Administration leaders should be aware of those views in order to respond to the issues that might be raised in Congress. Data that may help get the stakeholders to support the proposal should be emphasized in testimony and in the President's Budget documents.

Conclusion

While understanding the budget process and how to prepare a budget justification is important, the role of have a well-written product cannot be over-emphasized. In addition, keeping up to date with changes to OMB circulars and both Executive and Legislative Branch revisions to budget procedures is critical to keeping your department or agency current with the policies and procedures of the administration. In the competition for resources, failure to produce clear, concise, and meaningful budget justifications could result in inadequate or no program funding.

Chapter 13

Preparation of Effective Emails

As in the private sector, email communication in the Government is ubiquitous. While reliable statistics on how often email is used are difficult to obtain, it is estimated that there are 2.2 billion emails users worldwide and 144 billion daily emails are sent each day.[1] While nearly 70% of these emails are spam, many daily emails require a response in writing.[2] How you craft or respond to emails impacts whether you are considered an effective communicator or not.

It is the efficiency associated with email communication that has made it an essential tool in the workplace but this efficiency also provides opportunities for missteps and blunders. This chapter will discuss problems that have evolved in the age of email and provide pointers on how to be a more effective communicator in this medium.

The World May Be Your Audience

When writing in any media, the writer must consider his/her audience. Because emails can so readily be forwarded on, your audience may be much larger than your originally intended recipient. Here are a few things to consider given your potential audience:

- **Confidential or Personal Information:** Email is a poor communication tool for conveying sensitive information. This applies to tidbits of a personal

---

[1] Internet 2012 in Numbers, http://royal.pingdom.com/2013/01/16/internet-2012-in-numbers/ accessed October, 2013.
[2] Ibid.

nature such as family gossip, Social Security numbers, bank accounts, etc. It also applies to strategic or proprietary business information. It only takes one recipient with poor judgment to hit the "forward" button.

- **Inability to Retract:** Once an email has been sent, it is impossible to take back. In the wake of the British Petroleum (BP) oil spill in the Gulf of Mexico, a congressional investigation obtained emails sent among various BP employees. Those emails revealed significant concerns with the safety of their oil rig operations and that corners were cut in their drilling operation in the interest of time.

- **Permanent Record:** When considering the people in your audience, also consider the timing of your message. When an email is sent and received, copies are kept on the sender's computer and the recipient's computer (and copies are often kept on computer servers also). These copies can be removed, but beware: an information technology expert may be able to find copies of deleted messages long after they were initially sent.

Tips for Effective Emailing

Communication by email has evolved into a very specific type of written communication. While the basic tenets of effective writing apply, there are many other considerations:

- **Consider a Phone Call or Personal Visit:** Before the email is sent, make certain it is the vehicle by which you want to convey your message. Often times, it is preferable to talk in person or on the phone. Even though email is quick, a miscommunication because the wrong medium was chosen may cost you valuable time in the long run.

- **Use the Subject Line:**[3] When communicating with busy people, the subject line will often determine whether or not your messages are given any attention, or even opened. A common mistake is to use a vague or non-descriptive subject line. For example, rather than writing in the subject line "Working Lunch?" write the specific nature of the lunch meeting: "The Dominguez Study, follow up meeting." In addition, use the subject line to convey the level of urgency of your message: "Urgent: The Dominguez Study, follow-up meeting." Do not leave the subject line blank; it is a sure way to get your message ignored or deleted.

- **Separate Points, Separate Emails:** Do not be afraid to send several emails in a row to the same person. Each email should have an individual purpose and point. If you include multiple points in one message, something is likely to be missed. Separate emails permit the recipient to address matters one at a time thus increasing the likelihood of a thoughtful response or follow-up action.

---

[3] Writing Effective Emails, http://www.mindtools.com/email.html accessed June, 2010.

- **Clearly State the Response or Action Needed:** Don't be shy. State clearly what actions you expect your message to precipitate. Emails are often read in a hurry, and if you are not clear about what you are seeking and the action to be taken, the effort could be meaningless. If this is not made clear, you will find that by default nothing happens.

- **Be Clear about Who is Copied, and Why:** All email programs provide the sender the option to carbon copy (cc:) or blind carbon copy (bcc:) other intended recipients. If you are copying people that the main recipient may not know (or cannot immediately make a logical connection as to why others are copied), make a note of it in your message. For example, "I have copied Matthew Miller from the GSA Motor Pool because you will likely need his assistance to get your agency's trucks back online." If appropriate, you may ask your recipient to "reply to all" so all of the relevant people remain in the loop.

- **Reply to All is Dangerous:** The "reply all" button allows users to send a reply to everyone that received an email. This saves you the time and effort of manually entering email addresses. Because it is so convenient to hit the "reply all" button, people often do not take the time to check and see to whom they have sent a message. The result can range from embarrassing to disastrous. Imagine intending to reply to a coworker to say "the boss's expectations are not realistic on this issue," but you unintentionally copy the boss. Always check every single email address before pushing "send."

- **Stay on Top of Your Inbox:** If you want people to respond to your emails, respond to theirs. Email is so commonly used now that people rely on it and assume that messages are received. It is good policy to check your email a minimum of twice per day. If you don't have time to respond in detail, let the sender know that. For example, "I received your question but will not be able to give it due consideration and response until tomorrow afternoon." If you do not acknowledge receipt, the sender may assume you are ignoring him/her.

- **Maintain Formality:** Because email is so common and quick to use, writers often forget that emails are written documents. Treat each one just as you would a memorandum to your boss. Save the cute emoticons, text abbreviations, and slang for emailing with your friends and family; they are not appropriate at work.

- **Unintended Emotion:** When you talk with someone in person, or to some extent on the phone, you have the benefit of reading their inflection and body language. It may be obvious that someone is sarcastic, undecided, or enthusiastic, to name a few emotions. Do not assume that someone should infer your emotion from an email. If you want your audience to know how you feel, be explicit, not subtle. For example, "I am concerned there may be a personality conflict between Steve in Accounting and Dave in Engineering."

Not the sarcastic comment, "Oh, yeah right; they get along great." Obviously the latter is unclear and leaves a lot of room for interpretation.

- **ALL CAPS:**[4] If you type in all CAPS, your readers will think YOU ARE YELLING AT THEM.

- **Spell Check and Proofread Every Time:** Take the time to check your work and you'll be surprised how many typos and errors you may find. You wouldn't send a memo that you know has misspellings, would you? Many e-mail accounts include a spelling and grammar check function that will run a check and give you a chance to make corrections.

- **Describe Your Attachments:** Attachments are a great way to pass documents along to others quickly. If you send someone an attachment, view your email as a cover note. Mention that you have included an attachment and tell the reader why. It is useful to highlight the main points of the attachment in your "cover" email. For example, "The attached report concludes that there is a strong correlation between public opinion in Peoria, Illinois and nationwide public opinion. I recommend we adjust our budget accordingly based on this conclusion."

By following these simple pointers, you will ensure that your audience gets your message.

---

[4] Ibid.

Chapter 14

Prepartion of Effective PowerPoint Presentations

PowerPoint has become a staple of Government and corporate presentations and can be a very powerful tool if used properly. In this chapter, we will discuss how to create an effective PowerPoint presentation. PowerPoint provides several presentation formats and has many unique features that can be utilized to enhance a presentation. Before PowerPoint was developed, lectures and presentations generally required the use of chalk, transparencies, or slides. This all changed in 1987 when the Forethought Company from Sunnyvale, California published PowerPoint 1.0. In August of 1987, Microsoft acquired Forethought and took over production of PowerPoint. PowerPoint version 2.0 was released in 1990 and the tool has been significantly updated throughout its existence.

Tips for Creating an Effective PowerPoint Presentation

Make Sure your Presentation has a Good Flow: A good PowerPoint presentation should tell a story. You do not want your presentation to turn into a random assortment of bulleted lists. Your presentation should have the flow of a book or movie. To create a logical flow for your presentation, consider using the outline feature built into Microsoft Word to organize the structure of your PowerPoint before you begin to build it. This preparatory step will help determine the main topics of the presentation and their related subordinate topics. Thus, main topics should have subordinate topics.

Make your Presentation Easy to Read: You want to make sure that your slides are easily read from various vantage points in the room. To ensure this:

- Use a minimum of 28 point type;
- Use no more than 6 words in a line;
- Use no more than 6 lines in a slide;
- Limit punctuation marks;
- Avoid abbreviations and acronyms;
- Avoid long sentences;
- Use larger font to indicate more important information;
- Use bold font or color to emphasize a point;
- Be sure that text contrasts with background; and
- Avoid using all capital letters.

Use Appropriate Fonts: For title slides, it is best to use a sans serif font (i.e., Arial, Verdana, Helvetica, etc.) and a serif font for bullets or body text (i.e. Times New Roman, Garamond, Goudy, etc.). Most books are typeset this way because it makes them more readable.

Avoid Paragraphs or Long Blocks of Text: If you need to use a long text block to present information, put the text block by itself on a single slide. Focus on breaking paragraphs down to the bare essentials.

Your PowerPoint Slideshow is Not the Presentation, it is an Aid: PowerPoint should not take center stage in a presentation. You must not forget that PowerPoint is a tool designed to augment your presentation, not be your presentation. Many people forget this and think that their PowerPoint slides will do the speaking for them. If you don't do an effective job of preparing for the presentation, PowerPoint can't save you.

Do Not Read Your Presentation: Reading a presentation word-for-word – either from very detailed slides or from a prepared written speech – is monotonous and puts the audience to sleep. The less comfortable you are in the language in which you are presenting the material, the more you may have to rely on a written text, but avoid reading it word for word.

Keep it Simple:

- It is easier for the audience to see and understand the slides when they are not cluttered;
- These rules apply to both slides with text and slides that use charts, graphs, and tables; and

- Page numbers are very helpful because of the need to refer to slides during and after the presentation; however, identifying logos and dates are best reserved for the first and, perhaps, last slide.

Bullets are Better than Complete Sentences:

- Use bullets to highlight the most important items in your presentation;
- Avoid using complete sentences whenever possible; and
- Bullets should be mainly comprised of words and phrases that are used as a memory tool for you to emphasize your points and "stay on track" during the presentation.

Have an Easy to Understand Organization:

- The title slide should have your name and the title of your presentation;
- A second slide should be a table of contents; and
- The rest of the slides following the table of contents in an order which clearly states the high points in storyboard form.

Use Color:

- Color can highlight key phrases and draw the audience's attention to important concepts.
- The color wheel (also known as the chromatic wheel) is a helpful tool in graphic design and should be applied to text, background, and lines. The wheel helps define what colors are complimentary and which colors clash with each other. PowerPoint has color themes that can be applied to the entire presentation.
- Avoid color combinations with colors on opposite sides of the color wheel.
- Dark text on a light background looks more pronounced than light text on a dark background.
- The easiest combination to read is black text on white background.

Use Charts, Graphs, and Tables:

- These visual aids assist the audience in understanding the information presented more quickly.
- Most people find it more pleasing to learn from a graphic , rather than textual, presentation of information.

Chapter 15

Preparation of Effective Performance Appraisals

The performance appraisal is the method that federal organizations use to measure the performance of the staff within their organization. Staff is most commonly measured in terms of quality, quantity, time, and the cost associated with their output. Performance appraisals must be tangible, measurable, definable, and specific. They identify those who are deserving of awards, special recognition, and advancement within their organization.

Performance appraisals are used to:

- Identify training needs for employees.
- Give performance feedback to employees.
- Facilitate communication between upper management and the employee.
- Document criteria to allocate organizational awards/rewards.
- Help management identify employees deserving of salary increases or promotions, as well as disciplinary action.
- Provide opportunities for organizational diagnosis and development.
- Validate selection techniques and human resource policies to meet Federal Equal Employment Opportunity requirements.

Appraisal System versus Appraisal Program

An appraisal system describes the general policies and parameters for the administration of performance appraisal programs in the agency. An appraisal program is the specific procedure, method, and requirement for planning, monitoring, and rating performance. Programs have to be designed within the boundaries of the merit protection system but can be tailored to the needs of the organization. Federal employee appraisal law requires that Federal agencies establish one or more appraisal systems. If an agency finds a need to describe different general policies and parameters for different groups of employees who are not in the Senior Executive Service (SES), it can develop more than one appraisal system. Agencies can also authorize the development of separate appraisal programs under the framework of their appraisal system. Employee coverage, appraisal period length, and a pattern of summary levels for ratings of record all must have their own single definition within each program.[1]

Requirements for Performance Appraisals

Performance appraisals can be written on paper forms or submitted electronically. The regulations read "written, or otherwise recorded." Oral appraisals do not meet statutory requirements. The statute requires that employees be appraised based on their performance standards[2] and that they are not appraised by "presuming" they are meeting those performance standards. However, this requirement "to rate" should not be interpreted as a requirement to produce lengthy written justification of elemental appraisals and summary level assignments. Most agencies typically do a performance appraisal on an annual basis.[3]

Performance Elements

Under the Federal Employee Performance Appraisal Regulations[4], performance elements are work assignments or responsibilities that are used to plan, monitor, and appraise employee and group performance.

The regulations specify three types of performance elements:

- Critical elements;
- Non-critical elements; and
- Additional performance elements.

A "critical element" is a work assignment or responsibility of such importance that unacceptable performance would result in a determination that an employee's overall

---

[1] *Performance Management Overview*, http://www.opm.gov/perform/overview.asp accessed June 2010.

[2] 5 CFR 430, http://ecfr.gpoaccess.gov/cgi/t/text/text-idx?c=ecfr&tpl=/ecfrbrowse/Title05/5cfr430_main_02.tpl accessed June 2010.

[3] Performance Management Overview, http://www.opm.gov/perform/overview.asp accessed June 2010.

[4] Appraisal Program Requirements, http://www.opm.gov/PERFORM/faqs/progflex.asp accessed June 2010.

performance is unacceptable. The regulations require that employees have at least one critical element in their performance plans. Critical elements must address performance at the individual level only.

A "non-critical element" is a dimension or aspect of individual, team, or organizational performance, exclusive of a critical element, that is used in assigning a summary level. It may include, but is not limited to, objectives, goals, program plans, work plans, and other means of expressing expected performance. Its use is optional but, if used, it must be expressed as an element, be included in the employee's performance plan, and be used in assigning a summary level for the rating of record. However, a non-critical element cannot be used as a basis for taking performance-based action. Other features of non-critical elements include:

- They cannot be used in two-level appraisal programs (i.e., pass/fail);
- They can be given more weight than critical elements when assigning a summary level above "Unacceptable;" and
- They must have performance standards written for at least one level. The written standard does not need to describe the "Fully Successful," or equivalent, level.

Figure 15.1 provides a description of the various topics encountered in federal performance appraisals.

Figure 15.1 – Performance Appraisal Topics

A Topics		
Topic	**Description**	**Legal Citation Link**
Additional Performance Element • Goals • Stretch goals • Extra credit	A type of performance element that does not affect the summary rating level but can be used to help focus employees on goals and achievements that are important to the organization.	• 5 CFR 430.203 (definitions) • 5 CFR 430.206(b)
Additional Service Credit • Crediting performance in a Reduction in Force (RIF) • Performance in RIF • RIF credit • Performance credit • Retention credit	Additional years of service credit added to an employee's actual years of service when determining retention in a reduction in force. The credit is usually based on the 3 most recent ratings of record within the last 4 years.	• 5 CFR 351.504 • 5 CFR 430.208(d)(5)

A Topics (contin)

Topic	Description	Legal Citation Link
Appraisal • Assessment • Evaluation • Rating performance	The evaluation of performance in comparison to the elements and standards in an employee's performance plan.	• 5 CFR 430.203 (definitions) • 5 CFR 430.207(b) • 5 CFR 430.208(b)
Appraisal Period • Appraisal cycle	The period of time covered by a specific performance plan, during which performance will be evaluated against elements and standards and for which a rating of record will be prepared.	• 5 CFR 430.203 (definitions) • 5 CFR 430.206
Appraisal Program	The specific procedures and requirements established by the organization for evaluating employee performance.	• 5 CFR 430.203 (definitions) • 5 CFR 430.205
Appraisal System (for operating procedures see Appraisal Program)	The agency-established framework of policies and parameters within which performance appraisal programs are designed. The Office of Personnel Management reviews and approves appraisal systems.	• 5 CFR 430.203 (definitions) • 5 CFR 430.204 • 5 CFR 30.209(a) • 5 U.S.C. 4301(2)
Appraisal System Approval • System approval • OPM approval	The review of an agency's established parameters and flexibilities to ensure that they comport with the intent of law and regulations. An agency must submit a description of its appraisal system to OPM for approval, using OPM Form 1631.	• 5 CFR 430.209 • 5 CFR 430.210

Appraising Official • Rating Official • Rater	The person who evaluates an employee's performance and assigns the element rating(s) and rating of record.	• 5 CFR 30.207(b) • 5 CFR 30.208(b)

A Topics (contin)

Topic	Description	Legal Citation Link
Award • Gain-sharing • Goal-sharing • Honorary Award • Incentive • Informal Recognition • Merchandise Awards • Nonmonetary Awards • Recognition • Reward	Something given or a ceremony or event held to recognize someone, either as an individual or a member of a group, for a specific achievement that the agency values, or as payment of a promised incentive that is often based on predetermined criteria, such as productivity or performance goals.	• 5 CFR 451.102 (definitions) • 5 CFR 451.104(a)-(c)
Awards Limitations • Limits • Prohibitions • Restrictions	Awards in excess of $10,000 per individual must be approved by the Office of Personnel Management. Awards in excess of $25,000 require Presidential approval. Awards may not be given during a Presidential election period (June 1 of an election year to January 20 of the following year) to certain employees in the excepted service or the non-career Senior Executive Service. Cash awards may not be given to employees in certain Executive level positions when appointed by the P resident with Senate confirmation.	• 5 CFR 451.106 (b) • 5 U.S.C. 4502 (b) • 5 CFR 451.105 • 5 U.S.C. 4508 • 5 CFR 451.105 • 5 U.S.C. 4509

C-G Topics		
Topic	**Description**	**Legal Citation Link**
Cash Award • Bonus • Variable Pay	A lump-sum payment made to an employee in recognition of an achievement or incentive, a payment.	• 5 CFR 451.104(a)-(c) • 5 U.S.C. 4503
Critical Element • Contribution • Critical incidents • Critical results • Expectations • Objectives • Performance elements	Those aspects of a job for which an employee can be held individually accountable and that must be done successfully in order for the organization to complete its mission.	• 5 CFR 430.203 (definitions) • 5 CFR 430.206(b)
Employee Involvement • Union representation	Seeking and including employee ideas and opinions in the development of awards programs, performance systems and programs, and employee performance plans.	• 5 CFR 430.204(c) • 5 CFR 430.205(d) • 5 CFR 430.206(b) (1)
Forced Distribution • Peer comparison • Ranking • Quotas	Limitation on the use of particular summary appraisal levels. This practice is prohibited when doing performance ratings or ratings of record.	• 5 CFR 430.208(c)
Government Performance and Results Act • GPRA • Results Act	Law requiring agencies to set organizational goals pertinent to the agency mission as well as means to accurately measure them. Such goals should be cascaded through the organization and linked to the development of employee elements and standards.	• 1993 Government Performance and Results Act

I-N Topics

Topic	Description	Legal Citation Link
Invention Award	An award given for an invention developed by one or more employees. May take the form of a cash, honorary, informal recognition, or time-off award.	• 5 CFR 451.104(a)
Marginal Performance	The level of performance below "Fully Successful" but above "Unacceptable" that is sufficient to be retained in the position. However, agencies should assist employees to improve their performance whenever it falls below the "Fully Successful" level.	• 5 CFR 430.207(c)
Minimum Period	The period of time specified in an organization's appraisal program that must be completed before a performance rating may be prepared.	• 5 CFR 430.207(a)
Monitoring Performance • Measuring performance • Ongoing appraisal • Providing feedback • Improving Performance	Reviewing employee performance to check progress and identify any problems.	• 5 CFR 430.207(b)
Non-critical Element	Aspects of an employee's job that are not critical but will impact the summary rating level. Can include aspects of shared accountability, such as group or team elements.	• 5 CFR 430.203 (definitions) • 5 CFR 430.206(b)

P Topics		
Topic	**Description**	**Legal Citation Link**
Performance Award • Rating-based award • Bonus	An award based on the employee's most recent rating of record of Level 3 (Fully Successful or equivalent) or higher. Performance awards may only take the form of cash.	• 5 CFR 451.104(a) • 5 U.S.C. 4505(a)
Performance-Based Actions • 432 Actions • Reduction-in-grade • Removal	Allows for the reduction in grade or removal of an employee based solely on performance.	• 5 CFR, part 432 • 5 CFR 430.207(d)(2) • 5 U.S.C. 4302(b)(6)
Performance Management	The integrated processes of planning, monitoring, developing, rating, and rewarding employee performance.	• 5 CFR 430.102(a)
Performance Standards • Behaviors • Competencies • Contributions • Customer Service • Goals • Objectives • Outcomes • Quality • Results • Standards	The expression of how well an employee needs to perform on the associated element in order to be appraised at a specific level. Standards should be attainable and verifiable.	• 5 CFR 430.203 (definitions) • 5 CFR 430.204(a)(1)(i) • 5 CFR 430.206(b)(7) • 5 CFR 430.207(b)
Performance Plan	The written or automated document that communicates to the employee what is expected in the job. The performance plan includes the critical and non- critical elements and standards, plus any additional elements on which the employee will be evaluated.	• 5 CFR 430.203 (definitions) • 5 CFR 430.206(b)

P Topics (continued)		
Topic	**Description**	**Legal Citation Link**
Performance Rating • Rating • Interim rating • Special rating • Off-cycle rating	Appraisals done at other times than at the end of the appraisal period.	• 5 CFR 430.203 (definitions) • 5 CFR 430.208
Presidential Awards	The President has the authority to grant awards to Federal employees. OPM must approve most cash awards over $10,000. The President approves all awards of more than $25,000.	• 5 CFR, part 451, subpart B • 5 U.S.C. 4502 (b) • 5 U.S.C. 4504
Progress Review • Interim Review • Mid-year review • Monitoring • Feedback	Communication with an employee about progress on the elements in the employee's performance plan. There is no limit on the number of progress reviews a supervisor can hold during a cycle, but at least one formal progress review is required.	• 5 CFR 430.203 (definitions) • 5 CFR 430.207(b)

Q-R Topics

Topic	Description	Legal Citation Link
Quality Step Increase • Base pay award • QSI • Additional step increase	An increase in base pay given to recognize excellence in performance. Must be based on the highest rating level used by the appraisal program (Level 5, "Outstanding," if used), and meeting agency-established criteria when the program does not use Level 5.	• 5 CFR, part 531, subpart E • 5 U.S.C. 5336
Rating of Record • Appraisal • Evaluation • Summary rating	The evaluation of an employee's performance as compared to the elements and standards for performance over the entire appraisal period.	• 5 CFR 430.203 definitions) • 5 CFR 430.208
Recordkeeping • Documentation • Employee Performance File (EPF) • Official Personnel Folder (OPF)	Instructions on how to record and report ratings of record and awards as well as how long to retain information in official files.	• 5 CFR 430.209(b), (e), and (f)
Reduction In Force Credit • Additional service credit • Performance in RIF • Performance credit • Retention credit	Additional years of service credit added to an employee's actual years of service when determining retention in a reduction in force. The credit is usually based on the 3 most recent ratings of record within the last 4 years.	• 5 CFR 351.504 • 5 CFR 430.208(d) (5)

S-W Topics

Topic	Description	Legal Citation Link
Second Level Review • Higher Level Review • Approval	Review of a rating or award recommendation by someone at a higher level in the organization than the person recommending the rating or award. Required for "Unacceptable" ratings of record. Not required for other ratings of record or awards.	• 5 CFR 430.208(e)
Special Act or Service Award • Cash award • Honorary awards • Informal recognition • Nonmonetary award • On the Spot Award	An award given in recognition of an employee achievement or contribution or as payment as an employee incentive. May be given to individual employees or groups of employees.	• 5 CFR 451.104(a) • 5 U.S.C. 4503
Suggestion Award	An award granted to an employee or group of employees for an accepted suggestion.	• 5 CFR 451.104(a)
Summary Levels • Levels 1-5 • Unacceptable level • Fully Successful level • Pass/Fail (two-level) • Outstanding level	The designators assigned to the summarization of the element appraisals of employee performance, done by comparing actual performance to the elements and standards in the employee's performance plan.	• 5 CFR 430.208(b) and (d)
Summary Pattern • Patterns A-H	The aggregation of summary appraisal levels used in a particular appraisal program. Each pattern must include summary Levels 1 ("Unacceptable") and 3 ("Fully Successful").	• 5 CFR 430.208(d)

S-W Topics (continued)

Topic	Description	Legal Citation Link
Superior Accomplishment Award • Performance Award • Rating-Based Award	An award based on the employee's most recent rating of record of Level 3 (Fully Successful or equivalent) or higher. Performance awards may only take the form of cash.	• 5 CFR 451.104(a)
Time-off Award	An award given to an employee or group of employees that takes the form of paid time off. May be based on performance as reflected in a rating of record or as a specific contribution.	• 5 CFR 451.104(a) and (f) • 5 U.S.C. 4502(e)
Within-grade Increase • Step increase • WGI or WIGI • Pay progression	A periodic increase in an employee's pay based upon a Level 3 (Fully Successful or equivalent) or higher rating of record and completion of specific waiting periods. The General Schedule method of pay progression within an employee's current grade.	• 5 CFR, part 531, subpart D • 5 U.S.C. 5335

Chapter 16

Preparation of Effective Executive Summaries

All Government reports, including strategic plans, white papers, scientific/technical reports, and annual performance and accountability reports, have an Executive Summary. It provides the context, summary of the subject matter discussed, and conclusions inclusive of recommendations/next steps and give the report's target audience a clear understanding of the substance of the report. Since Executive Summaries are typically directed toward senior executives, it should be optional whether they study the detailed information included in the body of the document. Remember, their reading time is constrained by their schedule and other responsibilities.

To be an effective writer of summaries, you must focus on two things:

1. The Substance:

    • The issue or problem addressed;
    • The strategy or process to which they apply; and
    • The findings.

2. The Recommendation:

- What is the background?
- What alternatives are available?
- Who should take action?
- What benefit will ensue?

The Executive Summary should not direct the reader to specific items in the report for clarification. The Executive Summary must be a standalone document.

This chapter explains the purpose of Summaries, their typical structure, criteria for style, suggestions for different audiences, and requirements within the Federal Government.

Purpose

An Executive Summary provides a brief overview of the content and substance of a report; it should be no more than 1,000 words.[1] This short statement – four pages at most – delivers the report's most pertinent information for the targeted official to read and completely comprehend on the first "pass." Through it, writers present the recommended course of action and the alternatives to that course. If the Executive Summary does not understand the relevance of the analyses, the methods employed, the solutions recommended, and the advice provided by the Summary, it will not be well received.

Structure

Introduction

The opening paragraph should be brief, concise, and powerful. Describe in 25 words or less the nature of the task. Follow this with an illustrative statement that supports this assertion. This idea should be developed and supported with quantitative and qualitative findings that show the reader the extent of the problem. This paragraph should end with an indication of the implications of failing to act on the problem.

Supporting Data

This second paragraph supports the document's major findings and recommendations. State, for example, the most significant three to five findings resulting from the research. Maintain focus on actual results rather than on the process and assumptions on which the findings are based. The objective is to state the direction of the report without forcing the reader to read the entire report. The next objective is to shift the focus to the conclusions drawn from these findings.

---

[1] Writing Executive Summaries, Massachusetts Institute of Technology: Department of Urban Studies and Planning, 2002.

Clarification

In the following paragraph, provide additional insight into the problem. Note any trends that are uncovered by the report's findings that constrain the possible courses of action. Further, note the facts that preclude or favor a particular approach. The paragraph should ensure a clear understanding of the report's criteria for choosing among possible solutions. This must also be obvious and logical.

Recommendations

The recommendations section must establish a strong linkage between the conclusions drawn and the course of action recommended; thereby providing the rationale as to why the alternative solutions are not recommended. Such rationales are logically and conceptually related to the criteria developed in the conclusions. Be specific when making recommendations concerning the appropriate course of action. Stylistically, using bullets to make the recommendations stand out is effective. This paragraph should end with an indication of the benefits that will ensue from the recommended course of action.

Criteria for Style[2]

A basic approach to style is discussed below. Overall, keep your work simple and approach it with neutrality.

- Do not let your emotions or biases discredit your written product.
- Edit to highlight the substance of the material.
- Be careful with your choice of words and the positioning of both controversial and routine information.
- Objectivity and dispassionate professionalism should be obvious to your audience.
- Organize your document simply and logically where ideas appear in descending order of importance.
- Edit your document several times with a focus on avoiding overwriting and overstatement. Reread, revise, and eliminate excess verbiage as necessary.
- Do not take shortcuts at the cost of clarity and do not truncate to the point of understatement.

Considerations for Different Audiences

The audience is the driving force of any document (see Chapter 18 for more on understanding your audience). Understanding the "hot button" for your audience is critical to the effectiveness of your document. The "hot button" is the item which adds the greatest value to your Summary. For instance, when writing a pro forma

---

[2] The Elements of Style, Strunk and White, 2000.

business plan, potential investors are most interested in the project's cash flow and the rate of return on their investment. Thus, these items are presented immediately in the Executive Summary. Alternatively, the Executive Summary in a report to Congress that discusses the efficacy of a recently enacted regulation will highlight the changes that have occurred and any possible shifts in policy that will improve the policy's effectiveness. Thus, depending on the contents of the document, the Executive Summary must highlight the facts and analysis related to those hot buttons.

Unique Government Writing Considerations

OMB advises highlighting the following elements in Executive Summaries for several federal reports:[3]

- **Strategic goal or strategic objective:** A statement of aim or purpose.
- **Performance goal:** A target level of performance over time that is measurable.
- **Performance measures:** The metrics or statistics used to gauge program performance.
- **Target:** Measurable characteristic that indicates the level of desired performance.
- **Outcome measures:** Outcomes describe the intended result of carrying out a program or activity.
- **Output measures:** Outputs describe the level of activity that will be provided over a period.
- **Efficiency measures:** Indicators that capture skillfulness in program execution, implementation, and the results.
- **Program assessment:** An objectively measured analytical tool for capturing the extent to which federal programs achieve intended results.
- **Performance budget:** A budget presentation that links performance goals with costs for achieving a target level of performance.

---

[3] OMB Circular A-11, Section 200.

Chapter 17

Preparing Effective Procurement Documents

Writing Effective Procurement Documents

The government makes key decisions implementing its statutory mission when it contracts for goods or services from the private sector. Further, government executives responsible for drafting documents which result in the delivery of goods and services understand that a lack of clarity impacts attainment of performance objectives. This aspect of program operations is intensely scrutinized within the Executive Branch. The Inspectors General, Government Accounting Office Investigators, and Congressional Investigating Committee staff evaluate the Departments' performance. Their reports seek improvements requiring corrective actions. When instructions, requirements, and expectations are written clearly, concisely, and transparently, many of the "routine" and "usual" issues do not occur.

Success, in attaining government acquisition objectives in partnership with the private sector, occurs when:

- The scope of goods/services the government requests are articulated in plain English, based on an acquisition plan;

- The technical specifications associated with the goods or services to be provided are clearly stated;
- The comprehensive budget for the procurement is accurately formulated, justified, outlayed and monitored pursuant to government's internal controls;
- The government's selection criteria associated with the goods or services being procured are concise and transparent;
- The requirements on which to judge the sufficiency of responses to Requests for Proposals (RFP) are clear to government team members evaluating proposals; and
- The correspondence between the government and its stakeholders is factual, concise, and transparent.

Acquisition Plan

It is integral to accurately and thoroughly define your requirements early so you can communicate them to all of the stakeholders throughout the entire contracting process (from requirements determination to closeout).

The purpose of Acquisition Planning is to:

- Anticipate problems;
- Save time;
- Save money and resources;
- Stay on schedule and reach milestones;
- Communicate to higher management;
- Generate commitment; and
- Ensure compliance with FAR.

Procurement Authorization

The Office of Management and Budget (OMB) Circular A-76 establishes the method by which procurement decision-making authority is delegated. The circular also requires that resources are available to be obligated prior to contracting with the private sector. OMB Circular A-123 establishes management's responsibility for internal controls in the Departments. It also provides guidance to Federal managers on improving accountability and effectiveness of Federal programs and operations. Both qualitative and quantitative factors should be analyzed so that the costs versus benefits are clear. Cost/Benefit analysis is an objective basis for approving contracts for goods and services.

Written requests for procurement authority, or purchase requests, must be consistent with the government's budgeted requirements:

- Procurement objectives are clearly defined, realistic, are within budget constraints, and reflect agency performance requirements;
- Requests are written to safeguard against requirements which have not been evaluated sufficiently; and
- Requests are written to clearly state the program objectives to be achieved and articulate that obligations and costs are in compliance with federal procurement laws.

Example of a well written Procurement Authorization[1]

General

The FHA shall: provide for a procurement system of quality and integrity; provide for the fair and equitable treatment of all persons or firms involved in purchasing by the FHA; ensure that supplies and services (including construction) are procured efficiently, effectively, and at the most favorable prices available to the FHA; promote competition in contracting; and assure that FHA purchasing actions are in full compliance with applicable Federal standards, HUD regulations, State, and local laws.

Specific

This requests authorization to procure 50 Samsung model 1213 digital cameras to photograph condors in their habit. The FY2014 Appropriation articulates performance criteria and assumes $1,400 to be expended for this purpose.

Approve _____   Disapprove_____

Program Announcement

The Program Announcement, or pre-solicitation considerations, should not deviate from the wording of information included in the RFP. The announcement should be written to articulate: (a) the reason that the government is soliciting services; (b) an overview of the services to be provided; (c) delineation of detailed program information; (d) process requirements governing the preparation and submission of both preliminary and formal proposals inclusive of all schedules and forms; (e) the criteria against which proposals will be evaluated; and (f) guidance associated with emphasis and priorities. The Program Announcement should be an objective, concise, and informative document associated with the solicitation.

Each Department's Program Announcement should include written guidelines that state what goods and services are being requested and should include:

---

[1] HUD Handbook 7460.8 REV 2, dated 2/2007.

- The target date, font size, and page limit;
- The program objective clearly articulated;
- The technical specifications;
- Budget constraints and requirements for matching funds;
- Review criteria that emphasizes differences between one procurement and another if there are multiple RFPs that are similar within a program area;
- Clear differences in specific versus general requirements; and
- Format requirements.

Example of a well written Program Announcement [2]

Gulf War Illness Research Program

Clinical Trial Award with Multiple-PI Option

Funding Opportunity Number: W81XWH-13-GWIRP-CTA-MPIO

Catalog of Federal Domestic Assistance Number: 12.420

SUBMISSION AND REVIEW DATES AND TIMES

• **Pre-Application Submission Deadline:** 5:00 p.m. Eastern time (ET), August 28, 2013

• **Invitation to Submit an Application:** October 2013

• **Application Submission Deadline:** 11:59 p.m. ET, November 25, 2013

• **Peer Review:** January 2014

• **Programmatic Review:** March 2014

Types of Government Solicitations

Invitation for Bid (IFB): This solicitation is associated with procurements of more than $100,000 in value. The government specifications are clear as to when and how the products and services are to be delivered. The award is generally based on price.

Example of a well written Invitation for Bid [3]

(A) The highest responsible bidder who accepts the stipulations specified in the Invitation for Bids will be declared the purchaser. The purchaser will be required to sign a timber sale contract at which time he will pay the full purchase price and post a performance bond equaling seven (7) percent of the sale price. Both of these amounts

---

[2] http://cdmrp.army.mil/funding/pa/13gwirpctampio_pa.pdf; DoD FY13 GWIRP Clinical Trial Award.
[3] State of Tennessee; Department of Agriculture Division of Forestry; July 8, 2010.

shall be in the form of certified or cashier's check, payable to the Tennessee Department of Agriculture, Division of Forestry.

(B) Should the highest bidder not accept or meet the requirements or stipulations in the Invitation for Bids or General Provisions, then the next highest responsible bidder will be declared the purchaser.

(C) Should two bids be identical in amount, the winner of a coin toss will determine the purchaser.

Request for Quote (RFQ): This solicitation is used to determine current market pricing.

The written clarity of each component below is critical to receiving appropriate responses to solicitations:

- Preparation of requests to departmental management for authority to solicit goods and services;
- Preparation of the program announcement to acquire goods and services;
- Preparation of RFPs for goods and services;
- Preparation of selection criteria to guide vendors who provide goods and services; and
- Preparation of evaluation requirements for departmental team members who select from vendor's responses to RFPs.

Example of a well written Request for Quote[4]

This is a solicitation for Ammunition. Please see attached combined synopsis/ solicitation for all information.

Basis for Award: Award will be made to the vendor that submits the lowest firm-fixed priced quotation which meets the requirements. The socio-economic status of the offeror could be decisive if two or more offerors are considered equal. In this situation the government may consider the socio-economic status of the offeror in the following descending order of priority: Small business concerns that are also labor surplus area concerns, other small business concerns, other business concerns.

Request for Proposal (RFP): This solicitation is written when the government is seeking a proposal to meet a requirement for goods or services and provide the associated cost estimate to meet the requirement.

---

[4] Social Security Administration; Office of Acquisition and Grants; SSA-RFQ-12-1851.

Request for Proposals

A pivotal part in the procurement process is completing the RFP. The RFP will present the requirements for the solicitation and will instruct vendors of the exact structure and format that their responses should follow. A Program Announcement will provide prospective bidders and stakeholders on the details for preparing RFPs. The following information should be considered when drafting RFPs:

- Clearly articulate what the RFP process is;
- Provide descriptive narratives that are readable, well-organized, and specific;
- Allow adequate time to redraft specifications based on questions from offerors and offerors preparing bids; and
- Identify all evaluation criteria and their importance to selection of vendors.

RFP Categories

The RFP categories are listed below and are mandated by the Federal Acquisition Regulation (FAR).

Category I.   Instructions, Conditions, and Notices to Offerors

Example of a well written Instructions, Conditions, and Notices to Offerors section[5]

4. NUMBER OF AWARDS

It is anticipated that multiple awards will be made to multiple successful offerors as a result of this solicitation. What this means is that the award will include the design, development and delivery of that specific offering. OPM reserves the right to award to one vendor for the full scope of the project. However, multiple vendors may be deemed acceptable for multiple delivery dates. All content must cover the Key Results/ Objectives for Modules as outlined below and must be agreed upon by the program evaluation team.

5. DATE OF AWARD

It is anticipated awards will be made on or about February 10, 2012.

6. PERIOD OF PERFORMANCE

The specific periods of performance for award are itemized in the SOW, Attachment 1.

Category II.   General Instructions to Offerors

---

[5] Office of Personnel Management; Solicitation No. OPM26-12-R-0002; January 17, 2012.

Example of a well written General Instructions to Offerors section[6]

The first page of the quotation must show:

(i) The solicitation number;

(ii) The name, address, and telephone and facsimile numbers of the offeror (and electronic address if available);

(iii) A statement specifying the extent of agreement with all terms, conditions, and provisions included in the solicitation and agreement to furnish any or all items upon which prices are offered at the price set opposite each item;

(iv) Names, titles, and telephone and facsimile numbers (and electronic addresses if available) of persons authorized to negotiate on the offeror's behalf with the Government in connection with this solicitation; and

(v) Name, title, and signature of person authorized to sign the quotation. Quotations signed by an agent shall be accompanied by evidence of that agent's authority, unless that evidence has been previously furnished to the issuing office.

Category III.   Instructions for Preparing the Technical Portion of the Quotation

Example of well written Instructions for Preparing the Technical Portion of the Quotation[7]

The offeror shall include in its quotation a discussion of the offeror's proposed technical approach to respond to the requirements in the statement of work (SOW), Sections II and III. Present clear and convincing evidence that you understand the scope of work as described in the SOW, and that your technical approach to accomplishing this work is sound. Include:

- A narrative describing your understanding of this requirement.
- A description of your technical expertise for meeting the requirements of this solicitation. Your narrative should, at a minimum:
- Indicate the initial plan to gain an understanding of OPM's curriculum needs;
- Discuss the anticipated methodology to complete the work described in section 2 of the SOW; and
- Provide realistic time and skill level estimates.

Category IV.   Instructions for Preparing the Business Portion of the Quotation

Example of a well written Business Portion of the Quotation[8]

---

[6] Office of Personnel Management; Solicitation No. OPM26-12-R-0002; January 17, 2012.
[7] Office of Personnel Management; Solicitation No. OPM26-12-R-0002; January 17, 2012.
[8] Office of Personnel Management; Solicitation No. OPM26-12-R-0002; January 17, 2012.

Offerors shall submit a detailed breakdown of estimated labor hours and rates by tasks to be performed as itemized in the statement of work. In addition, a summary total amount shall be furnished for the entire project.

The business portion of the quotation must contain sufficient information to allow the Government to perform a basic analysis of the proposed price of the work.

Prices quoted shall be fixed unit prices (per labor hour) per labor category (i.e, design, facilitation, session delivery, and other line items from the statement of work).

Category V.   Past Performance Instructions

Example of well written Past Performance Instructions[9]

Offerors shall submit a list of 3 references. Contracts listed may include those entered into by the Federal Government and/or agencies of state and local governments. Offerors that are newly formed entities without prior contracts should list contracts and subcontracts as required above for all key personnel.

The reference list shall include the following information for each contract and subcontract:

    a.   Name of contracting activity;
    b.   Contract Number (if known);
    c.   Contract Type;
    d.   Total Contract Value;
    e.   Contract Work;
    f.   Contracting Officer and telephone number;
    g.   Program Manager and telephone number;
    h.   Administrative Contracting Officer, if different from item f; and
    i.   List of major Subcontractors:

Category VI.   Evaluation Factors for Award

Example of well written Evaluation Factors[10]

In determining which offer represents the best value and results in the lowest overall cost alternative (considering price, special features, administrative costs, etc.) to meet the Government's needs, the Government shall evaluate responses using the following evaluation criteria that are listed in descending order of priority:

- Proposed technical approach;
- Subject matter knowledge/Staff Credentials;

---

[9] Office of Personnel Management; Solicitation No. OPM26-12-R-0002; January 17, 2012.
[10] Office of Personnel Management; Solicitation No. OPM26-12-R-0002; January 17, 2012.

- Availability;
- Past Performance (with references)

  o Experience conducting writing seminars.
  o Experience working with Federal government audiences.

- Price.

Category VII. Attachments to the RFP (Statement of Work; Key Results/Objectives Specific Clauses; FAR Clauses)

Example of a well written Statement of Work[11]

The Offeror, also referred to as the Contractor or Vendor, selected for this project will design, develop, and deliver a hands-on, four-day, training seminar on effective writing in the Federal government.

Selection Criteria

Evaluating a RFP is a complex part of the procurement process and is one of the most important. A well written evaluation plan can make this process less complicated and result in a contract agreeable to both the agency and offeror.

In this section, potential offerors are instructed how bids will be selected. Effective selection requirements should be written precisely and provide specific details on the selection criteria.

Example of well written Selection Criteria[12]

Threshold Eligibility Criteria. These are requirements which if not met by the time of initial proposal submission will result in elimination of the proposal from further consideration for funding. Only proposals that meet all of these criteria will be ranked against the evaluation criteria (see Section V) of this announcement. Applicants deemed ineligible for funding consideration as a result of the threshold eligibility review will be notified within 15 calendar days of the ineligibility determination.

1. Applicant Eligibility: Applicants must meet the applicant eligibility requirements described in Section III. A.

2. Priorities: Projects must protect and restore the water quality (including aquatic habitat) in the San Francisco Bay and its watersheds.

---

[11] Office of Personnel Management; Solicitation No. OPM26-12-R-0002; January 17, 2012.
[12] U.S. Environmental Protection Agency Region 9; San Francisco Bay Area Water Quality Improvement Fund (FY2013 Funds).

3. EPA Strategic Plan: Proposals must support Strategic Plan Goal 2 of EPA's Strategic Plan as specified in Section I.C.1.

4. Fifty (50) % Match: Applicants must demonstrate how they will provide a minimum 50% match of the total project cost as described in Section III. B.

5. CCMP Consistency: Proposals must describe how the proposed activities are consistent with SFEP's CCMP by reviewing Attachment A and identifying relevant CCMP objective(s) and action(s) to be implemented by the project.

6. Substantial Compliance: Proposals must substantially comply with the proposal submission instructions and requirements set forth in Section IV or else they will be rejected. However, where a page limit is expressed in Section IV with respect to the proposal narrative, pages in excess of the page limitation will not be reviewed.

7. Project Location: Projects must occur within one or more of the nine Bay Area counties (Marin, Napa, Sonoma, Solano, Contra Costa, Alameda, Santa Clara, San Mateo, and San Francisco).

Evaluation Requirements

Federal Agencies award grants on a competitive basis. Proposals are evaluated by Agency experts in their related disciplines. The reviewers are chosen on the basis of their capability to comprehend the written criteria and thereby assess how the responses match up to the emphasis, priorities, and technical criteria articulated in the RFP.

The peer review panel provides a written critique of each response. Further, some reviewers prepare a numerical score as well as a written amplification on the score as a part of their responsibility on the panel. One of the panel members writes a compilation and summary of the panels information. The results are provided to the Program Manager making the selection.

During the review and selection process, confidentiality must be maintained. Reviews are not disclosed to persons outside the Agency except to the Principal Investigator. At the end of the review process, the Principal Investigator is sent the written reviews with the names and affiliations omitted. Reviews are forwarded whether the RFP is funded or not. All reviews are confidential. The Agency releases abstracts and other information about funded RFPs only.

Any correspondor seeking information in these areas should clearly state what can be stated versus what is not permitted.

The following information should be considered during the evaluation process[13]:

---

[13] General Service Administration's Source Selection Plan.

- Evaluate proposals against the agency's written RFP requirements;
- Ensure proposals are evaluated individually and not compared to one another;
- Make sure comments clearly relates to the evaluation factor;
- Allow adequate time to give each proposal the same considerations;
- Provide detailed comments and accurate references;
- Give comments that are clear and written in plain English; and
- Prepare comments that are concise, clear and professionally stated.

The following examples illustrate the writing style that is most effective during the written evaluation process[14]

What Not to Write	• *Offeror X's approach is not nearly as effective as Offeror Y.* • *Offeror Y is equally capable as Offeror Z.* • *This proposal was significantly stronger than all the others.*
What To Write	• *Offeror X's approach does not meet CMMI Level 2 technical requirements as defined in Section C.1.2 because…* • *Offeror Y offers their employees 2 weeks of paid time off to attend training sessions every year. This encourages retention and staff growth.*
What Not to Write	• *Offeror X's, page 5, not where we are going (this is unclear).*
What To Write	• *Offeror X's, page 5, para 4. The Offeror does not appear to understand the direction of the program or the intent of the RFP and has specified an approach which has been proven unsuccessful on this program in the past.*
What Not to Write	• *Offeror X offers great resumes (too vague – how are they great?).*

---

[14] General Service Administration, Acquisition Services Division's Source Selection Plan.

What To Write	• The key Personal resume presented by Offeror X offers the Government a strong technical staff member with 13 years of TRICARE experience and 20 years of management experience.
These mistakes can lead to a RFP protest	• Rating an idea as a positive in one proposal and the same idea as a negative in another. • Rating based on criteria not included in the RFP.

Example of a well written Evaluation Criteria[15]

Initial proposals and full proposals will be evaluated and scored by reviewers using the applicable criteria listed below. Each initial proposal may receive up to 100 points and each full proposal may receive up to 100 points. Applicants should explicitly address these criteria as part of their submittals. Initial Proposal Evaluation Criteria (100 pts)

Points	Initial Proposal Evaluation Criteria
45	**1. Scope/Approach:** Under this criterion, proposals will be evaluated based on whether they present: • a technically/scientifically sound approach for addressing one or more of the program priorities in Section I, Part B. **(20 pts)** • a description of the environmental significance of the project, including institutional change to further ongoing water quality improvements. **(15 pts)** • activities based on plans and assessments, such as watershed plans and TMDLs and/or associated analysis to ensure that priority activities are being undertaken that will lead to water quality objectives and the protection of beneficial uses within a specific time-frame. **(10 pts)**

---

[15] U.S. Environmental Protection Agency Region 9; San Francisco Bay Area Water Quality Improvement Fund (FY2013 Funds).

45	**2. Environmental Results—Outputs and Outcomes:** *Under this criterion, proposals will be evaluated based on how well they demonstrate:* • *that significant environmental results, including specific (quantitative) water quality and related environmental outcomes, will be achieved by the project.* ***(25 pts)*** • *an effective plan for tracking and measuring progress toward achieving expected project outputs and outcomes, including those identified in Section I.* ***(20 pts)*** *Note: EPA will consider the quality and scope of the monitoring component to measure environmental results under this criterion. If monitoring is not an appropriate project activity necessary to achieve and document results, proposals will not receive a lower rating under this criterion.*
10	**3. Budget Summary:** *Under this criterion, proposals will be evaluated based on whether the budget as presented in Form 424(A) is reasonable given the project scope and environmental results proposed.* ***(10 pts)***

Procurement Resource Sources

This section provides information associated with the procurement processes in various Government Departments.

Office of Federal Procurement Policy Guides

- Contracting Guidance to Support Modular Development (June 14, 2012);
- Emergency Acquisitions Guide (January 14, 2011);
- Update to FAC Manager's Guide to Competitive Sourcing: 2nd Edition (February 20, 2004);
- Managers' Guide to Competitive Sourcing (October 2, 2003);
- Performance-Based Service Acquisition, Contracting for the Future (July 2003); and
- Best Practices for Collecting and Using Current and Past Performance Information - Guidelines agencies should follow on contractor performance information (May 2000).

Government Procurement Resources

- Acquisition.gov;
- Acquisition Community Connection;
- Chief Acquisition Officers Council (CAOC);
- Defense Acquisition University (DAU);
- Federal Acquisition Institute (FAI);
- Federal Acquisition Regulatory Council;
- Federal Procurement Data System (FPDS);
- The Federal Register;
- Mission Support Contracting Community of Practice; and
- Office of Federal Procurement Policy (OFPP) Act.

Sample Executive Branch Departmental Procurement Manuals

Department/Manual	Procurement Manual
Department of Commerce (DOC)	Commerce Acquisition Manual (CAM)
Department of Defense (DOD)	Defense Acquisition Circulars DoD Directives and Instructions DCAA Contract Audit Manual (CAM)
Department of Education (ED)	Department of Education Acquisition Regulation (EDAR)
Department of Energy (DOE)	Acquisition Guide, Directives, and Policy Flashes
Department of Health and Human Services (HHS)	Health and Human Services Acquisition Regulation (HHSAR)
Department of Homeland Security (DHS)	Homeland Security Acquisition Regulation (HSAR)
Department of Housing and Urban Development (HUD)	Department of Housing and Urban Development (HUDAR)
Department of Justice (DOJ)	Justice Acquisition Regulation
Department of Labor (DOL)	Department of Labor (DOLAR), Department of Labor Manual Series (DLMS)
Department of State (DOS)	Department of State Acquisition Regulation (DOSAR)
Department of the Interior (DOI)	Acquisition Policy Releases (DIAPR)
Department of the Treasury	Department of Treasury Acquisition Procedures (DTAP)

Department of Transportation (DOT)	Transportation Acquisition Regulation (TAR) Transportation Acquisition Circulars (TACs) Transportation Acquisition Manual (TAM)
Department of Veterans Affairs (VA)	Department of Veterans Affairs Acquisition Regulation (VAAR)
Environmental Protection Agency (EPA)	Comprehensive Procurement Guidelines
General Services Administration (GSA)	Comprehensive Procurement Guidelines
Office of Management and Budget (OMB)	Circulars: Procurement

Chapter 18

Preparation of Correspondence

The Government prepares correspondence on two bases: controlled and non-controlled. Controlled correspondence has been determined important enough to warrant tracking and a suspense date by which a response must have been generated while non-controlled correspondence warrants no such concerns.

For the Government official, the majority of controlled correspondence is received from members of Congress and congressional committees and subcommittees. But correspondence referred by or transmitted from the White House, the Office of the Vice President, other federal agencies, and state and local agencies is considered to be controlled correspondence. The final category of controlled correspondence is Freedom of Information Act (FOIA) and Privacy Act requests. Letters of inquiry from the general public, if directed to the Director or Secretary of a Government office or agency, are often non-controlled but do require a response.

Non-controlled correspondence and "Action as Appropriate"[1] correspondence are essentially the same. This category of correspondence may or may not require a written response. Other non-controlled correspondence would include general letters of comment from the public that do not ask a question and any type of correspondence that was received as part of a mass mailing or a form letter.

---

[1] *Washington Office Correspondence Manual*, National Park Service, October 1999 – 3.9.

Chapter 18: Preparation of Correspondence

The correspondence unit in all departments is managed by the Executive Secretariat or its equivalent. The Executive Secretariat receives, screens, distributes, tracks, and files correspondence from the public, academia, all Government agencies, Congress, the White House, and foreign heads of state and their representatives. Many Executive Secretariats use an electronic document management system to track the status of the actions generated to reply to the correspondence received. All correspondence is generally handled on the basis that the Government should respond within 30 days. The most sensitive correspondence is distinguished by having a 7 to 14 day suspense date. The Executive Secretariat reviews, edits, and clears all correspondence prior to the final draft and signature of any correspondence.

Four Types of Correspondence

There are many different writing techniques that will help you achieve your correspondence and communication goals. The most common are: logical organization with the reader in mind; writing in an active voice; using short sentences and paragraphs; and using everyday words and easy to follow design features.

There are four types of correspondence that you will prepare or encounter while working in the Government: interim correspondence, procedural correspondence, policy correspondence, and correspondence dealing with FIOA.

Interim Correspondence

An interim response simply acknowledges receipt of a letter and informs the sender that you have received their letter and are working on the issues raised within that letter. If an interim letter is needed you should generate one as quickly as possible to inform the sender of the status of their request. An interim letter does not buy you an indefinite amount of time to respond to a letter, but rather it is a professional way to inform the sender that their request will take a little longer to complete.

An interim letter is short but informs the reader when to expect a full response. When drafting an interim response, be sure to include: the date the letter was received and a confirmation of what information is requested. This gives the sender of the interim response an opportunity to state what the complete response will address and eliminates discrepancies. This also helps to ensure that retrieval of the wrong information does not occur. Be sure to include a line at the end of the response with carbon copies for all the departments and staff that will be involved in the preparation of the complete response.

Procedural Correspondence

Procedural correspondence responds to inquiries that raise questions or issues concerning the manner, method or techniques your agency uses to resolve issues. Agency processes are generally prescribed in regulations and formal guidance documents. Effective correspondence would be a summary of the process milestone focused on the area highlighted in the incoming. This summary should be followed by a reference to the applicable regulations and/or guidance document.

Policy Correspondence

Complete correspondence is used when you are addressing an issue within a letter you received and the information is known. You can respond to the letter in the suggested time frame with the policy or information that was requested.

FIOA Requests

FOIA requires federal agencies to make their records promptly available to any person who makes a proper request. Agencies within the Executive Office of the President and independent regulatory agencies are subject to the provisions of the FOIA. However, state Governments, municipal corporations, the courts, Congress, and private citizens are not subject to the FOIA.

FOIA requests can be made by any person, partnership, corporation, association, and any foreign or domestic Government. Requests may also be made through an attorney or other representative on behalf of a person. FOIA requests can be made for any reason and requesters generally do not have to justify or explain their reasons for making a request. The FOIA specifies only two requirements for requests:

1. The request must reasonably describe the records being sought; and
2. The request must be made in accordance with the agency's published FOIA regulations.

The fact that a FOIA request is very broad or burdensome does not entitle an agency to deny a request. The key factor is the ability of an agency's staff to reasonably ascertain exactly which records are being requested and their ability to locate them. Each federal agency publishes in the Federal Register its procedural regulations governing access to its records under the FOIA. These regulations inform the public of:

- Where and how to address requests;
- Its schedule of fees for search, review, and duplication;
- Its fee waiver criteria; and
- Its administrative appeal process.

The procedures for a FOIA request vary from agency to agency. Occasionally, an agency may waive some of its published procedures for reasons of public interest, speed, or simplicity. An agency may not impose any additional requirements on a requester beyond those prescribed in its regulations however, a requester's failure to comply with an agency's procedural regulations governing access to records may be considered as a failure to properly request information and therefore can be denied. An agency does not have to begin a search until it receives a proper FOIA request and all fees for the request have been paid by the requester. Once an agency receives a proper request it has twenty working days in which to make a determination on the request. In unusual circumstances, an agency can extend the twenty-day time limit for processing a FOIA request if it tells the requester in writing why it needs the extension and when it will have a determination on the request.

General Correspondence Rules to Follow

Before you begin to draft your letter give some thought to your audience or reader. You want the reader to stay interested in the material being presented and the best way to do that is to grab their attention and then write directly to them. Give the reader information that is pertinent to them. Readers are generally interested only in material that applies to them in some shape or form. If necessary, you may need to tell the reader why the information you are providing is important to them by providing examples. Identifying the audience upfront will do more than ensure that you write clearly, it will also help you focus on the reader's needs which will make the correspondence you are drafting more effective.

Organize your letter in way that is easy to follow. Tell the reader what they're going to read about and they'll be less likely to need to re-read the paragraph. Think ahead to some of the questions the reader may have and address those questions in the letter in the order in which they may arise. Establish a good context for the reader before you provide them with details. Chronological organization is the best process for information that requires a series of steps. General information is usually presented first with exceptions, conditions, and specialized information to follow. Limit the levels of information to three or fewer as documents or letters with more levels of information can make it overwhelm the reader. If what you need to present requires you to detail several processes consider dividing your letter or document into sections and presenting the information that way.

Keep your letter clear and concise. Writing in an active voice makes it clear to the reader who is supposed to do what. This helps to eliminate the uncertainty of who is responsible for any action that may need to take place. Express only one idea in a sentence. Avoid words connoting arrogance, clichés, technical jargon and bureaucratic writing full of legalisms as they do little to enhance your letter and can give it a negative appeal. Use short simple and easy to understand words when communicating. It is important to understand that you shouldn't leave out any necessary technical terms, but make sure your other language is as clear as possible. Going beyond necessary technical terms to write in jargon can cause misunderstanding or alienation.

Avoid long paragraphs because they can become convoluted. Short paragraphs, on the other hand, are easy to read and understand. Writing experts recommend that paragraphs be no more than 150 words in three to eight sentences. Generally speaking, paragraphs should never be longer than 250 words. Although not done often, there is nothing wrong with the occasional one-sentence paragraph. Pay close attention to your grammar, punctuation and consistency throughout the letter. Also, whenever possible limit your letter to one page but if it is necessary to carry a document over to a second page be sure to have at least two additional lines of text on the following page.

All documents must have a closing paragraph. When closing your letter, state what action you would like the reader to take if applicable. If you are looking to schedule a meeting or a follow-up phone call, request it during this section of this letter. Discuss briefly what it is you hope to accomplish in the meeting or phone call and make it as appealing to the reader as possible. Include the contact information for the person or persons the reader may contact should they have any questions or concerns. Close the paragraph by thanking the reader for their time and reassure them that their request is being handled.

The presentation of your correspondence is just as important as the content. Your letter should be presented on the letterhead of the organization you are representing. The document should be generated on a computer using a word processing software program. Margins should be set at 1 inch on all four sides. The most common font type used for business correspondence is Times New Roman set at either 11 or 12 point; however Arial font type is acceptable. The address heading should begin no less than 4 lines from the start of the document. There should be 5 line spaces between the complimentary closing (which should be formal in professional correspondence such as "Sincerely") and the signature line.[2]

---

[2] *Letter Elements*, Available at: http://www.kcitraining.com/styleguide/letelem.html accessed June 2010.

Chapter 19

Preparation of Advocacy Documents

Advocacy is the act of arguing on behalf of a particular issue, idea, or person. Individuals, organizations, businesses, and Governments advocate their agendas under specific rules and circumstances. Advocacy is meant to affect or influence a decision-maker's viewpoint on an issue. Decision-makers include elected officials, career civil servants, and industry executives.

There are many methods associated with advocating a position. This chapter discusses preparation of written documents. When your target audience does not have specific knowledge on an issue and receives a written document which provides knowledge and is deemed valuable, the presentation is effective. Advocacy instruments provide the audience with ideas, proposals, and solutions to facilitate the decision-making process. Branches and divisions within agencies and private companies use this instrument to educate and persuade their management to support a particular decision or approach to an issue.

Before drafting an advocacy document, it is necessary to plot out a precise strategy. Advocacy documents bring the strategy to life. They must clearly state the advocate's position and provide substantive support that is more persuasive to the decision-maker than other documents with a different approach.

Categories of Advocacy

When it comes to advocacy, we oftentimes think of concerned citizens, special interest groups, or professional advocates contacting or working with elected officials and staff to resolve an issue of concern (i.e., private sector to Government lobbying). However, Government officials also advocate at all levels within the Government and the private sector. Advocacy categories include: intra-agency; inter-agency; Executive to Legislative Branch and vice versa, and Legislative to Legislative. Similarly, categories for the private sector are: private sector to Executive Branch; private sector to Legislative Branch; and Government to private sector. It is important to note that while Government advocacy is focused on preparation of "educational" and other factual responses to inquiries, the Administration's policies are generally advocated in their written documents.

The following part discusses the major categories of advocacy and outlines key criteria when writing other parties in the advocacy process. This chapter also provides general writing guidance that applies to all types of advocacy.

Private Sector to Government[1]

Each year thousands of people advocate before the federal, state and local Governments. Such advocacy can be as simple as a citizen writing a letter to your Congressman. However, advocacy documents can also be complex, involving an elaborate strategy with multiple parties working to resolve an issue that stands to impact an entire industry or profession.

When preparing advocacy documents for the Government, it is important to remember that each year the Executive and Legislative Branches receive tens of thousands of advocacy documents including emails, papers, reports, and letters. To be effective, the decision-maker must believe that reading your document is time well spent. Your focus is to equip them with substantive information supporting your idea or proposal.

There are several key considerations for the private sector advocate to keep in mind when preparing an advocacy document:

- **Persistence:** Successful advocacy involves approaching more than one office or agency or approaching the same office more than once. Prepare documents with your immediate and foreseeable future audiences in mind. A successful advocacy effort may take months or years to bear fruit. Thus, being strategically persistent in all documents is critical.

---

[1] Distribution of advocacy documents is deemed lobbying under the law if the private sector is trying to persuade legislators to propose, pass, or defeat legislation or to change existing laws. See, http://www.senate.gov/pagelayout/legislative/g_three_sections_with_teasers/lobbyingdisc.htm accessed June 2010.

- **Education:** Much of the Government's policy and programs are incredibly complex and extraordinary. Your audience often has no working knowledge of the subject matter. Drafting a series of advocacy documents for your target audience is often required. Initially, the job is to draft documents that educate the audience. Once the audience understands the subject matter, the crux of your advocacy position can be written.

- **Timing:** Pay particular attention to informal and formal deadlines. The utility of an advocacy document is extremely time-sensitive. Make sure that advocacy documents are prepared well in advance of decision-making sessions, hearings and deadlines. A well written document has little or no value if the reader has already made their decision.

- **Keep it Short:** State your objectives concisely and do not provide unnecessary information that confuses or clutters the document.

- **Competing Interests:** Be aware that your opponents are presenting documents that contradict your position. It is always advantageous to preemptively confront opposing viewpoints and distinguish your viewpoint as the optimal choice. A well-written document should not result in the decision-maker asking why your viewpoint is optimal.

- **Provide Substantive Solutions:** Give your audience something of value. Provide substantive options and real-time solutions to the decision-maker. The best idea in the world may be of little value to a decision-maker unless it is accompanied by substance that can be integrated or implemented.

- **Explain the Value of Choosing Your Viewpoint:** Be explicit as to how the decision-maker benefits from choosing to concur with the ideas presented in your advocacy document. The decision-maker needs to know why concurring with your advocacy message is advantageous and what is gained as a result.

- **Stakeholders:** Describe your stakeholder base as broadly as possible. Any group of people or any entity or industry that stands to benefit from the implementation of your proposed idea is a stakeholder. Present the stakeholders in the most positive light (spin). Emphasize the positive and, if possible, tie your proposed idea to the masses by explaining how the idea will positively impact the everyday citizen.

Government to Government

The Government's complex democratic system does not discourage differing viewpoints within the Government as a whole. Key players will often have different interests and considerations that drive their decision-making. This is to be expected given the fact that there are two major political parties that differ ideologically. It is often necessary for the Administration or other agency stakeholders to advocate to other Government stakeholders to avoid a stall in the Government processes.

There are several subcategories of Government to Government advocacy, including:

- **Intra-agency:** Government agencies are responsible for managing hundreds of programs and issues. Agencies are made up of multiple divisions or working groups that are assigned specific programs and issues. Because of this division of labor, it is commonplace for individuals working in a Government agency to educate and advocate to their colleagues. Also, because of the hierarchical structure in Government agencies, it is also oftentimes necessary for subordinate officials to educate or persuade their superiors on a particular position.

- **Inter-agency:** There is a lot to be gained from state, local and federal agencies communicating and working with one another; sometimes, it is even required by law. Within the Federal Government, the laws and regulations that are drafted today often implicate multiple Government agencies or divisions and require their participation or oversight. When multiple Government agencies are involved, it is not uncommon for there to be competing positions or interests that surface. Therefore, effective advocacy is the way to ensure quick resolution so that a suitable compromise can be realized.

- **Legislative to Legislative:** Any member of the House or Senate can introduce a Bill, but the sponsor(s) must secure substantial support from both House and Senate members for the bill to become a law. Thus, it is often necessary for Members of Congress to advocate their position. Furthermore, it is common for members to advocate on behalf of their constituents for spending allocated through earmarked congressional directives.

- **Executive to Legislative:** Under current law, the Executive Branch cannot lobby the Congress. However, the Executive Branch has managed to develop several advocacy "tools" to influence legislative proposals. For example, the Administration regularly issues Statements of Administration Policy (SAP).[2] The Executive Branch informs Congress of its views on each bill through these statements. The SAP states whether the Administration supports the bill, recommends changes to the bill as written, or whether the President's advisors would recommend a veto. In the budget context, SAPs are often used to communicate a preference for a House or Senate position.

  Furthermore, House and Senate members often call upon members of the Executive Branch to provide testimony to their committees. While this practice is often used to facilitate oversight, there are times that this provides

---

[2] See, Understanding the Budget of the United States Government, 11th Edition, The EOP Foundation, March 2007.

the Executive Branch an opportunity to advocate its position or display its expertise on a matter.

- **Legislative to Executive:** Members of Congress are charged with the responsibility to represent their constituency. As chief advocates for their Congressional district or State, Members often write letters to the Administration discussing funding, programming, and their constituents' needs and requests. Drafting an advocacy document is the best way to communicate a particular position or persuade another Government stakeholder about your position. Here are several key considerations for preparation of a Government-to-Government advocacy document:

- **Institutional Knowledge or Expertise:** Make it clear that you and the office you represent have a specific expertise or knowledge that makes you an authority on the issue being addressed. Particular agencies generally are privy to institutional knowledge that puts them in a unique position to speak intelligently on select subject matters. Institutional knowledge is a collective of facts, concepts, experiences, and know-how held by a group of people.

- **Provide Substantive Support for Your Position:** A good advocacy document always provides adequate data or substantive evidence that supports the stated position. Charts, graphs, and other visual aids can be especially helpful in supporting a position because they summarize large amounts of data and introduce information in a simple and uncluttered manner.

- **Be Respectful:** Avoid insensitive or strong language when drafting a document for another Government actor. Persuasive tones are the trademark of an advocacy document, but always remember that an advocacy document is offering solutions, not demanding them. If you had authority to commandeer the target audience, an advocacy document would not be necessary.

- **Maintain Your Credibility:** Be careful not to make attenuated arguments in an advocacy document that may damage your credibility. Providing constructive and substantive support for your arguments will almost always eliminate the possibility of damaging your credibility.

- **"Political Awareness:"** When working in Government, it is incredibly important to be aware of the political landscape. An issue that was overlooked yesterday may become a controversial issue tomorrow. Most Government decision-makers analyze political ramifications associated with the Administration's policies before taking a particular position.

- **Use Your "Political Capital" Wisely:** Each Government stakeholder has a limited amount of "political capital;" that is, the opinion of another person or group of people about you and/or your organization. This capital is institutional, *not* partisan. Expend your "political capital" on advocacy when it is necessary and feasible. Generally, your "political capital" is only at issue when advocating a controversial or politically-sensitive position.

Government to Private Sector

There are many occasions in which the Government can benefit from advocating to the private sector. The private sector has a vast array of resources and commodities on which the Government depends. State and local Governments, as well as some of the federal departments, have economic development agencies that work with the private sector to establish operations in their locale. The Government regulates or encourages the private sector to implement significant policies and processes. The Government's success in its work with the private sector generally requires advocacy.

Several key considerations for the Government to keep in mind when preparing an advocacy document for the private sector are:

- **State the Financial Benefit(s) or Incentives:** Government officials must make it clear to the private sector how a proposal is going to benefit their organization or industry. Most private enterprises are driven by bottom-line considerations. Thus, stating the financial benefits or incentives associated with a business proposal or proposed policy is critical.

- **Candid, Candid, Candid:** Be completely candid about all of the negative factors associated with your position or proposal. It is better to disclose these factors up front rather than have the decision-maker find out through his own research or contradictory fact surfacing from an inquiry.

- **State the Intangible Benefit(s):** Private entities are aware that it is beneficial to have a solid relationship with the appropriate Government departments. Make it clear that you would appreciate their support. Also, clearly state your willingness (if true) to provide assistance to, or maintain an ongoing relationship with their organization.

- **Present Multiple Options When Possible:** The private sector is accustomed to working in an environment where they get to make independent decisions that are driven by market forces and other considerations. Whenever possible, present multiple scenarios or options that further your goal or position. Private entities feel more comfortable in the decision-making process when they have choices.

- **Provide Substantive Support for Your Position:** Directors of private entities must be informed when making decisions.[3] Basic corporate law doctrine requires directors to have adequate information available before making a

---

[3] See, the ABA Model Business Corporation Act, http://www.abanet.org/buslaw/library/onlinepublications/mbca2002. pdf accessed June 2010.

decision. They owe a duty of care to the enterprise and can be held liable for mismanagement if they proceed negligently. Therefore, a good advocacy document provides adequate data or substantive evidence that the corporate decision-maker can rely upon in the decision-making process.

- **Win-Win for Everyone:** Whenever possible, state that everyone comes out a winner if your position is adopted. This is not always possible, but when it is, make sure to clearly advertise it to the reader.

Preparing for Advocacy Writing

Strategic Goal

Regardless what you write, your immediate goal is to achieve the desired result. The first step is to identify that desired result and to assess its feasibility. After the strategic goal is identified, the document should be written to realize that goal.

Developing a Title

The title should be a specific, informative statement describing the document's content. A clear idea of what the title is will integrate your work, as inspired by the strategic goal. Keep your title in mind as you write every section of your document. If, by the time you finish writing your draft, you feel your document does not reflect your title, you have two options: revise the whole document or change the title.

Be Conscious of the Audience

- **Identifying Your Audience:** The most critical step in successful advocacy is identifying your audience and understanding what they know, their current position (or lack thereof) on the issue(s), and how the audience benefits from the proposal(s) in your document.

  Generally, it is easy to identify the audience. It will likely be a Congressional member from a particular district or an agency official. However, the decision on who is receiving the document should be thoughtful. Furthermore, it is important to consider the foreseeable unintended audience so that any statements that might offend the unintended audience are avoided.

  It is important to plan, research, and write with the intended audience in mind. We all have many ways of talking and writing. We can be formal or informal, concise or detailed, technical, specialized, or general. We choose a writing strategy based on our audience. Knowing your audience makes the writing process easier because it simplifies the aforementioned issues. Knowing the audience also promotes unity and purpose in the document. Moreover, it permits you to involve the audience more directly in your argument.

- **Recognize the Stage in the Process:** It is critical to assess the audience's level of understanding of the issue(s) and subject matter(s) that will be covered in the advocacy document. Initially, it may be necessary to provide documents that educate the audience. However, do not bore your audience with unnecessary material that has no relationship to the desired outcome.
- **Write for an Adverse Audience:** Notwithstanding your knowledge of the audience's position on the pertinent issue(s), advocacy documents should challenge an adverse audience. In practice, this means that all major points should be persuasive and assume that you need to change your audience's position.

Be Conscious of the Stakeholders and their Needs

Be conscious of the stakeholders' interests represented in your document and present solutions or proposals to address them. Sometimes, a compromise is required if you are representing more than one party with similar interests. It may be necessary to get these similarly situated parties to compromise or reach an agreement before constructing your advocacy document. You need to present a unified front in your advocacy document.

Brainstorming Process

Most writing focuses on the end product. However, an astute writer should not neglect the process by which words are chosen (the mental aspects of writing). The process determines the quality of the product. Many professionals damage their final work product by skimping at this stage and on outlining. A bridge without a detailed plan could not be constructed! Writing must be approached in the same manner.

Once you know your general goal, you can begin to brainstorm. Brainstorming is a strategy for exploring ideas based on the free expression of thoughts. Brainstorming can result in rejecting certain lines of thought; if you can see clearly enough to reject an idea this early, it has been time well spent.

In the initial stages, do not constrain your thought patterns. Take the time to write down some sporadic ideas about the project. These sporadic ideas will eventually lead to substantive points or arguments. An excellent way of maneuvering though this process is to use a non-linear outline. Start by simply jotting down all of your ideas. These ideas will eventually be incorporated into an annotated outline.

Research

With a goal, title, and audience in mind, you have the focal point of your document. You have a focus, a goal, a purpose – in essence, the bones of your document. But now you need substance; that is where research comes in. The research step is important because it allows you to gather some proof for your audience about your proposal or idea. This step forces you to immerse yourself in a pool of outside knowledge so that you can integrate it with your own ideas that developed during brainstorming.

Do not narrow yourself too much at this point. A very clear strategic goal gives you enough direction to keep you on task, but still leaves you open to new angles on the subject.

Outlining

Effective writing requires structure. Effective structure does not simply happen. Before you begin to write, you should have a clear plan in mind for your entire document; a little time here will save you a lot of time later. Before writing in earnest, figure out how many issues there are and what they are.

When it comes to outlining, most people think of Roman numerals, capital letters, and the like. It does not really matter what format you choose as long as the outline is broken up into numerous parts (headings and subheadings) that represent the main points or arguments you plan to make.

Using much the same strategy as you did in your brainstorming session, begin to fill in the information under the appropriate heading or sub-heading; do not worry about complete sentences or paragraph structure at this stage. As you write, remember that an outline is a hierarchal structure (ordered by level of importance) that illustrates the relationship of ideas.

Drafting Advocacy Documents

Writing for an Audience

It is a mistake to assume that your audience already agrees with you or comprehends the material you're trying to convey. Provide enough information to educate and persuade your audience.

Use Plain Language

You achieve plain English when you use the simplest, most straightforward expression of an idea. You can still choose interesting words but avoid using fancy ones that have everyday replacements meaning precisely the same thing.[4] Plain English is a clear, straightforward expression, using only as many words as are necessary. It is language that avoids obscurity, inflated vocabulary, and convoluted sentence construction. It is not simplified version of the English language. Writers of plain English let their audience concentrate on the message instead of being distracted by complicated language. They make sure that their audience understands the message easily.

---

[4] Garner, Bryan, from *Legal Writing in Plain English*, 2001, pp xix. See, http://press-pubs.uchicago.edu/garner accessed June 2010.

Turning your Theme into Concise Point Headings

The first step in writing is to create clear points that summarize the different arguments or solutions that are to be conveyed to the audience. Point headings should convey the big picture. The different point headings frame the main substantive issue(s) and your proposed solution(s). Point headings should persuade and indicate that there is only one answer. Your most important points must come first in an advocacy document (a hierarchal document).

When presenting complex ideas or arguments, it may be necessary to further subdivide your substantive thoughts or proofs with subheadings. Subheadings should clearly and concisely support the appropriate heading.

The First Draft

The text of the draft should serve as justification for the point headings and proposals. Write a draft straight through, without stopping to edit – use your outline as your guide. While you develop your first draft, focus on one idea at a time, but link ideas together, clearly explaining how each step brings the reader closer to your conclusion. Let it sit awhile before editing. Polishing the document at an early stage is a waste of time.

A Strong Summary

The summary should be written after the first draft is completed. Every advocacy document should make its primary point(s) within 90 seconds of reading time.[5] The summary should outline the issue(s), the resolution(s), and the reasons for the particular resolution(s). The reasoning should weave facts into the issues and correlating resolutions to make them concrete.

Emphasizing in the Conclusion

The nature of the conclusion depends upon the specific arguments or ideas that you are presenting, but in general your conclusion should emphasize the information you want your reader to have learned from your document.

Style, Spin, Credibility, and Polishing

Clear and Concise Writing

Advocacy writing, because it conveys complex information, must be organized, precise, and clear; otherwise, your reader may misinterpret, devalue, or completely miss your point. Because a reader should never have to struggle to figure out what you are saying, you must employ a writing strategy that ensures the efficient, accurate flow of information.

---

[5] Ibid.

Spin

Spin is not a dirty word. It can be either positive and constructive or negative and destructive. Remember that the arguments and ideas presented are to convince the decision-maker that your position is optimal. This means that positive, constructive spin should be your approach in advocacy writing.

The number one rule of spin is to "never lie." The use of emotional trigger words is appropriate when used in a constructive manner. Since the people who make or influence the key decisions are typically busy, the proposal has to be stated in a simple, concise manner. Emotional trigger words (also referred to as "buzz words") or shorthand ways to describe the proposal often can be useful if the program is a major initiative and likely to be scrutinized. Examples of such descriptions would include the following, "War-on-Terror," "death tax," and "terrorist surveillance program." If the proponents do not develop appropriate "buzz words," opponents will develop ones to disparage the program.

Credibility

Check every citation, quotation, and reference; your credibility depends on it! Make sure that your citations are accurate and give credit to the originator of the ideas or analysis documented. Moreover, the use of credible sources also adds value to your document. It is beneficial to show that you are not the only party that holds your position or has studied your issue(s) and came to the same conclusion.

Proof and Tweak

No one can expect to write a finished essay in a single draft, and no one except a novice ever tries. Although students and professionals have been told the virtues of second and third drafts from the time they learned to write, they are still reluctant to take the trouble to act on the advice. The results can be disastrous.

Proof carefully; and then have several others proof carefully. Most writers can benefit from a fresh pair of eyes. If you have seen the page several times, you are likely to assume that things are as you expect them to be, not as they actually are. Lastly, make sure you have the most up-to-date information in the document.

Chapter 20

Preparation of Media Instruments

Developing and maintaining an effective relationship with the media is a critical responsibility that the Federal Government must recognize and improve. The media has the responsibility to communicate both the Government's successes and failures to the American public. However, the media's reporting can only be as good as the information they rely on and the credibility of their Government sources.

Government officials, both political and career, often criticize the media and its personalities for publishing or reporting issues that are misleading or inaccurate. The worst charge Government officials assert is that reporting is so biased that it diminishes the Government's capability to effectively perform its responsibilities. On the other hand, Government executives must recognize that if their responses to the media engender anger/hostility or defensiveness/paranoia or represents stonewalling and avoidance, the Government's media coverage will not improve. Further, these actions will result in greater suspicion and mistrust of the Government and its representatives than the public currently holds. A 2013 Pew Research poll indicated that only 26% of Americans trust the Government, an all time low.[1]

---

[1] Available at: http://www.pewresearch.org/daily-number/trust-in-government-in-government-in-washington-remains-low/.

Government officials must change their attitude, behavior, and approach with the media to improve its "branding" with the citizenry. The media asserts its reporting would greatly benefit all stakeholders and be more objective if the media had consistent, accurate, and factual information; transparency at all levels of Government; better education on a Department's issues and events; and observance of mutual respect between both political parties.

Government executives must embrace the concept that the media should not be denied information associated with Government operations, activities, and program information unless it is truly classified, subject to executive privilege, or represents incomplete work product. Other than the aforementioned categories, it is unacceptable to deny media access to information.

Finally, the Federal Government must adopt enhanced communication methods. The objective is to improve the Government's written materials and associated scripts. The results would ensure that the public's right to know is given a higher priority and thereby should improve relations with the media.

To stay relevant in today's global 24/7 news atmosphere, the Government must adapt to the emerging technologies that are changing the way Americans receive their news with the objective of enhancing communication methods. The result would be that the public's right to know is deemed a higher priority and thereby should improve relations with the media. The shifting paradigm for Government and its media relations is a focal point of this chapter.

There are additional recognized perspectives on the most appropriate actions which Government executives should employ to be more effective with the media and industry. These perspectives are documented below:

Public Relations—The Public

- The first step in enjoying good public relations and favorable public response is to realize who the public is and what your responsibilities are. For example, local disaster coordinators is a "who" that is multiple. The general public, private and public agencies, public officials, law enforcement officers and other disaster workers, and mental health professionals are among the "who" in your public relations campaigns. You must be sensitive to the fact that all groups of people in your community are stakeholders that the media similarly serves.
- What are your responsibilities? Your responsibilities cover two aspects of public information: (1) timely responses to requests and (2) effective and politically sensitive public education. Minimally, you must respond to a request which is clearly information releasable to the public and therefore the media. Any request should be viewed as an opportunity to educate the public in the right manner.

- Proactive public education is an essential component to be credible with the media. By not waiting for news to happen to you, you can control the overall impact of the news on your general public. For example, the public can be prepared for disasters; thus, minimizing the physical and emotional damage that result from a disaster. Not only is the Government well served to do so but failure to do so will result in media criticisms.
- Conduct "outreach" campaigns within the agency. The media would take notice and see an illustration of approaches to providing effective Governmental services to the public.

Public Relations—The Media

- The second step in developing good public relations is to develop contacts among the media covering your agency. They want to accurately report on the effectiveness of good programs. However, the integrity of the programs must be transparent.
- Government must expand its knowledge of and acknowledgment of media professionals to include more than "beat" reporters. These include: photographers, managing editors and radio/television program directors, sales staff, commentators and owners.
- Comprehend and acknowledge the media's expectations as a Government official.

  o Ensure that the person authorized by your agency to speak for a program is the one the media is dealing with. Confusion occurs when too many people try to serve as the spokesperson.
  o Make it easy for reporters to contact the spokesperson. Make sure that all media outlets covering your agency or program know both the cell phone and office telephone numbers, have a reliable email address, and the name and number of a back-up person to contact when your spokesperson is unavailable.
  o Publish the deadlines for the appropriate media outlets within your agency in order to plan ahead. The media's deadlines are your deadlines.
  o Media professionals appreciate news releases, public service announcements and other materials that are focused to meet their specific needs. There are examples provided in this chapter which provide guidance for preparation purposes. Always provide printed or high quality copies of the aforementioned materials.
  o Correct errors in the Government's written instrument carefully and quickly. Mistakes made by the media should be evaluated and only the most severe should be a focal point for correction. For minimal mistakes, no comment is usually necessary.
  o Seek the reason a policy pronouncement or event was not covered; it could have been cut at the last minute for something else of more value. Further, feedback on whether there was something wrong with the story so that it

can be corrected in future stories is appropriate. The key is not to overreact.
- o Express your appreciation every time you submit material, regardless of whether the material is used.

What is Considered News?

- News is anything the media chooses to print, film, or broadcast as "news." It is the media's choice, not yours. The Government does not control the media; nor should it. Understanding this principal will serve any Government official well.
- News is also anything enough people are interested in reading, seeing, or hearing about. Media outlets are both sensitive to their audience and competitive. This is generally the best arbitror of the news.
- As the Government considers their approach, consider the audience you want to reach and how to generate interest within that audience. Many events related to your job, while ordinary for you, are newsworthy, exciting and unusual events for people outside your agency.
- Think in terms of two types of news--spot news and feature stories. Spot news is perishable news. A feature story can be used any time. A feature story is the human interest angle that gives the media's audience more than the surface facts.
- If you are responsible for setting up an interview with a reporter, help set the climate for the interview. Review the kind of questions that are likely to be asked and prepare a written response to assist the Government's spokesperson to be more comfortable with the upcoming interview. Provide a brief backgrounder on your agency's spokesperson.

Effective Communication

Communication between career and political executives is the most important factor associated with achieving agency objectives. It is the cornerstone of their relationship. Communication is structured around the following products and performance-related criteria:

- Effective Government writing;
- Neutral competence-based analysis;
- Accurately discussing the stakeholders' positions on the issues and gaining the political executives confidence;
- Demonstrating respect for opposing points of view and knowing where the line is between advocacy and lobbying;
- Giving articulate, effective testimony, inclusive of sufficient responses to all questions; and
- Understanding differing views of what constitutes success between political and career executives.

Effective Government Writing

Career executives communicate with political executives routinely in writing. The primary instruments transmitted to political executives are:

- Briefing papers;
- PowerPoint presentations;
- Short emails discussing issues of interest;
- Issue papers;
- Decision documents;
- Budget and regulatory proposals;
- Program guidance documents;
- Murder board review documents; and
- Media/editorial board review documents.

In addition, effective writing is crucial to career and political executives' ability to build coalitions. There are specific written instruments to explain policy alternatives, vet policy choices, justify policy decisions, seek Congressional buy-in, explain policy changes to industry and other interested stakeholders, and to use the media to promote why those policy decisions reflect effective governance. These written instruments are drafted by the career service staff and address either issues internal to the agency or issues internal or external to the Executive Branch.

Instruments drafted for internal purposes include:

- Policy and technical white papers;
- Options papers;
- Decision memoranda;
- Briefing memoranda; and
- Policy memoranda.

Instruments drafted for external purposes include:

- Guidance documents, Executive orders and regulations;
- Budget justifications;
- Testimony and Q&A responses;
- Capability statements;
- Correspondence; and
- Press releases.

Neutral Competence-Based Analysis

Political executives must be particularly sensitive to the career executive's duty to ensure objectivity and promote professionalism within the entirety of the career service.

This includes gathering the right information in order to produce critical thinking. This requires developing reasoned performance metrics. It also means discussing the issues on a comprehensive basis.

The practicality of neutral competence-based analysis is critical to all aspects of a career executive's performance. Neutral competence means that, at the end of the day, there is an issue that needs to be dealt with in a manner that is not subjective, but objective. The career executive staff outlines the logic associated with the respective written instruments:

1. State the issues so that it can be answered with pros and cons. The issue needs to be described in one to two lines. If it cannot be described in one to two lines, then it needs to be broken up into two or more separate issues.
2. Discuss the background, relying on the history and the facts bearing on the issue.
3. Formulate the options and alternatives, including those often overlooked because of the sources, by thinking them through and articulating all of the possible options and alternatives that those within the "power cluster" and stakeholders are concerned about.
4. Use the pros and cons to distinguish all of the positive and negative factors and impacts associated with the issue.
5. Base the conclusion on the substance and logic of the analysis.

After a neutral competence-based analysis has been performed, career executives ensure objectivity, apply political sensitivities, and strategize as to how to be successful when addressing the challenges and opportunities identified previously.

Career executives must be objectively analytical. Analytical does not always mean "quantifiable." Qualitative factors could be more instructive in certain cases. Career executives, above all, must be balanced, applying the political intelligence gathered throughout the process. Telling the truth, as one believes it to be, based on the analysis he or she has on hand: this is what in Government is called "neutral competence."

The Right Perception

Career and political executives know that, often times, management views perception as reality. Managing perception is an art. Here are some ideas that might help:

- *Be patient* during the policy-making process, because the more institutional knowledge that is applied, the more likely being able to manage perception will be.
- *Be consistent* during all encounters with stakeholders. Any deviation from strategy or from associated opportunities for internal or external participation,

in either the decision-making or implementation phases will result in false perceptions due to inconsistency.

- ***Be conservative*** with commitments at all levels internally, and ensure clarity associated with personal, time-related, organizational, policy or program commitments, both internally and externally. This is the most important factor relative to achieving the right perception with stakeholders.

Advocacy versus Lobbying

Career executives must be able to assert that their advocacy is more about educating stakeholders than lobbying them. Influence should be actualized with empirical data, impartial reports, balanced testimony and expert opinions, and with a respect for the institutional memory of the bureaucracy. Political executives are less bound by this constraint, given that they are expected to reflect and successfully implement the Administration's political agenda.

Remember, career executives already have the benefit of Administration positions and the history associated with how those decisions were made. Thus, within the actualization of their professionalism, senior executives can educate stakeholders in a comprehensive fashion, without lobbying them.

Career executives' credibility will be lost if the stakeholders encountered on issues within their authority see them as a lobbyist or cheerleader rather than a professional bureaucrat. Again, this is a polar difference to be acknowledged in the perspective of the political executive.

This often means that career executives will have to acknowledge facts that do not support the Administration's position. In other words, this means that career executives will have to acknowledge that there are other approaches that could work. However, when these factors are applied to the challenges and opportunities identified earlier, the chances of success go up.

Articulate Testimony

Both the career and political executive's testimony is the primary opportunity to demonstrate the demeanor, tone, sales pitch, and rationale for the Administration's approach versus another. It also provides both types of executive with an opportunity to discuss who they have partnered or built a coalition with so as to demonstrate support beyond the Administration.

The testimony of Government executives represents their only opportunity to educate and advocate the Administration's position without being interrupted or immediately challenged by Members of Congress. It is, also, an opportunity for Government executives to build credibility with their other stakeholders. Simple acknowledgement of their perspective gains the respect of adversaries.

Finally, the testimony of Government executives should be prepared from all of the information and data available related to the agency's policies and programs of interest.

Respect for Opposing Perspectives

The final technique involves acknowledging all of the alternatives presented by other stakeholders and demonstrating respect for opposing points of view.

The goal is to bring other stakeholders' alternatives that are evaluated as meritorious to a higher management level in order to seek their inclusion during negotiations.

The objective is to achieve quick resolution of the issues so that the Government executive can move forward, continuing to build trust with his or her stakeholders. The secondary objective would be to use the differences articulated by other stakeholders that are not evaluated as meritorious to support the executive's position as he or she responds to their alternatives.

Adopting this technique can result in an executive gaining credibility with appropriate elements within his or her "power cluster."

Respect, from an executive's standpoint, is about demonstrating that he or she has taken an objective look at what other stakeholders proposed and providing a thorough response, given the Administration's position. Assuming these efforts are made, it may be possible to negotiate alternatives to the Administration's position and be successful.

Social Networking

Changing the way the Government communicates with the global media has become a much higher priority in recent years. The Government bureaucracy's normal response is to resist radical change. The newest model to facilitate more effective communication is centered on instant news and press releases via social networking sites such as Twitter and Facebook.

Social Networking is a concept and approach which many in Government are unfamiliar. Academia and media professionals agree that social networking techniques work in building online communities of stakeholders who share interests and/or activities, or who are interested in exploring the interests and activities of the Government. Social networking services provide a variety of ways for users to interact, including e-mail, blogging, and live chat (instant messaging) services. This allows Government users to interact by employing a bi-directional model. Bi-directional theory holds that communication can take place between two people or two groups at the same time. Social networking requires that new methods to communicate and share information be optimized. Social networking websites are being used routinely by millions of people.

Just as private companies have embraced social media to manage their company brands, Government must adapt and follow suit.

Press Offices act as "brand ambassadors" for the Government when they promote the Government's goods and services. In the Government's case, the goods and services are programs and activities authorized by statute.

The technological renaissance within the Federal Government took shape during the Bush Administration but is being fully deployed by the Obama Administration. By using the Internet as a tool to reach the public, Government accomplishes two extremely important objectives. The first is unprecedented transparency. In the past, finding a Government report, press release, budget justification, or bill language was an arduous task. It often meant purchasing from report at the Government Printing Office or requesting by mail, Government documents that could reach into the thousands of pages. Now the global media can access recently passed or proposed legislation or a White House press release, etc. by visiting a web page. However, this means that the public is inundated with information. The challenge is to ensure the quality, accuracy, and significance of materials the Government releases to these outlets. This highlights the importance for Government officials to be sure these materials exhaust the focus and sensitivity their audiences demand.

Social networking and the associated social software have numerous Government applications. These include information-sharing within and among agencies; communicating more easily and cost effectively with international partners and U.S. diplomats stationed in remote countries; and most importantly, public outreach.

Congressmen are now tweeting messages (140 character messages sent out to subscribers or "followers") in real time during floor debates at the Capital building (twitter is described in more detail later in this chapter). Doing so gives them a distinct advantage over other members of Congress who have not invested in social networking. Each tweet or Facebook status update has the chance to reach thousands, if not millions of interested parties. This gives elected officials a unique opportunity to gauge public sentiment and adapt their rhetoric and political positioning immediately.

It is also a great way for Members to reach their constituents on a daily basis without sending out mass mail or having staff make thousands of calls around election time. Rep. John Culberson (R-Tex.), whose experimentation with social software (including Twitter), prompted changes to Congressional rules. The changes authorize members to act as bi-directional ambassadors, bypassing traditional media to directly connect Congress with constituents, and vice versa.

The Executive Branch and career officials are also more frequently utilizing social networking sites. NASA has taken advantage of a few social networking tools, including Twitter and Flickr (a website where users can share thousands of pictures with the public). They are using these tools to accomplish their strategic goals. In-Q-Tel, a

CIA subsidiary, has been using Facebook as a way to share open source information with other intelligence groups.[2] EPA's Facebook network, for example, has tens of thousands of members. Anyone with a Facebook account can become a member of the group. It gives EPA a platform for announcing major environmental news, links to petitions to get laws passed, and volunteer links such as the following from EPA's Facebook page: Find information about volunteering along the Florida Peninsula and the Keys as part of the Deepwater Horizon oil spill planning efforts.[3]

While press releases, fact sheets, and television commercials have not been completely replaced; they are unidirectional, thus limited. Unidirectional, as implied and unlike bidirectional communication, is just one way communication; e.g., reading a newspaper.

The Government has always relied on polls and tracking negative phone calls to get a feel for what their constituents and stakeholders are feeling about various issues. Now, through social networking, members of Congress gauge their constituent's perspectives through open information sharing platforms on a day-to-day basis. An increasing number of public relations executives are predicting that the old approaches will be financially unfeasible soon, if not obsolete entirely. Citizens are increasingly becoming familiar with what the Government is doing because Government staff is sitting at their computers and entering real time information associated with their agency programs utilizing social networking tools. By keeping their agencies' mission and goals in mind, the career service is able to complement the agencies' public affairs infrastructure by engaging relevant groups in real time about what the agency is trying to accomplish and how the public can help. USA.gov has started a Facebook page for Really Simple Syndication (RSS) feeds, videos, photos, and other relevant Government news. The public is welcome to become a "fan" of that page and keep up with and participate in Government. An example of something the Government posts on their Facebook page to share with their followers is: National HIV Testing Day is June 27.[4]

Press Releases

Press Releases are a summary of facts about a policy, program, or decision to be reported by the media. Governmental departments use a standardized format. The principle criterion for a good press release is that it contains news that people want to know about. Press Releases dispense information to the broadest audience of stakeholders. However, the broader the audience, the simpler the document must be. Like other Government publications, Press Releases should be written in a manner that is clear, concise, and simple. Editors, reporters, and the public should be able to review the Release quickly and comprehend the subject matter with relative ease.
Prior to writing a Press Release, federal media officials should ask themselves the following six questions:[5]

---

[2] Available at: http://www.wired.com/dangeroom/2009/10/exclusive-us-spies-buy-stake-twitter-blog-monitoring-firm/.
[3] Available at: http://www.facebook.com/#!/EPA?v=wall&ref=ts.
[4] For additional information on testing site near you, visit http://go.usa.gov/3Rl.
[5] *Press Releases, Media Advisories, and Fact Sheets: A Closer Look,* U.S. Department of State.

- Why the subject of the press release is important and why does the agency believe it makes news?
- What are the Government's key messages conveyed in the press release and are they consistent with the Administration's policy and Government advocacy?
- Is the research and the data supporting the position in the press release in our Government base document?
- Is the background information easily accessible by the public?
- Have we provided names and files of Government officials who are authorities on the topics discussed in the press release?
- Is a Fact Sheet necessary to provide supplemental information?

When federal officials prepare a press release for media outlets, the following six questions must be addressed:

- ***Who*** *is the subject of this news?*
- ***What*** *is this news about?*
- ***Where*** *did this news occur?*
- ***When*** *did this news occur?*
- ***Why*** *is this news relevant?*
- ***How*** *is the Administration's point of view best articulated?*

The basic format for writing Press Releases is articulated below:

- <u>Print the press release on plain departmental stationery</u>: The agency's seal, name, and address should be printed at the top. Each Government agency has its own stationery or template with the seal, motto, and address at the top of the document. This serves to prevent any confusion surrounding which agency issued the press release.
- <u>Format with wide margins</u>: The margins should be at least one inch around; there should be at least one inch of blank space surrounding all sides of the text. This gives users ample space to make notes for their purposes.
- <u>Print release on one side</u>: Do not print double sided.
- <u>Provide accurate contact information</u>: This includes the name of the right contact person in the press office or the Agency's issue expert. Also, the email address and the best phone number should be provided, e.g. direct dial office phone and cell phone numbers.
- <u>Print the time of the Release</u>: Print the time below the title, usually in the local time where the news occurs. This allows readers to know the Government's release time.
- <u>Capitalize the headline</u>: Note the following example: *President Obama Lays Out Strategy For American Innovation.*
- <u>Use capitalized dateline preceding the first paragraph</u>: This appears below the title and above the time.
- <u>Place the word "more" at the bottom of the page</u>: If the Release exceeds one page; center "more" at the bottom of the page.

- <u>Signify the end of release with #### or --30--</u> : This is shorthand for indicating that the Release is completed and there is no additional information: This is the last item seen on the Release and appears centered, at the bottom.

Media Advisories

Media Advisories are official written announcements to entice reporters to come to an event that Government officials desire to have covered by the press. An advisory answers the same six questions as stated in the Press Release section. However, advisories are more brief and concise. Government press offices often list this information in bold type and then follow the bold entries with more detail. The issuing Agency hopes to attract attention for the upcoming event by utilizing the bold print headers. Media Advisories follow the same style and format as Press Releases.

Editorial Board

An editorial board is a group of publication editors and contributors who dictate the tone and direction the publication's editorial policy will take. Editorial boards meet on a regular basis to discuss the latest news and opinion trends and discuss what the newspaper should say on a range of issues through the writing of editorials published in their newspapers. They decide who will write what editorials and for what day. When such an editorial appears in a newspaper, it is considered the institutional opinion of that newspaper. Thus, their opinion is of high interest to the Government. The Press Office prepares the information for an editorial board. The Department's Press Secretary usually offers one of its political executives to appear at a meeting of the editorial board to respond to questions raised by the presentation. The presentations are a mixture of Fact Sheet and Testimony.

Op-Ed

An op-ed, abbreviated from opposite the editorial page, is an article prepared by Government officials to put forth the Administration's position on a relevant topic. They are related to Government press releases. They are prepared by an agency's press office and state/advocate the Administration's position. A senior level Government executive is usually the named writer. As such, authors of op-eds are unaffiliated with the newspaper's editorial board. Press Offices often submit op-eds hoping that newspapers will publish them. The higher the level of the Government official submitting the op-ed, the more likely it will be used.

Fact Sheets

Fact Sheets, or Backgrounders, give more detail than Press Releases and Media Advisories. They are also provided as supplemental information associated with the press release or advisory. Fact Sheets are designed to provide media outlets with a written version of the information disseminated during press conferences. A secondary purpose is to ensure that a Government executive's time constraints impacting how long an executive can remain at the press conference does not negatively impact the media's story on the issue as additional information can be contained in the Fact Sheet. Finally, Fact Sheets help to ensure that all reporters receive the same information and thus facilitate objective reporting.

Fact Sheets are to be written in as clear and concise a form as possible. The format follows:

- Print the title in bold font: **Fact Sheet on Presidential Memorandum.** Underline subtitles in bold font and use bullets to provide data and information supporting each subtitle.
- Include the release date: The release date should be printed on the right, immediately above the title and immediately below the contact information. This allows readers to track policy implementation activities for an Administration.
- Provide accurate contact information: Contact information should be printed on the right above the title and immediately above the date and should include both a telephone number and email address.
- Print --30-- or #### to indicate the sheets end: This is the last item that appears on the Fact Sheet and appears centered and at the bottom of the last page.

OPM and other agencies offer customized Government training of this subject including a seminar affiliated with this book that OPM offers. The private sector offer trainings similar to the areas which are discussed in this chapter. Generally, the private sectors training philosophy assumes that the mass media is accountable to make the political system and the Government as a whole more "transparent." The three most important reasons associated with this philosophy is that: Mass media provides information explaining program operations in a manner that regular citizens can comprehend, the public holds political and program decision-making to a higher standard and should be comprehendible to the public, and the public holds Government officials more accountable by accurately reporting what they say and do. However, private sector training opportunities are seeking to enhance opportunities for industry to profit and help the economy whereas Government exists to perform its authorized purpose to the taxpayer without profit.

The Government has a number of mass media outlets which are funded and staffed by the Government. They include:

- **C-SPAN** – a private, non-profit company that provides public access to the political process through cable television stations.
- **Government E-mail Newsletters** – Subscribe to free Government e-mail newsletters.

- **U.S. Government International Radio and Television Broadcasting** – Learn about the federal agency responsible for all U.S. Government and Government sponsored, non-military, international broadcasting.
- **USA.gov News and Media** – Browse press releases, radio ads, video clips, public service announcements, RSS feeds, podcasts, newsletters, e-mail subscriptions, etc. at www.usa.gov.
- **Government RSS Library** – Library of RSS feeds from across the Government.
- **Blogs from the U.S. Government** – Read blogs from various U.S. Government sources.
- **Federal Agency News and Press Releases** – Browse this list of news and press release websites throughout the U.S. Government.
- **Federal News, Articles, and Tweets** – Can be found at GovExec.com, which aggregates Government news by agency.
- **Federal News Radio** – Management, procurement, technology, security, policy, pay, and benefits news for Federal Government and those who do business with the Government.
- **Foreign News Service** – Browse this online news service compiled from thousands of non-U.S. media sources.
- **Government Podcasts** – Listen to podcasts from various U.S. Government sources.
- **Videos from the U.S. Government** – Videos from USA.gov and across the U.S. Government.

Government Media

The Government's organizational structure unit for coordinating the Government's perspective with the media is a Press Office.

Press Offices

Press Offices are headed by Press Secretaries who are typically Presidential Appointees. As the link between heads of Government agencies or other executive level Federal Officials, they are judged by tenor of the press corps around them. They are responsible for finalizing all written instruments that will be provided to the press. Much of the material they draw on is generated by the career service and therefore presumed to be credible and accurate.

The staffs within the Press Office are typically career communication specialists. The staff is responsible for disseminating information and they are the most efficient means of dispensing large volumes of information to a broad and decentralized audience. The written instruments used most commonly by Press Offices are Press Releases, Media Advisories, Briefings, and Fact Sheets. Each year, the Federal Government prints thousands of these documents. The written instruments explain the Administration's position, announce events, provide the facts and data relied upon to support decision-making, and discuss and convey key policies and programs.

White House Press Corps

The White House Press Corps is the most well known group of journalists focused on the Executive Branch and the President. This group of journalists and correspondents are tasked with covering and reporting all news pertaining to the White House. They are typically stationed at the White House to cover White House press briefings and press releases. Reporters covering the White House get daily news releases and briefings from the White House Press Secretary. The journalists are then given the opportunity to ask questions to members of the Administration or to the President. The Administration spends hours writing and later rehearsing answers to possible questions they think reporters may ask. In addition, an Administration official may speak to a reporter only on background without attribution. This is the well known off-the-record interview which a reporter agrees to keep confidential.

Congressional Correspondents

Congressional correspondents are tasked with covering the daily activities and reporting all news pertaining to the United States Congress, both House of Representatives and the Senate. Many of the media networks change their White House correspondents with new Administrations. However, the most established correspondents stay on due to their individual credibility and popularity with the media outlets audience.

Bureau of Public Affairs

The Bureau of Public Affairs is located within the State Department and is used to disseminate relevant Government policy issues regarding foreign affairs with the global public. They are tasked with providing press briefings for the domestic and foreign press corps; pursuing media outreach, enabling Americans everywhere to hear directly from key Department officials through local, regional and national media interviews; and managing the State Department's web site at state.gov and developing web pages with up-to-date information about U.S. foreign policy to name a few.

Government Press Offices must coordinate their message with all of the mass media outlets summarized below:

Television

- Many different kinds of mass media can simulate transparency. But the dominant medium of political communication in our age – and therefore the dominant medium of political transparency – is television. To understand how television simulates transparency, we must understand how television shapes what we perceive. When we use television to understand politics, we see things in the way that television allows them to be seen. At the same time, television creates new forms of political reality that exist because they are seen on television. The House of Representatives first allowed television coverage in 1979, and the Senate followed by allowing C-SPAN to cover its proceedings in 1986.

Radio

- Radio, along with newspapers, was the main way that Americans received their news prior to the advent of the television. President Franklin Roosevelt held "fireside chats" to promote his political agenda through the radio. The radio, like the newspaper, has seen a steady decrease in the number of people listening to it to hear their news. However, radio is making a huge comeback with the rise of talk radio personalities such as Rush Limbaugh and Bill Maher who have built up a large fan base who use their forum for receiving news while driving in a car or sitting in a cubicle at work.

Newspapers

- Though the newspapers subscription base has steadily declined over the last decade due mainly to online competition and increased costs, many Americans still rely on the newspaper as their main source for getting news. Newspapers are most often published on a daily basis (budget cuts have forced some to print weekly), and they usually focus on one particular geographic area where a majority of their readers are located. Despite recent setbacks in circulation and profits, newspapers are still the most conventional and relevant outlet for news and other types of written journalism. Newspapers, like television, influence Americans views on many critical issues.

Magazines

- Magazines are another way that we receive news. Magazines cover many different political topics and there are magazines suited for every possible political leaning. Magazines are printed on a regular schedule, i.e. once a week, once a month, etc. and are typically financed through subscriptions and advertising.

Internet

- Websites are used by Government agencies/departments to provide information to the public about what it is they do. The primary website affiliated with the United States Government is www.usa.gov. However, the White House, individual agencies, and congressional offices all have their own websites. Some of the topics covered on Government websites include:

- Mission statements;
- Contact information;
- Relevant news pertaining to the official agency/department;
- An "About" section detailing what they do;
- An organizational chart; and
- Places to print out relevant information that is open to the public, i.e. stats and figures.

Tricks to Analyze Your Audience via the Internet

You should use an assortment of means to learn about and analyze your audience, including the following:

- Usability testing and research: Even though participant numbers are typically small, you can include open-ended questions during testing to gather demographic information and general impressions of your website.
- Customer satisfaction surveys: You can include open-ended questions to ask who your visitors are (e.g. academics, industry researchers, media, etc.), why they come to your site, and what they want to accomplish while visiting your site.
- Focus groups: Though participant numbers may be tiny, you can learn about what some typical visitors think about your site.
- Market research: There are lots of polling firms, media research companies, and non-profit and academic research centers that collect and analyze data about web users and behavior on the web.
- Web server logs: Server logs can provide some data about your visitors, such as country of origin.
- Email, phone calls, letters, and other contacts with the public: Find out the top requests coming into your agency by phone, email, and in-person service centers. If you have a central agency phone number (like a 1–800 number), get regular reports from the operators to find out what your audience is asking for and who they are.
- Input from other web content managers: Compare common audience groups with other agencies. This may help you develop the same kind of content from your agency and compliment what other agencies are doing.
- Analyze search data: Find out the terms your visitors are typing into your search engine. Make sure the terms they use are the same terms and labels you're using on your site. And make sure the most requested items are easily accessible from your homepage.

- **Commercial products that provide demographic data about your website visitors**: There are a variety of products that will collect and analyze demographic data about your website visitors.

Personas (Audience Profiles)

Personas have become an increasingly popular technique to help design websites based on audience needs and expectations. They are also sometimes called "customer profiles" or "audience profiles." Personas are hypothetical "stand–ins" for actual users that can help you envision real users, their goals, and expectations. Personas can help you synthesize all the information you collect about your users into clear, vivid portraits of your typical site users. Having these portraits is one way to help you (and your whole team) create web sites that really connect with your audience.

Blogs

A blog, short for weblog, is a website that contains entries by the author on a particular topic. Blogs are a forum for an individual to post opinions and provide news coverage and analysis on the bloggers topic of interest. They are organized in a reverse chronological order. Blogs are beginning to uproot traditional media reporting due to low overhead costs and accessibility. Blogs often combine texts, images, and links to other web pages or blogs that relate to the bloggers subject area. Blogs make Government more transparent by allowing more interaction between Government and its citizens. It is now common to see Members of Congress blogging on websites such as The Hill Blog (blog.thehill.com). The importance and popularity of blogging is emphasized below:

- Blogging was the number one technology trend of 2005, according to Fortune Magazine.
- In April 2007, blog search and measurement firm Technorati was tracking over 70 million blogs and reported seeing about 120,000 new blogs created each day. That's 1.4 blogs every second.
- According to the Pew Internet and American Life Project, 12 million Americans were blogging in 2006, with about 57 million reading blogs. Fifty–four percent of bloggers are under the age of 30.

Podcasts

Podcasting is a way of publishing MP3 audio files on the web so they can be downloaded onto computers or portable listening devices. Podcasting allows users to subscribe to a feed of new audio files using "podcatching" software (a type of aggregator), which occasionally checks for and downloads new audio files automatically. Any digital audio player or computer with audio-playing software can play podcasts. The benefit of podcasts is that users can listen to them whenever they want. Putting together a podcast is relatively easy and inexpensive and allows Government to communicate more effectively with the public. Many Government agencies are now using podcasts as a way of getting information out to the public in an audio format to supplement text.

The Government's resources which routinely deal with the media follows:

USDA

Director of Communications
Rm 402-A,
Whitten Building
Washington, D.C. 20250-1301

Commerce Department

1401 Constitution Ave., N.W.
Washington, D.C. 20230
202-482-4883

Contact: Office of Public Affairs
Phone: 202-482-4883
Fax: 202-482-5168
Web: http://www.commerce.gov/

Department of Defense

Media with queries during normal business hours should call (703) 697-5131.
The Press Desk Hours of Operation are 8:00 a.m. to 5:00 p.m. Monday - Friday

Public Inquiries
Questions from the public should be directed to Public Inquiries at (link to www.defense.gov/landing/comment.aspx) or call (703) 571-3343.

Department of Education

Reporters and education writers may contact the U.S. Department of Education press office by phone at (202) 401-1576 or by mail at

U.S. Department of Education Press Office,
400 Maryland Avenue, SW,
7E-247,
Washington, D.C. 20202.

Department of Energy

To subscribe to DOE's press release distribution list, send a plain-text email to listserv@vm1.hqadmin.doe.gov with the following command in the body of the email: Subscribe DOENEWS first-name; last-name.

Department of Energy Headquarters Press Office
Press Officer
U.S. Department of Energy
PA-20/Forrestal Building
1000 Independence Ave., SW.
Washington, D.C. 20585
Phone: 202-586-4940
Fax: 202-586-5823

Department of Health and Human Services
Public Affairs
Phone: 202-690-7850
Fax: 202-690-6247

Public Affairs
Room 647-D,
200 Independence Ave., S.W.,
Washington, D.C. 20201

Department of Homeland Security

Media Inquiries Headquarters

- Office of Public Affairs: 202-282-8010
- Office of Inspector General (OIG): 202-254-4100
- US-VISIT: 202-298-5200

Department of Housing and Urban Development

Office of Public Affairs
202-708-0980, ext-6628

Department of Interior

1849 C Street, N.W.
Washington, D.C. 20240
Phone: (202) 208-3100
E-Mail: feedback@ios.doi.gov

Department of Justice

Mail-Correspondence to the Department, including the Attorney General, may be sent to:

U.S. Department of Justice
950 Pennsylvania Avenue, NW
Washington, D.C. 20530-0001

Phone-Department of Justice Main Switchboard - 202-514-2000
Office of the Attorney General Public Comment Line - 202-353-1555
Email-AskDOJ@usdoj.gov

Department of Labor

Office of Public Affairs
U.S. Department of Labor
200 Constitution Ave. NW, Room S-1032
Washington, D.C. 20210
(202) 693-4676

Department of State

The Bureau of Public Affairs (PA)
(202) 647-2492
Office of Press Relations
Room 2109U.S. Department of State
Washington, D.C. 20520-6180

Department of Transportation

1200 New Jersey Ave, SE
Washington, D.C. 20590
202-366-4000

Department of Veteran Affairs

810 Vermont Ave., NW
Washington, D.C. 20420
(202) 461-7600

Department of the Treasury

1500 Pennsylvania Avenue, NW
Washington, D.C. 20220

General Information: (202) 622-2000
Fax: (202) 622-6415

Chapter 21

General Elements of Government Writing

Introduction

The vast majority of career, political, and elected Government officials prepare written materials on a daily basis. This implies that Government officials must possess the necessary writing skills to perform their official responsibilities.

OMB is particularly well-placed to judge effective Government writing. OMB evaluates written materials from all departments and agencies across the Government for a single constituent, the President of the United States. OMB is the only Governmental institution that has oversight responsibility in every area of federal governance: budget, management, finance, regulation, legislation, and policy. Indeed, OMB reviews more department/agency, Government. To write effectively, OMB implements the principal of neutral competence[1] in the review of written presentations, regardless of the instrument.

Neutral competence is the administrative objective of a merit-based bureaucracy. Such a bureaucracy should be "neutral" in the sense that it operates by objective, and not partisan standards. It should be "competent" in the sense that its employees are hired and retained on the basis of their talent and expertise.[2] The application of neutral competence in Government writing is straightforward: factual and objective in stating issues. This includes explaining differing positions, alternatives, and motives as a U.S. Government official and in recognition of the agency's institutional memory.

The importance of effective Government writing and key objectives for this book were discussed with former career senior executives from OMB. What follows are the observations from lessons learned during their careers. Don Gessaman, OMB's former Deputy Associate Director for National Security Division stated, "The official that writes well advances faster in the work place," but cautioned that, "the author of a poorly written document is often remembered as being incompetent and loses credibility as a result." Joseph Hezir, OMB's former Deputy Associate Director for Energy and Science made a different, equally important point: "Written communication is often the only way career staffers and managers have to relay information. Written communications are often incomplete because officials presume there will be follow up discussions and leave out essential information. Therefore, written communications must be concise and comprehensive in scope." He went on to say, "As an engineer and former analyst, presenting science and technology issues must be accurately written in plain English so that policy officials understand the decision criteria and can act without further briefings." Barry Anderson, former Deputy Director of both the OMB and the Congressional Budget Office (CBO), brought it all together when he stated, "In a world of ever-expanding sources of information, making your points succinctly is critical. Unfortunately, many education systems do not place sufficient emphasis on writing in a clear, concise, and to-the-point manner. But Understanding Effective Writing in the Federal Government can help Government staff and all those who deal with Government improve their abilities to communicate both inside and outside the Government."

Grammar and Style

The Government generally subscribes to the rules of grammar most of us learned during our youth. However, Government writing varies from basic grammar in certain situations. In addition, there are also differences in style depending on the instrument and purpose of the presentation.

---

[1] The concept of neutral competence was perhaps best described by the late American writer Herbert Kaufman as, "The ability to do the work of government expertly, and to do it according to explicit, objective standards rather than to personal or party or other obligations and loyalties."

[2] Patterson, Thomas E., "The American Democracy."

The following chart, Table 21.1, is a brief review of the most common grammatical rules which illustrates the different grammatical rules between Government and regular writing. It is important to note that there are many books which discuss grammar in detail. Do not rely on this brief summary alone. If you have more complex questions; refer to one of the common grammatical primers to address your needs.

Table 21.1

Grammatical Primer

General Rules	Chicago Style Manual	The Elements of Style	GPO Style Manual	DOD Manual for Written Material	DOJ Bureau of Justice Statistics Style Guide
Brackets: To enclose interpolations that are not specifically a part of the original quotation.	✓	✓	✓		✓
Capitalizations: Proper names, titles of people, organized bodies, legislative, administrative and judicial bodies, laws, religious terms, scientific names, and the first word of sentences.	✓		✓	✓	✓
Colons: Join two independent clauses with a colon if the second interprets or amplifies the first.	✓	✓	✓	✓	✓
Commas: Used to indicate a break in sentence structure.	✓	✓	✓	✓	✓

General Rules	Chicago Style Manual	The Elements of Style	GPO Style Manual	DOD Manual for Written Material	DOJ Bureau of Justice Statistics Style Guide
Compounds: Words are usually combined to express literal or non-literal unit ideas that would not be as clearly expressed in unconnected succession.	✓		✓		✓
Dashes: Used to mark a sudden break or abrupt change in thought.	✓	✓	✓		✓
Ellipses: Three asterisks or periods are used to denote an ellipsis within a sentence.			✓		✓
Exclamation points: Marks an outcry or an emphatic or ironic comment.	✓	✓	✓		✓
Hyphens: To connect the elements of compound words.	✓	✓	✓		✓
Italics: Used for emphasis, foreign words, and titles of publications.	✓		✓	✓	✓
Numerals: Percentages, decimal fractions, dates, time, and money are expressed in numbers.	✓	✓	✓		✓

General Rules	Chicago Style Manual	The Elements of Style	GPO Style Manual	DOD Manual for Written Material	DOJ Bureau of Justice Statistics Style Guide
Parentheses: To set off material that is less closely related to the rest of the sentence.	✓	✓	✓		✓
Periods: Used at the end of a declarative or an imperative sentence.	✓	✓	✓	✓	✓
Question marks: Used to mark a direct question and to express doubt.	✓	✓	✓		✓
Quotation marks: Used to enclose direct quotations.	✓	✓	✓	✓	✓
Semicolons: Used to separate clauses containing commas.	✓	✓	✓	✓	✓
Spelling: Webster's Third New International Dictionary.	✓				✓
Specific Government Rules					
Brackets: In transcripts, Congressional hearings, the Congressional record, testimony in court work, and used to enclose material that is not specifically a part of the original text.			✓	✓	✓

General Rules	Chicago Style Manual	The Elements of Style	GPO Style Manual	DOD Manual for Written Material	DOJ Bureau of Justice Statistics Style Guide
Capitalizations: A common noun title immediately following the name of a person or used alone as a substitute for it is capitalized. [e.g. President of the United States: the President]					
Titles of head or assistant head of National Government unit. [e.g. the Secretary]	✓		✓	✓	✓
Proper noun [e.g. the United States: the Republic; the Nation; the Union; the Government; Administration; also Federal and Federal Government]					

Editing

Editing and re-editing written presentations are critical to an effective final product, regardless of the instrument. Primary considerations for editing a document are:

General Review Strategies

- Read the text aloud.
- Read slowly to assess the likelihood of a positive reception of the text from your audience.
- Evaluate the flow of the text to ensure that your audience is not expected to either guess about a point or fill in a blank with logic.
- Proofread for one type of mistake at a time (for example, spelling first, then punctuation, then spacing).
- Proofread the body of the text and the heading separately.

Title

- It should state the purpose and rationale for the paper.
- It should be brief and clear.

Introduction

- It should clearly state the objectives to be achieved.
- The first paragraph should enable the audience to understand the progression of the presentation.

Areas of focus

- Sentences and phrases

  o Sentences should be clear and logical.
  o Sentence tone should be consistent throughout the presentation.
  o Sentence fragments should be completed.

- Vocabulary

  o Position important words where they are more effective.
  o Develop and use active and descriptive vocabulary.

- Nouns

  o Avoid adjective-noun strings [such as, employee compensation level evaluation procedure].
  o Avoid using vague nouns and verbs [such as, area, things, got, and get].

- Spell words correctly.[3]

---

[3] Landsberger, Joe, "Study Guide and Strategies," June, 2007 http://www.studygs.net/writing/revising.htm accessed June, 2010.

Chapter 22

Understanding your Stakeholder Audience

Introduction

Each federal department and agency prepares its written instruments for different audiences. In general terms, the audience will always include specific members of Congress, state and local elected, appointed, and career officials that have a clearly defined *stake* in the materials being written. In most, cases, there will be little overlap with non-Governmental organizations (NGO's) interested in your programs.

Agencies' websites are also taking on increased importance. To get the most utility from your Agency website, collecting information associated with who your audience is and what they are looking for when visiting your website is an important analysis. It is important to continuously analyze current website hits and your prospective audience. This information is critical when designing and writing your website for your audience.

This chapter explores the audiences associated with your department/agency's work. It begins by discussing Government's audience, or, power cluster, which is comprised of the stakeholders that are integral in making policy decisions within specific issue areas. The chapter focuses on who the key players are and the role they play within each power cluster as related to both policy and operational activities. It is also important to understand the comprehension level of your stakeholders, and this chapter closes with how to write to those various comprehensive levels.

Identifying Power Cluster Audiences

The Government's "audience" can also be defined as power clusters. "The Power Cluster Theory," was developed by Dr. Dan Ogden in 1971.[1] Ogden argued that public policy is not made in a vacuum, but is influenced by various groups that have a stake in the outcome.

Power clusters are composed by occupations, geographic regions, subject areas, issues, and the consideration of the issues of today. There are, for example, power clusters which deal with education, agriculture, defense, labor, manufacturing. Power clusters evolve around a subject area (e.g., energy, defense, etc.), around a geographic area, e.g. corn power clusters in the plains states, manufacturing in the north, etc. and specific areas of interest (e.g. Gulf of Mexico clean up following the BP oil spill). These clusters work to identify the issues, outline policy alternatives, propose new legislation, and implement policy.

Power clusters are constructed with the goal of shaping public policy and are nonpartisan in nature. Even though public officials are elected to a partisan party, i.e. Republican or Democrat, once in office, they participate in power clusters as public officials and work together with other stakeholders to form bipartisan public policy. People who are involved usually remain in a power cluster for a lifetime. Turmoil occurs when an outsider is thrown into a power cluster. Many of the difficulties that former Secretary of Agriculture, John Block, faced were due to the fact that he did not come through the ranks of the environmental-interior power cluster. Block, who was part of the agriculture power cluster, but at a very low level, was plucked from there and moved to the top of the agriculture power cluster. Since Block had not been anointed by the people at the top of the agriculture power cluster, they were unwilling to work with him.[2]

It is important when preparing documents to write to and respect all stakeholders within the power cluster. When writing Government documents that power clusters read, always:

- Demonstrate respect for all points of view;
- State how the Government has considered the positions of power cluster stakeholders; and
- Demonstrate the analytical progress the Government utilized to reach their perspective.

[1] Flinchbaugh, B.L. Who Makes Public Decisions? Who Makes Policy? Avaialbe at: http://www.jcep.org/reports/decisions.htm#power accessed June 2010.
[2] Ibid.

The groups comprising a power cluster include:

1. Executive Agencies;
2. Legislative Committees;
3. Special-Interest Groups;
4. Professionals;
5. Volunteers;
6. Attentive Public; and
7. Latent Public.

These groups, and the role they play in policymaking, are explored in detail below:

Executive Agencies

- The executive agencies include departments, administrations, bureaus, services, and commissions at each level of Government. Officials within these agencies become highly involved in specialized issues and are powerful forces in the policy decision-making process.

- Budget examiners from OMB, an executive agency, are involved in power clusters due to their specialization within particular policy issues such as agriculture or energy. Oftentimes the budget examiner will stay a part of the power cluster long after they have stopped working at OMB.

Legislative committees

- Legislative committees become part of the power cluster system due to the fact that they specialize in policy issues within their committee.

- Members of Congress seek assignments to committees that are most important to their constituents back home.

- Each appropriations subcommittee in Congress identifies itself with the power clusters of that policy issue and they work hand-in-hand with these clusters.

- The power clusters from these committees consist of Members of Congress, professional staff of the members that deal with the power cluster issue, and the professional staff of the standing committees and appropriations subcommittees.

- Senators are allowed to be a part of two standing committees and one minor committee. Senators use this opportunity to play a major role in the power cluster of their choosing.

- Members of the House of Representatives are limited to one standing committee but still seek committee assignments that will help their constituents thus enabling them to stay in power.

- Professional staff of the standing committees and appropriations subcommittees become major players in power clusters and gain political power due to their knowledge of the clusters issue. Though it does happen, committee professional staff are rarely transferred from one power cluster to another.

- Active participants of power clusters know the key committee staffers and many times work closer with them than with the Members themselves.

Special interest groups

- Every power cluster has a wide array of special interest groups affiliated with them.

- Special interest groups consist of large membership *service groups*, such as AARP that focus on issues that are important to their members, as well as *goal groups*, such as, the National Wildlife Federation, Sierra Club, etc., that are organized to protect special interests through some sort of political action.

- Power clusters also consist of *trade associations*; organized to protect and advocate for the public policy interests of service groups. Examples include the Nuclear Energy Institute, which works on behalf of nuclear power producers, and the National Automobile Manufacturers Association that advocates the interests of American car companies. Many times trade associations are composed of corporations, although some are not. The big trade associations have offices in Washington, D.C. so that they can be involved in the day to day interactions of the power clusters.

- Service groups, goal groups, and trade associations usually create a spin-off called a *political action committee* (PACs). PACs are responsible for raising money to donate to candidates running for public office and hence create additional influence within the power cluster for the group they represent.

The three groups mentioned above (executive agency personnel, legislative personnel, and the interest group personnel) made up the traditional "Iron Triangle."[3] Ogden added several other participants to the triangle to better describe who participates in the negotiations and the final decision-making process. The other components of a power cluster include:

---

[3] Grasty, Charles. Forces at War in Peace Conclave.http://query.nytimes.com/mem/archive-free/pdf?_r=2&res=9407E 1D71339E13ABC4052DFB7668382609EDE&oref=slogin Accessed July 2010.

Professionals

- Professionals are considered to be the people who make a living selling their expertise to the power cluster. These professionals include lawyers, lobbyists, and consultants. Many law firms in Washington, D.C. are established to specialize in a particular issue, such as environmental law, and work exclusively in that power cluster.

Volunteers

- Volunteers participate in power clusters in two main roles. First, there are a select few of highly influential volunteers who participate at the highest levels of policymaking. These are typically former members of Congress, wealthy businessmen, or ex-cabinet officers. The other groups of volunteers consist of those who volunteer their time and energy to influence public programs. An example would be Greenpeace, who uses volunteers to promote their message broadly to the public. These volunteers make up an important aspect of the power cluster.

Attentive public

- Power clusters are influenced greatly by informed citizens who typically pay close attention to one particular public policy area. Many times it is the cluster by which they make a living, i.e., farmers pay attention to agricultural policy.

- The attentive public can be easily mobilized to defeat a certain policy, e.g., the gay/lesbian community's attempt to secure same-sex marriage rights.

Latent public

- Most power clusters typically ignore the latent public which makes up the largest segment of the public. These are the people who feel that they have no voice in the public policy arena and stay out of the politics of shaping policy in America. With the right amount of effort, a key player in the power cluster can shift from the latent public to the attentive public. An example would be the People for the Ethical Treatment of Animals (PETA) which attempts to sway opinion in favor of animal rights.

Government and Public Relations

Public relations and publicity are not synonymous, but many public relations campaigns include provisions for publicity. Publicity is the distribution of information to gain public awareness for a product, person, service, cause, or organization, and can be seen as a result of effective public relations planning. Public relations is a field concerned with maintaining public image for high-profile people, commercial businesses and organizations, non-profit associations or programs. More recently in Government public relations, press offices are using technology as their focal tool to get their messages across to their target audiences. With the establishment of social networks and blogs, the Government's public relations professionals are able to send direct messages through these mediums that attract their target audiences. Methods used to find out what is appealing to target audiences include the use of surveys, conducting research, or focus groups. Tactics are the ways to attract target audiences by using the information gathered about that audience and directing a message to them using tools such as social media (e.g. Twitter, Facebook, Blogs, etc.).

Audience Targeting

A fundamental technique used in Government public relations is to identify the target audience, and to tailor every message to appeal to that audience. It can be a local, nationwide or worldwide audience, but it is more often a segment of a population. A good elevator pitch can help tailor messaging to each target audience. Marketers often refer to socio-economic-driven "demographics," such as "white males 18-49," but in public relations an audience is more fluid, being whoever someone wants to reach, or, in the new paradigm of value-based networked social groups, the values based social segment, e.g., the tea party movement.

An alternative and more simplistic approach uses stakeholders theory to identify people who have a stake in a given institution or issue. All audiences are stakeholders (or presumptive stakeholders), but not all stakeholders are audiences.

Sometimes the interests of differing audiences and stakeholders common to a public relations effort necessitate the creation of several distinct, but complementary, messages. This is not always easy to do, and sometimes – especially in politics – a spokesperson or client says something to one audience that creates dissonance with another audience or group of stakeholders.

Understanding your Audience's Reading Level

Understanding who that audience is, is important as demonstrated above in the cluster/stakeholder discussions. However, once identified you need to write effectively to each group's level of understanding. There is no precise method for testing your audience's comprehension level but writers can make informed guesses based on their audience's knowledge of the issue, age, education level, and profession.

Flesch-Kincaid

There are several tests for determining the readability of your writing, however, the most common is the Flesch-Kincaid test. The *Flesch–Kincaid readability tests* are designed to indicate comprehension difficulty when reading a passage of contemporary academic English. There are two tests, the *Flesch Reading Easiness*, and the *Flesch–Kincaid Grade Level*. Although they use the same core measures (word length and sentence length), they have different weighing factors, so the results of the two tests correlate approximately inversely: a text with a comparatively high score on the Reading Ease test should have a lower score on the Grade Level test. Both systems were devised by Rudolf Flesch.

In the Flesch Reading Ease test, higher scores indicate material that is easier to read; lower numbers mark passages that are more difficult to read. The formula for the Flesch Reading Ease Score (FRES) test is:

(total words/total sentences) – (total syllables/total words)

Scores can be interpreted as shown in the table below.

Score	Notes
90.0–100.0	easily understandable by an average 11-year-old student
60.0–70.0	easily understandable by 13- to 15-year-old students
0.0–30.0	best understood by university graduates

Political Savy and Politics

Closely related to tailoring your message to your audience's reading level is the ability to compose the message that will gain the most positive reception by that audience. A Government official employing "Political Savvy" when writing to a specific audience understands and utilizes the dynamics of power, organization, and decision-making to achieve objectives.

When elected officials or career bureaucrats make a speech or issue a press release on behalf of their department, they need to use political savvy and understand who their intended audience is comprised of and then be able to adjust their writing style to the audience that will be reviewing the written instrument.

Key behaviors attributable to someone with political savvy:

- Understands the process of how decisions are made.
- Identifies the key decision-makers and the people who influence them.

- Identifies ways to increase visibility and influence by participation in formal and informal activities.
- Understands the interests, motivations, and agendas of others.
- Promotes the interests of other key decision-makers and influencers in order to obtain support for one's own agenda.
- Understands the roles people play in an organization and uses that understanding to achieve objectives.
- Establishes alliances with people of power and influence in order to influence decisions and outcomes.
- Accurately anticipates changes in the political climate and plan and execute strategy and tactics based on that anticipation.

Proficiency levels associated with someone with political savvy:

- **Expert:** Models, leads, trains, and motivates multiple levels of personnel to be excellent in political know-how.

- **Advanced:** Even in the most difficult or complex situations, understands how decisions are made and who makes and influences them, understands and promotes the interests of others to obtain their support, understands the roles people play in an organization and uses that understanding to achieve objectives, and establishes alliances to influence outcomes.

- **Intermediate:** Usually understands how decisions are made and who makes and influences them, understands and promotes the interests of others to obtain their support, understands the roles people play in an organization and uses that understanding to achieve objectives, and establishes alliances to influence outcomes.

- **Basic:** Sometimes understands how decisions are made and who makes and influences them, understands and promotes the interests of others to obtain their support, understands the roles people play in an organization and uses that understanding to achieve objectives, and establishes alliances to influence outcomes.

- **Awareness:** Demonstrates common knowledge or an understanding of political know-how, but may avoid or miss opportunities to understand and utilize political dynamics to achieve objectives.[4]

The days of saying different things to different audiences are over. In the past, politicians would have several different speeches prepared for different audiences. Though this still takes place, it should not. With voice/video recorders on cell phones being the norm these days, politicians and bureaucrats need to be cognizant of the fact

---

[4] Available at: http://hhsu.learning.hhs.gov/competencies/leadership-political_savvy.asp accessed June 2010.

that whatever they say or do, can and will end up on YouTube and the 24 hour news cycle for the world to see and hear.

When politicians do not understand their audience, they make political gaffes. It happens all of the time. A few political blunders follow:

- President Barack Obama had to repair the damage from remarks caught on tape that he made at a private California fundraiser during his primary campaign in 2008. President Obama, in describing why he was having difficulty winning over working-class voters, said economic woes had led some voters to get "bitter and cling to guns or religion or antipathy to people who aren't like them."

- At George W. Bush's final White House press conference as President, he made the following ill advised comment: "Why did the financial collapse have to happen on my watch? It's just pathetic, isn't it, self-pity?"

- In 2001, talking energy policy at the Annual Meeting of the Associated Press in Canada, former Vice President Dick Cheney said, "Conservation may be a sign of personal virtue but it is not a sufficient basis for a sound, comprehensive energy policy."

- In a "Today Show" interview in April of 2009, Vice President Joe Biden, speaking about tips for avoiding swine flu, caused a lot of unnecessary fear when he said, "I wouldn't go anywhere in confined places now. ... When one person sneezes it goes all the way through the aircraft. That's me. I would not be, at this point, if they had another way of transportation, suggesting they ride the subway."

- After being asked whether he follows NASCAR racing in February of 2012, President hopeful Mitt Romney said, "I have some friends who are NASCAR team owners."

Chapter 23

Sources of Resource Information and Bibliography

This chapter provides sources of information which can be found online to enhance the quality of written instruments. It also articulates how social networks expand outreach to stakeholders and facilitates receipt of feedback from those stakeholders. The United States Government condones the use of the internet to advertise position, promote interagency collaboration, and maintain job related connections between geographically dispersed organizations. The Government also encourages federal employees to locate up-to-date subject matter to improve the quality of their written instruments. Even though the Departments and Agencies have their own internet/social media related policies, the following guidelines below generally apply:

- **Official Agency Business** – social media is employed to implement or to articulate policy interests in writing.
- **Professional Interest** – social media is used to enhance an employee's job responsibilities and professional duties by preparing written communication on an externally driven site. For instance, a Facebook page is a vehicle that can be written to inform employees and stakeholders of new developments.
- **Personal Interest** – social media is also used to address personal interests. Such interests are not necessarily related to an employee's job responsibilities. The government permits personal activities given its sensitivity to an employee's

rights under Article 1 of the Constitution. For instance, an employee checking their Facebook account, tweeting with their Twitter account, or watching a video on Youtube during one of their designated breaks during work hours is permissible. They are also permitted to maintain blogs associated with a hobby outside of work hours.

- **Third-Party Privacy Policy** – a requirement that third-party websites engaged with stakeholders must consider the third-party's privacy policy to ensure that the website or application is appropriate for government use; further, any changes to the third-party's privacy policy should be monitored to ensure any new risks are evaluated.
- **External Links** – employees using a *pop-up* to alert a stakeholder of a link directed to a non-government website must be explained to stakeholders that the link is government policy.
- **Embedded Applications** – third-party applications incorporated or embedded on an official government domain must be disclosed in the event that there is third-party involvement. The government activities must be clear and approved in a memorandum of agreement disclosing privacy policy.
- **Agency Branding** – branding must distinguish the government's activities from those of non-government stakeholders by adding the agency's seal or emblem to its profile page on a social media website.
- **Information collection** – information collected by a third-party website or application is limited only to information necessary for the proper performance of governmental responsibilities.

If more specific *Do's and Don'ts* are required, Departments and Agencies have exhaustive guidance in this area.

INTERNET SEARCH ENGINES

Search Engine - A web search engine is a software program that search documents for specified keywords and returns a list of the documents where the keywords were found. Search engines are a general class of programs; however, the term is most often used to specifically describe systems like Google, Bing, and Yahoo! Search engines utilize automated software applications (referred to as robots, bots, or spiders) that travel along the Web, following links from page to page, site to site. The information gathered by the spiders is used to create a searchable index of the Web.

Web Portal - Web portals are organized gateways that help to structure the access to information found on the Internet. Much more than a simple search engine, they usually include customizable access to data such as stock reports, local, regional, and national news, and email services. Most of the better-known portals are commonly identified as search engines, although they offer much more than simply the ability to search the Internet. Examples of popular web portals are: Facebook, YouTube, Wikipedia, and MSN.

While there are many web portals designed for general use by consumers, there are also portals that are created for the use of authorized personnel only. This is the case with the corporate or business portal. Where access is limited to those with login credentials issued and managed by the employer. This allows employees who are traveling to access corporate servers and connect with documents and other data saved on the server. Corporate portals may also be configured to allow consumers to browse, search, and purchase goods and services from the company.

Government Search Engines and Directories

Government portals are both search engines and portals. They are unique in that, as with the corporate model, users must have authorized access to the page in the form of login credentials, security clearance, and other proprietary access codes. This helps to ensure that employees can only gain access to data that is considered within their scope of responsibility, and effectively prevents the use of proprietary data by unauthorized individuals.

Government personnel use the search engines to access web portals through which actual resource information is collected. There are a number of government portals that are of invaluable assistance to government employees preparing: White papers, testimony, decision memoranda, etc.

Government employees should be aware that some internet sources are unreliable. The following are unreliable sources because they require confirmation with a reliable source:

- Wikipedia, although this site is a good starting point for finding initial ideas about a topic, some of their information and attached resources may not be reliable,
- Blogs, tweets.
- Personal websites.
- Forums.
- Questionable sites created by organizations that may have political or biased agendas.
- Self-published sources.
- Online sources with an Uniform Resources Locator (URL) that ends in (Hyper Text Markup Language (html), which is the basic building blocks of web pages.

Some online sources with an URL that ends in .com typically are websites of companies that conduct their business over the internet. Some of these sites are unreliable because they have hidden agendas.

Reliable search engines or web-portals are invaluable information sources to improve the quality of written instruments and are listed and described below:

I. National Archives and Records Administration (NARA)[1]

The National Archives and Records Administration (NARA) is the official records archive for the U.S. NARA is responsible for the preservation and documentation of government and historical records. In addition, NARA maintains the official acts of Congress, presidential proclamations and executive orders, and federal regulations. However, of all the documents created by the U.S. Federal Government less than 5% is deemed important for legal or historical reasons that they are kept by NARA forever.

II. USA.gov[2]

USA.gov is the official web portal of the United States Federal Government. USA.gov provides links to every federal agency website. The site is maintained by the Office of Citizens Services and Innovative Technologies in the General Services Administration (GSA) and also includes the Spanish-language web portal GobiernoUSA.gov.

USA.gov's search engine supports transparency of government information by providing access to government web pages from U.S. federal, state, local, tribal, and territorial governments. Search engine results are provided by Bing but managed technically and editorially in-house. In addition, all U.S. government agencies can apply through the USA Services Affiliate Program to install the Search.USA.gov search capability on its own pages, thus allowing agencies at all levels to provide website searching for their own users.

USA.gov also provides resources for users to access information on an array of topics such as local, state, federal and tribal officials contact information; reference and general government information; environmental, energy, and agriculture issues; science and technology; public safety and law; jobs and education; government sales and auction and, many more resource options.

III. Agency Index[3]

Agency Index is a web portal managed as a courtesy of Washburn University School of Law. The portal provides links to Federal Agencies' homepages, publications, organizational charts, electronic forms, and administrative decisions. This allows users the ability to save time conducting research by eliminating excess digging for resource information on Agency web sites.

Agency Index provides a single page with all of the links to the Executive Office of the President, Federal Agencies, Administrative Law, Congress, Federal Courts, Supreme Court, Federal Legislation, and court updates. In addition, there is another single page that lists legal resources by subject, as well as legal journals, legal forms, legal institutes, legal indexes and access to legal publications.

---

[1] www.archives.gov
[2] www.usa.gov
[3] www.washlaw.edu

IV.   The Catalog of U.S. Government Publications (CGP)[4]

The Catalog of U.S. Government Publications (CGP) is the search engine for electronic and print publications from the legislative, executive, and judicial branches of the U.S. Federal Government. These publications encompass the National Bibliography of U.S. Government Publications. The CGP contains descriptive records for historical and current publications and provides direct links to those publications that are available online.

The CGP has access to more than 500,000 records generated since July 1976 and is updated daily. Eventually, the catalog will grow to include records for publications dating back to the late 1800s. The CGP site offers direct links to online versions of publications from cataloging records. The website also provides a "Locate a Library" feature within each record to find a nearby Federal depository where a particular publication or expert assistance can be found; a robust search engine; basic, advanced, and expert search options; and, searches can be narrowed to specific collections, or formats, such as maps, Congressional, or Internet publications.

CGP is the respected national source for descriptive and subject cataloging for Federal Government documents.

V.   GovSpot.gov[5]

GovSpot.com is a search engine that was designed to simplify the search for the best government resources online. This website is a non-partisan government information portal and offers a high-utility collection of top government and civic resources hand-selected for quality, content and utility.

GovSpot.com is efficient in providing the best government web sites and documents, facts and figures, news, and political information for its users. Site users can also access information on the federal government, local governments, state governments, world government, and government employees. GovSpot offers information on consumer information, government documents, grants, historical documents, statistics, education, defense, intelligence, elections, political parties, polls/opinion, political science, business, commerce, economics, government contracting, taxes, environmental issues, transportation, science and technology, world government, world leaders, and international affairs. These features provide a wealth of resource information for individuals seeking to enhance their knowledge of the Federal Government.

VI.   INFOMINE[6]

INFOMINE is a virtual library of Internet resources utilized regularly at various universities. It contains internet resources including databases, electronic journals,

---

[4] www.gpo.gov
[5] www.govspot.com
[6] www.infomine.ucr.edu

electronic books, bulletin boards, mailing lists, online library card catalogs, articles, and directories of researchers.

INFOMINE was formed by the librarians from the University of California, Wake Forest University, California State University, and the University of Detroit-Mercy. Librarians from other colleges and universities have also contributed to building INFOMINE.

INFOMINE uses the following categories to organize the information found on its site:

- Biological, Agriculture, and Medical Sciences.
- Business Economics.
- Cultural Diversity.
- E-Journals.
- Government Information.
- Maps & GIS.
- Physical Sciences, Engineering Computing, and Math.
- Social Sciences and Humanities.
- Visual and Performing Arts.

WEBSITES

A website is a set of related web pages served from a single web domain. A website is hosted on at least one web server, accessible via a network such as the internet or a private local area network through an internet address known as a uniform resource locator or also known as a URL. All publically accessible websites collectively constitute the World Wide Web.

DATABASES

A database is an organized collection of data. The data are typically organized to model relevant aspects of reality in a way that supports processes requiring this information. Here are a few databases that are used by the U.S. Government personnel.

I.   OPMs Data Analysis Group Information Resources

OPM through its Data Analysis Group (DAG) provides OPM management, the President, Congress, and many other customers such as, the Government Accountability Office, the Merit Systems Protection Board, the Congressional Research Service, the media, educational institutions, and many agencies with data and analysis from its Enterprise Human Resources Integration-Statistical Data mart (EHRI-SDM) and other data sources (113 process, Work Years, and Personnel Costs). This generally takes the form of sending customers raw data, summaries of the raw data, or special reports. Data available to OPM through its EHRI-SDM covers over 2 million Federal civilian employees and has information concerning occupations, agency of employment, salaries, promotions, awards, and many other transactions concerning Federal civilian employees. The Data Analysis Group produces special and recurring reports on a variety of subjects and those reports are available on this website. DAG also processes certain Freedom of Information Requests and customized requests received through its email boxes. DAG uses EHRI-SDM data to provide analysis of policy options (direct hiring authorities, accelerated promotions available to certain occupations, various aspects of hiring reform, veteran hiring, and diversity information), legislative changes, and trends in Federal employment.

II.   Federal Digital Systems[7]

The U.S Government Printing Office (GPO) operates Federal Digital Systems which provides publishing and dissemination services for the official and authentic government publications to Congress, Federal agencies, Federal depository libraries, and other stakeholders.

Federal Digital Systems uses resource information on the following topics:

- Code of Federal Regulations.
- Compilation of Presidential Documents.
- Congressional Bills.
- Congressional Documents.
- Congressional Hearings.
- Congressional Record.
- Congressional Reports.
- Constitution of the United States of America: Analysis and Interpretation.
- Economic Indicators.
- Federal Register.
- Public and Private Laws.
- United States Code.
- United States Courts Opinions.

III.   The Library of Congress-Thomas[8]

THOMAS was launched in January of 1995, at the inception of the 104th Congress. The leadership of the 104th Congress directed the Library of Congress to make federal legislative information freely available to the public. Since that time THOMAS has expanded the scope of its offerings to include the features and content listed below.

- Bills, Resolutions.
- Activity in Congress.
- Congressional Record.
- Schedules, Calendars.
- Committee Information.
- Presidential Nominations.

---

[7] www.gpo.gov/fdsys
[8] www.thomas.loc.gov

- Treaties.
- Government Resources.

IV.   The U.S. Congressional Serial Set/American State Papers[9]

The U.S. Congressional Serial Set (Serial Set) began publication with the 15th Congress, 1st Session. The Serial Set contains the House and Senate Documents as well as House and Senate Reports. The reports contained are from congressional committees dealing with proposed legislation and issues under investigation. Documents include reports of executive departments and independent organizations, reports of special investigations made for Congress, and annual reports of non-governmental organizations.

The serial number is a unique number applied to each book in the series of congressional publications running consecutively from the 15th Congress. The serial number may be useful for locating items, but not for reference. Documents and reports can be located using the volume or serial number but should be cited using the publication number and Congress and session number.

The documents and reports series have three numbers:

- An individual report or document-publication number;
- A volume number of each series for each session of Congress; and
- The serial number.

V.   Education Resources Information Center (ERIC)[10]

The Education Resources Information Center (ERIC) is an online digital library of education research and information. ERIC is sponsored by the Institute of Education Sciences of the Department of Education. ERIC provides a comprehensive, user-friendly, searchable, Internet-based bibliographic and full-text database of education research and information for educators, researchers, and the general public.

ERIC provides access to more than 1.3 million bibliographic records (citations, abstracts, and other pertinent data) of journal articles and other education-related materials, with new records added weekly. A key component of ERIC is its collection of grey literature in education, which is largely available in full text in Adobe PDF format. Approximately one quarter of the complete ERIC Collection is available in full text. Materials with no full text available can often be accessed using links to publishers and/or library holdings.

The ERIC Collection contains records for a variety of publication types, including:

- Articles from scholarly journals.
- Books.

---

[9] www.memory.loc.gov
[10] www.eric.ed.gov

- Research syntheses.
- Conference papers.
- Technical reports.
- Dissertations.
- Policy papers.

ERIC provides the public with a centralized web site for searching the ERIC Collection, managing search results, and submitting materials to be considered for inclusion in the collection. Users can also access the collection through commercial database vendors, statewide and institutional networks, and Internet search engines. To help users find the information they are seeking, ERIC produces a controlled vocabulary, the Thesaurus of ERIC Descriptors.

VI.   The Federal Reserve Archival System for Economic Research (FRASER)[11]

The Federal Reserve Archival System for Economic Research (FRASER) is a data preservation and accessibility project of the Federal Reserve Bank of St. Louis. FRASER's mission is to safeguard and provide easy access to the nation's economic history, particularly the history of the Federal Reserve System, through digitization of documents related to the U.S. financial system. FRASER offers digital access to historic policy documents and data to scholars, economists, analysts, students, and interested observers of the U.S. economy.

FRASER preserves and provides access to economic and banking data and policy documents. Various types of documents have been digitized, including:

- Publications of the Board of Governors of the Federal Reserve System.
- Publications of District Federal Reserve Banks.
- Statements and speeches of Federal policymakers.
- Archival materials of Federal policymakers.
- Statistical releases.
- Government data publications.
- Congressional hearings.
- Reports by various professional financial organizations.

LIBRARIES

Libraries are internally located in all Government Departments and Agencies. However, there are also libraries external to Departments and Agencies which are similarly available as information sources considered credible resources to improve an employee's written instruments.

---

[11] www.fraser.stlouisfed.org

Chapter 23: Sources of Resource Information and Bibliography

I. Federal Libraries[12]

The Federal Library and Information Network (FEDLINK) is an organization of federal agencies working together to achieve optimum use of the resources and facilities of federal libraries and information centers by promoting common services, coordinating and sharing available resources, and providing continuing professional education for federal library and information staff. FEDLINK also serves as a forum for discussion of the policies, programs, procedures and technologies that affect federal libraries and the information services they provide to their agencies, to the Congress, the federal courts and the general public.

The Federal Library provides resources from e-government to disaster planning to outsourcing and content management. FEDLINK and its members have developed and collected resources on those issues most critical for federal libraries and information centers. FEDLINK offers the following features:

- Bibliographic Framework Initiative (BFI).
- Shared Repository Collection.
- Federal Library Directory: A listing and map of U.S. federal libraries around the world Federal Government Strategic Sourcing of Information: A Federal Research Division Report and Report Archives.
- Affiliated Library Resources.
- Research Agenda.
- Handbook of Federal Librarianship.
- Content Management Resources.

II. Library of Congress[13]

The Library of Congress is the research library of the United States Congress. The Library's primary mission is researching inquiries made by members of Congress through the Congressional Research Service. Although the Library is open to the public, only Library employees, members of Congress, Supreme Court Justices and other high-ranking government officials may check out books. In addition, as the de facto Library of the U.S., the Library of Congress promotes literacy initiatives and American literature through several projects such as the American Folklore Center, American Memory, and the Center for the Book and Poet Laureate.

The Main Reading Room in the Thomas Jefferson Building is the principal reference and book service point for the Library's general collections. The general collections include books, pamphlets, and bound or non-current periodicals in all languages except some that use non-roman alphabets and in all areas of the classification scheme except:

- Law.
- Music.

[12] www.loc.gov/flicc/fedlink/index
[13] www.loc.gov/

- Maps and atlases.

III.   Academic Libraries[14]

Academic libraries are attached to an institution of higher education which serves two complementary purposes to support the school's curriculum, and to support the research of the university faculty and students. Academic libraries are identified by the post-secondary institution of which they are a part and provide the following:

- An organized collection of printed or other materials or a combination of the two;
- A staff trained to provide and interpret such materials as required to meet the informational, cultural, recreational, or educational needs of students and faculty;
- An established schedule in which services of the staff are available to students and faculty; and
- The physical facilities necessary to support such a collection, staff, and schedule.

Academic libraries must determine a focus for collection development since comprehensive collections are not -practical. Librarians do this by identifying the needs of the faculty and student body, as well as the mission and academic programs of the college or university. When there are particular areas of specialization in academic libraries these are often referred to as niche collections. These collections are often the basis of a special collection department and may include original papers, artwork, and artifacts written or created by a single author or about a specific subject.

IV.   Corporate Libraries[15]

Corporate libraries help to organize and disseminate information throughout the organization for its own benefit. They often times support areas in the company relating to finance, administration, marketing, and technical specialization. In terms of size, they are seldom very small. The information services provided by corporate libraries save employees time, and can aid in competitive intelligence work.

The Corporate Library offers annual historical data captures. Information can include:

- Corporate Board Structure and Independence;
- Director Positions and Committee Assignments;
- Executive Compensation;
- Director Compensation;
- Audit Fees;

[14]   Curzon, Susan; Jennie Quinonez-Skinner (9). "Academic Libraries". Encyclopedia of Library and Information Sciences. doi:10.1081/E-ELIS3-120044525. Retrieved 10 September 2013.
[15]   Prusak, Laurence, and Matarazzo, James M. "The Value of Corporate Libraries: The 1995 Survey." SpeciaList 18, no. 1 (1995): 9–15.

- Corporate Ownership; and
- Takeover Defenses.

OTHER INFORMATION SOURCES

I. Research Papers and Methodology

Booth, Wayne, Gregory G. Colomb, and Joseph M. Williams. *The Craft of Research.* Chicago, IL: University of Chicago Press (1995).

Research & Writing Skills Success in 20 Minutes a Day. New York, NY: LearningExpress (2003).

Lutz, Jean A. and C. Gilbert Storms. *The Practice of Technical and Scientific Communication: Writing in Professional Contexts.* Westport, CT: Ablex Publishing (1998).

Scanlan, Christopher. *Reporting and Writing: Basics for the 21st Century.* New York, NY: Oxford University Press, USA (2002).

II. Scientific Papers and Methodology

Blum, Deborah and Mary Knudson, eds. *A Field Guide for Science Writers: the Official Guide of the National Association of Science Writers.* New York, NY: Oxford University Press (1997).

Briscoe, Mary Helen. *Preparing Scientific Illustrations: a Guide to Better Posters, Presentations, and Publications.* 2nd ed. New York, NY: Springer Publications (1996).

Council of Biology Editors. *Scientific Style and Format: the CBE Manual for Authors, Editors, and Publishers.* 6th ed. Cambridge, MA: Cambridge University Press (1994).

Davis, Martha. *Scientific Papers and Presentations.* San Diego, CA: Academic Press (1997).
Day, Robert A. *How to Write and Publish a Scientific Paper.* 4th ed. Phoenix, AZ: Oryx Press (1994).

Porush, David. *A Short Guide to Writing about Science.* New York, NY: HarperCollins (1995).

Turk, Christopher. *Effective Writing: Improving scientific, technical and business communication.* 2nd ed. New York, NY: E&FN Spon (1989).

Lutz, Jean A. and C. Gilbert Storms. *The Practice of Technical and Scientific Communication: Writing in Professional Contexts.* Westport, CT: Ablex Publishing (1998).

III. Policy Analysis

Geffner, Andrea B. *Business English: A Complete Guide to Developing an Effective Business Writing Style.* 3rd ed. Hauppauge, NY: Barron's Educational Series (1998).

Hall, Mary S. and Susan Howlett. *Getting Funded: The Complete Guide to Writing Grant Proposals.* 3rd ed. Portland, OR: Continuing Education Press (2003).

Lauchman, Richard. *Plain Style: Techniques for Simple, Concise, Emphatic Business Writing.* New York, NY: AMACOM (1993).

Miner, Lynn E., Jeremy T. Miner and Jerry Griffith. *Proposal Planning and Writing.* 2nd ed. Phoenix, AZ: Oxford Press (1998).

Royal, Brandon. *The Little Red Writing Book: 20 Powerful Principles of Structure, Style and Readability*. Cincinnati, OH: Writer's Digest Book (2004).

Sant, Tom. *Persuasive Business Proposals: Writing to Win More Customers, Clients, and Contracts.* New York, NY: AMACOM (2003).

National Renewable Energy Laboratory (NREL) www.nrel.gov/analysis/policy_analysis.html

Policy Analysis Republican Study Committee (RSC) www.rsc.scalise.house.gov/policyanalysis

New NATO Policy Guidelines on Counterterrorism: Analysis. www.ntis.gov

IV. Budget, Finance and Pricing Metrics

Allison, Libby and Miriam F. Williams. *Writing for the Government (Technical Communication).* New York, NY: Longman (2007).

Bennion, Francis A. R. *Understanding Common Law Legislation: Drafting and Interpretation.* New York, NY: Oxford University Press (2005).

Kimble, Joseph. *Memorandum: Re: Guiding Principles for Restyling the Civil Rules. Committee on rules of Practice and Procedures of the Judicial Conference of the United States.* (February 21, 2005).

Myersm, Judith G. *Banishing Bureaucratese: Using Plain Language in Government Writing.* Vienna, VA: management Concepts (2001).

Page, Steve. *7 Steps to Better Written Policies and Procedures.* Westerville, OH: Process Improvement (2001).

Redman, Eric. *The Dance of Legislation.* Seattle, WA: University of Washington Press (2001).

A Manual of Style: A Guide to the Basics of Good Writing. Washington, DC: United States Government Printing Office (1993).

Budget Pricing Guide Estimating Techniques Used http://www.usbr.gov/uc/progact/salinity.

Arizona State Procurement Office. http://www.spo.az.gov/docs/ADMIN_POLICY. State Water Resources. www.swrcb.ca.gov.

This section provides information on useful writing resources which can be found online.

V. General Writing Resources

Free Writing Courses
http://www.writer2writer.com/courses.htm

Effective Writing
http://www.auroramae.com/blog/

Exercises from Legal Writing in Plain English
http://press-pubs.uchicago.edu/garner/

Paradigm: Online Writing Assistant
http://www.powa.org/

Writing Tips at Writing Center, Inc.
http://www.writingcenter.com/writingtips.htm

Writing for Change
http://www.fahamu.org/WFCEng/sitemap.html

Effective Writing Tips
http://chppm-www.apgea.army.mil/imo/DDB/writ-tip.htm

Help with Writing Research Papers
http://mason.gmu.edu/%7Emontecin/writ-pap.htm

VI. Government and Legal Writing

Federal Register: Writing Resources for Federal Agencies
http://www.archives.gov/federal-register/write/index.html

Plain Language: Improving Communications from the Federal Government to the Public
http://www.plainlanguage.gov/index.cfm

Alaska Department of Law Document Library - Drafting Manual for Administrative Regulations http://www.law.state.ak.us/doclibrary/drafting_manual.html

Learn How to Write Proposal and Get Proposal Writing Tutorials
http://www.captureplanning.com/

Online Writing Lab offered from universities in the U.S.

Purdue's Online Writing Lab (OWL)
http://owl.english.purdue.edu/owl/

University of Florida's Online Writing Lab
http://web.cwoc.ufl.edu/owl/index.html

Guide to Grammar and Writing
http://grammar.ccc.commnet.edu/grammar/

Chapter 24

Proper Use of Government Acronyms

The use of acronyms in the Federal Government has become more prolific over time. The Federal bureaucracy continues to invent acronyms everyday in order to shorten their written communication. As a result of this, no printed list of acronyms can ever truly be complete. Still, what is printed here is a broad list of the major acronyms encountered in Government writing. We have organized them into fourteen respective categories:

1. Federal departments, agencies and offices;
2. Boards and commissions;
3. Programs;
4. Laboratories;
5. Schools;
6. Partnerships;
7. Inter-agency groups;
8. Institutes;
9. Publications;
10. Councils;
11. Commands;
12. Networks;

13. Banks; and
14. Special terms.

Most of the acronyms listed here are unique to Government. Because senior career management has concurred with their acceptability, they may be used in the Government's written instruments. If you fail to find an acronym within the following chart,[1] there are several online sources that may be of help and these are listed at the conclusion of this chapter. Additionally, many Government departments and agencies compile and list their own unique acronyms on their websites.

There are few rules when it comes to writing with acronyms but if they are not followed, acronyms will inhibit a reader's ability to absorb information and lead to frustration with the document as a whole. To write effectively with acronyms:

- Spell out the entire title on first use in the document, or in the chapter/section for longer documents, and then introduce the acronym in parentheses. Once the acronym has been defined in this manner, the acronym may be used as a stand-alone symbol. Do not first present the acronym and then provide its meaning in parentheses. For example:

  o **Acceptable:** Standards for drinking water quality in the United States are set under the Safe Drinking Water Act (SDWA).
  o **Not Acceptable:** Department of Defense (DoD) press advisories can be obtained by contacting the Public Affairs office.

- If your document contains numerous acronyms, consider including a separate glossary so the reader can quickly and easily refer to a common source.

- When introducing an acronym for the first time, attempt to not make it possessive or plural as it will be more clear to the reader what you mean when you refer back to that acronym. For example, instead of writing, "The Department of Energy's (DOE's) budget for the upcoming fiscal year targets clean energy," write "The upcoming budget for the Department of Energy (DOE) focuses on clean energy."

- To make an acronym plural, add a lower case "s" to it. For example, "SSNs" for social security numbers. To make an acronym possessive, add an apostrophe "s" as in "DOE's budget."

---

[1] Please send any acronyms we have omitted to acronym@eopfoundation.org!

208

DEPARTMENTS

	Name	Acronym
1.	Department of the Army	DA
2.	Department of Economic and Social Affairs	DESA
3.	Department of Homeland Security	DHS
4.	Department of Health and Human Services	DHHS
5.	Department of Commerce	DOC
6.	Department of Defense	DOD
7.	Department of Defense Education Activity	DODEA
8.	Department of Energy	DOE
9.	Department of the Interior	DOI
10.	Department of Justice	DOJ
11.	Department of Labor	DOL
12.	Department of State	DOS
13.	Department of Transportation	DOT
14.	Department of the Treasury	DOTRES
15.	Department of Education	ED
16.	Department of Veteran Affairs	VA
	Subtotal	16

AGENCIES

	Name	Acronym
1.	UNITED States Arms and Controls and Disarmament Agency	ACDA
2.	Administration for Children and Families	ACF
3.	Administration for Children, Youth, and Families	ACYF
4.	Administration on Developmental Disabilities	ADD
5.	American Forces Information Service	AFIS
6.	Air Force Reserve Officer Training Corps	AFROTC
7.	Agency for Health Care Policy and Research	AHPCR
8.	Agency for Healthcare Research and Quality	AHRQ
9.	Agency for International Development	AID
10.	Agricultural Marketing Service	AMS
11.	Administration for Native Americans	ANA
12.	Administration on Aging	AOA
13.	Animal and Plant Health Inspection Service	APHIS
14.	Animal and Plant Health Inspection Service	APHIS
15.	Administrative Review Board	ARB

16.	Advanced Research Project Agency	ARPA
17.	Agricultural Research Service	ARS
18.	Bureau of Alcohol, Tobacco, and Firearms	ATF
19.	Bureau of Economic Analysis	BEA
20.	Bureau of Engraving and Printing	BEP
21.	Bureau of Health Professions	BHPr
22.	Bureau of Indian Affairs	BIA
23.	Bureau of Industries and Security	BIS
24.	Bureau of Justice Association	BJA
25.	Bureau of Justice Statistics	BJS
26.	Bureau of Land Management	BLM
27.	Bureau of Labor Statistics	BLS
28.	Bureau of National Affairs	BNA
29.	Federal Bureau of Prisons	BOP
30.	Bureau of Reclamations	BOR
31.	Bureau of Bonneville Power Administration	BPA
32.	Bureau of the Publishing Department	BPD
33.	Bureau of Primary Health Care	BPHC
34.	Bureau of Transportation Statistics	BTS
35.	Bureau of Export Administration	BXA
36.	Child Care Bureau	CCB
37.	Commodity Credit Corporation	CCC
38.	Center for Disease Control	CDC
39.	Center for Drug Evaluation and Research	CDER
40.	Community Development Financial Institute	CDFI
41.	Bureau of the Census	CEN
42.	National Center for Center Food Safety and Applied Nutrition	CFSAN
43.	Defense Advanced Project Agency	DARPA
44.	Defense Contract Audit Agency	DCAA
45.	Drug Enforcement Administration	DEA
46.	Defense Commissary Agency	DeCA
47.	Defense Intelligence Agency	DIA
48.	Defense Information Systems Agency	DISA
49.	Defense Legal Service Agency	DLSA
50.	Defense Mapping Agency	DMA
51.	Defense Securities Cooperation Agency	DSCA
52.	Defense Threat Reduction Agency	DTRA
53.	Employee Benefits Security Administration	EBSA
54.	Bureau of Education and Cultural Affairs	ECA

55.	Energy Information Administration	EIA
56.	Epidemic Intelligence Service	EIS
57.	U.S. Environmental Protection Agency	EPA
58.	Employment Standards Administration	ESA
59.	Economics and Statistics Administration	ESA
60.	Employment and Training Administration	ETA
61.	Federal Aviation Administration	FAA
62.	Federal Bureau of Investigation	FBI
63.	Farm Credit Administration	FCA
64.	Food and Drug Administration	FDA
65.	Federal Emergency Management Agency	FEMA
66.	Federal Housing Administration	FHA
67.	Federal Highway Administration	FHWA
68.	Federal Insurance Administration	FIA
69.	Federal Motor Carrier Safety Administration	FMCSA
70.	Federal Railroad Administration	FRA
71.	Forest Service	FS
72.	Farm Service Agency	FSA
73.	Federal Transit Administration	FTA
74.	Fish and Wildlife Service	FWS
75.	Family and Youth Service Bureau	FYSB
76.	Grain Inspection, Packers, and Stockyards Administration	GIPSA
77.	General Services Administration	GSA
78.	HIV/AIDS Bureau	HAB
79.	Health Care Finance Administration	HCFA
80.	Health Resource and Service Administration	HRSA
81.	Head Start Bureau	HSB
82.	International Atomic Energy Agency	IAEA
83.	International Broadcasting Bureau	IBB
84.	Indian Health Service	IHS
85.	Bureau for International Labor Affairs	ILAB
86.	Bureau for International Narcotics and Law Enforcement Affairs	INL
87.	Immigration and Nationalization Service	INS
88.	International Organization Affairs	IO
89.	Internal Revenue Service	IRS
90.	International Trade Administration	ITA
91.	Maritime Administration	MARAD
92.	Minority Business Development Agency	MBDA
93.	Maternal and Child Health Bureau	MCHB

94.	Multilateral Investment Guarantee Agency	MIGA
95.	Mine Safety and Health Administration	MSHA
96.	National Archives and Records Agency	NARA
97.	National Aeronautics and Space Agency	NASA
98.	National Cemetery Administration	NCA
99.	National Center for Infectious Diseases	NCID
100.	National Credit Union Administration	NCUA
101.	National Highway Traffic Safety Administration	NHTSA
102.	National Marine Fisheries Service	NMFS
103.	National Nuclear Security Administration	NNSA
104.	National Park Service	NPS
105.	National Security Agency	NSA
106.	National Telecommunications and Info Administration	NTIA
107.	National Weather Service	NWS
108.	Bureau of Oceans and International Environmental and Scientific Affairs	OES
109.	Office of Government Ethics	OGE
110.	Office of Personnel Management	OPM
111.	Occupational Safety and Health Administration	OSHA
112.	Public Buildings Service	PBS
113.	Peace Corps	PC
114.	Public Housing Agency	PHA
115.	Public Health Service	PHS
116.	Bureau of Population, Refuges, and Migration	PRM
117.	Pension and Welfare Benefits Administration	PWBA
118.	Rehabilitation Service Administration	RSA
119.	Research and Special Programs Administration	RSPA
120.	Substance Abuse and Mental Health Services Administration	SAMSHA
121.	Small Business Administration	SBA
122.	Secret Service	SS
123.	Social Security Administration	SSA
124.	Technology Administration	TA
125.	Transpiration Administrative Service Center	TASC
126.	Trade and Development Agency	TDA
127.	Transportation Securities Administration	TSA
128.	Transportation Security Administration	TSA
129.	Tennessee Valley Authority	TVA
130.	U.S Citizenship and Immigration Service	UCIS
131.	U.S Army Corp of Engineers	USACE

132.	Bureau of Reclamation	USBR
133.	U.S Customs Service	USCS
134.	U.S Geological Survey	USGS
135.	U.S Marshals Service	USMS
136.	U.S National Central Bureau of INTERPOL	USNCB
137.	U.S Postal Service	USPS
138.	U.S Secret Service	USSS
139.	Veterans Benefits Administration	VBA
140.	Veterans Health Administration	VHA
141.	Voice of America	VOA
142.	Western Area Power Administration	WAPA
143.	Women's Bureau	WB
	Subtotal	143

OFFICES

	Name	Acronym
1.	Office of the Under Secretary of Defense of Acquisition, Technology and Logisitics	AT&L
2.	Armed Forces Radio and Television Service	AFRTS
3.	Army High Performance Computing Research Center	AHPCRC
4.	Beltsville Agricultural Research Center	BARC
5.	Business Information Center	BIC
6.	Biology Informative Molecular Analysis Section	BIMAS
7.	Ballistic Missile Defense Organization	BMDD
8.	Center for Biology Evaluation and Research	CBER
9.	Chemical and Biological Defense Info Analysis Center	CBIAC
10.	Congressional Budget Office	CBO
11.	Center for Devices and Radiology Health	CDRH
12.	Child Exploitations and Obscenity Section	CEOS
13.	Chemical Emergency Preparedness and Prevention Office	CEPPO
14.	Center for Earth and Planetary Studies	CEPS
15.	Topographic Engineering Center	CETEC
16.	Civilian Health and Medical Program of Department of Veteran Affairs	CHAMPVA
17.	Critical Infrastructure Assurance Office	CIAO
18.	Consumer Information Center	CIC
19.	Cancer Information Service	CIS
20.	Center for Information Technology	CIT
21.	Center for Mental Health Services	CMHS

22.	Centers for Medicare Services	CMS
23.	Center for Minority Veterans	CMV
24.	Center for Nutrition Policy and Promotion	CNPP
25.	Office of Community Oriented Policing Service	COPS
26.	Defense Civilian Personnel Management Service	CPMS
27.	Correction Program Office	CPO
28.	Civil Right Center	CRC
29.	Congressional Research Service	CRS
30.	Center for Substance Abuse Prevention	CSAP
31.	Center for Substance Abuse Treatment	CSAT
32.	Office of Child Support Enforcement	CSE
33.	Center for Study of Intelligence	CSI
34.	Center for Scientific Review	CSR
35.	Cooperative State Research, Education, and Extension Service	CSREES
36.	Counter-Terrorism Center	CTC
37.	Division of Computer Research and Technology	DCRT
38.	Defense Distribution Center	DDC
39.	Defense Prisoner of War/Missing Personnel Office	DDMO
40.	Defense Energy Support Center	DESC
41.	Defense Finance and Accounting Service	DFAS
42.	Defense Logistics Information Service	DLIS
43.	Defense Manpower Data Center	DMDC
44.	Defense National Stockpile Center	DNSC
45.	DLA office Operations Research and Resource Analysis	DORRA
46.	Defense Reutilization and Marketing Service	DRMS
47.	Defense Security Service	DSS
48.	Defense Technical Information Center	DTIC
49.	National Institute of Early Childhood Development and Education	ECI
50.	Epidemic Intelligence Service	EIS
51.	Office of Environmental Management	EM
52.	Executive Office of Immigration Review	EOIR
53.	Executive Office of for U.S Attorneys	EOUSA
54.	Executive Office of Weed and Seed	EOWS
55.	Educational Resource Informational Center	ERIC
56.	Economic Resource Center	ERS
57.	Environmental Services Data and Info Management	ESDIM
58.	Federal National Mortgage Association	Fannie Mae
59.	Food and Agricultural Organization	FAO

60.	Federal Agricultural Mortgage Corporation	Farmer Mac
61.	Foreign Agricultural Service	FAS
62.	Foreign Broadcast Information Service	FBIS
63.	Federal Consumer Information Center	FCIC
64.	Federal Energy Technology Center	FETC
65.	Federal Judicial Center	FJC
66.	Federal Law Enforcement Training Center	FLETEC
67.	Federal Labor Relations Authority	FLRA
68.	Financial Management Service	FMS
69.	Food, Nutrition, and Consumer Services	FNCS
70.	Food and Nutritional Services	FNS
71.	Federal Procurement Data Center	FPDC
72.	Food Safety and Inspection Service	FSIS
73.	Federal Technology Service	FTS
74.	Government Accountability Office	GAO
75.	Government National Mortgage Service	Ginnie Mae
76.	Geographic Names Information Center	GNIS
77.	Government Printing Office	GPO
78.	Global Positioning Service	GPS
79.	Goddard Space Flight Center	GSFC
80.	Health Administration Center	HAC
81.	Health Insurance Regional Office	HIRO
82.	Health Information Resource Service	HIRS
83.	High Performance Computing and Communications	HPCC
84.	International Civil Aviation Organization	ICAO
85.	Information Integration Program Office	IIPO
86.	International Labor Service	ILO
87.	International Criminal Police Organization	INTERPOL
88.	International Organization for Migration	IOM
89.	Johnson Space Center	JSC
90.	Kennedy Space Center	KSC
91.	Minority Online Information Service	MOLIS
92.	National Counterintelligence Center	NACIC
93.	National Agricultural Statistics Service	NASS
94.	National Center for Biotechnology Information	NCBI
95.	National Coordinating for Telecommunications	NCC
96.	National Center for Complementary and Alternative Medicine	NCCAM
97.	National Center for Chronic Disease and Health Promotion	NCCDPHP

98.	National Child Care Information Center	NCCIC
99.	National Climactic Data Center	NCDC
100.	National Center for Environmental health	NCEH
101.	National Center of Educational Statistics	NCES
102.	National Center for HIV, STD, and TB Prevention	NCHSTP
103.	National Crime Information Center	NCIC
104.	National Center for Injury Prevention and Control	NCIPC
105.	Naval Criminal Investigative Service	NCIS
106.	National Center for Research Resources	NCRR
107.	National Center for Toxicological Research	NCTR
108.	National Drug Intelligence Center	NDIC
109.	National Earthquake Information Center	NEIC
110.	National Energy Research Scientific Center	NERSC
111.	National Environmental Satellite, Data, and Info Services	NESDIS
112.	National Geophysical Data Center	NGDC
113.	National Health Info Center	NHIC
114.	National Oceanographic Data Center	NODC
115.	National Ocean Service	NOS
116.	National Science and Technology Center	NSTC
117.	National Technical Information Service	NTIS
118.	Office of Antiboycott Compliance	OAC
119.	Office of Animal Care and Use	OACU
120.	Office of American Indian Trust	OAIT
121.	Office of Administrative Law Judges	OALJ
122.	Office of Aids Research	OAR
123.	Office for the Advancement of Telehealth	OAT
124.	Office of Community Development	OCD
125.	Office of the Chief Economist	OCE
126.	Office for Civil Rights	OCR
127.	Office of Civilian Radioactive Waste Management	OCRWM
128.	Office of Community Services	OCS
129.	Office of Child Support Enforcement	OCSE
130.	Office of Disability Employment	ODEP
131.	Office of Disease Prevention	ODP
132.	Office of Enforcement and Compliance Assurance	OECA
133.	Office of Electronic Government and Technology	OEGT
134.	Office of English Language	OELA
135.	Office of Educational Research and Improvement	OERI
136.	Office of Elementary and Secondary Education	OESE

137.	Office of Family Assistance	OFA
138.	Office of Foreign Assets Control	OFAC
139.	Office of Federal Contract Compliance Programs	OFCCP
140.	Office of Federal Housing Enterprise Oversight	OFHEO
141.	Office of Financial Management	OFM
142.	Office of the Federal Register	OFR
143.	Office of Government wide Policy	OGP
144.	Office of Groundwater and Drinking Water	OGWDW
145.	Office of Health and Safety Information System	OHASIS
146.	Office for Human Research Protections	OHRP
147.	Office of Homeland Security	OHS
148.	Office of the Inspector General	OIG
149.	Office of InterGovernmental and Interagency Affairs	OIIA
150.	Office of Juvenile Justice and Delinquency	OJJDP
151.	Office of Justice Programs	OJP
152.	Office of Laboratory Animal Welfare	OLAW
153.	Office of Labor Management Standards	OLMS
154.	Office of Marine and Aviation Operations	OMAO
155.	Office of Medical Applications of Research	OMAR
156.	Office of Management and Budget	OMB
157.	Office of Minority Health	OMH
158.	Office of Multifamily Housing Assistance	OMHAR
159.	Offshore Minerals Management Program	OMM
160.	Office of National Control Policy	ONDCP
161.	Office of Naval Research	ONR
162.	Office of Population Affairs	OPA
163.	Office of Postsecondary Education	OPE
164.	Organization of Petroleum exporting Countries	OPEC
165.	Office of Public Health Service	OPHS
166.	Office of Prevention, Pesticides, and Toxic Substances	OPPTS
167.	Office of Research and Applications	ORA
168.	Office of Risk Assessment and Cost-Benefit Analysis	ORACBA
169.	Office of Rare Disease	ORD
170.	Office of Rural Health Policy	ORHP
171.	Office of Research Integrity	ORI
172.	Office of Research Minority Health	ORMH
173.	Office of Refugee Resettlement	ORR
174.	Office of Research on Women's Health	ORWH
175.	Office of Small Business Programs	OSBP
176.	Office of Special Council	OSC

177.	Office of Child Support Enforcement	OSCE
178.	Office of Small and Disadvantaged Business Utilization	OSDBU
179.	Office of Special Education and Rehabilitative	OSERS
180.	Office of Space Flight	OSF
181.	Office of Surface Mining	OSM
182.	Office of Science and Technology	OST
183.	Office of Scientific and Technical Information	OSTI
184.	Office of Science and Technology	OSTP
185.	Office of Solid Waste and Emergency	OSWER
186.	Office of Technology Assessment	OTA
187.	Office of Tribal Justice	OTJ
188.	Office of Thrift Supervision	OTS
189.	Office of Transportation Technologies	OTT
190.	Office of Vocational and Adult	OVAE
191.	Office for Victims of Crime	OVC
192.	Office of Women's Business Ownership	OWBO
193.	Office of Workers' Compensation	OWCP
194.	Office of Women's Health	OWH
195.	Center for Population, Health, and Nutrition	PHN
196.	Public Health Practice Program Office	PHPPO
197.	Public Health Prevention Service	PHPS
198.	Office of Public and Indian Housing	PIH
199.	Program Support Center	PSC
200.	Patent Trademark Office	PTO
201.	Rural Housing Service	RHS
202.	Rural Information Center Health Service	RICHS
203.	Reserve Officer Training Corps	ROTC
204.	Rural Utilities Service	RUS
205.	Space Environment Center	SEC
206.	Socioeconomic Data and Applications Center	SEDAC
207.	Smithsonian Environmental Research Center	SERC
208.	Office of Strategic Industries & Economic Security	SIES
209.	Smithsonian Institution Traveling Exhibition Service	SITES
210.	Stanford Linear Accelerator	SLAC
211.	Scientific and Technical Information	STI
212.	Treasury Executive Office for Asset Forfeiture	TEOAF
213.	Office of Terrorism and Financial Intelligence	TFI
214.	Trade Information Center	TIC
215.	TRICARE Support Office	TSO
216.	U.S Employment Service	USES

217.	U.S Marshals Service	USMS
218.	U.S Patent and Trademark Office	USPTO
219.	U.S Trade Representative	USTR
220.	Veterans' Employment and Training Service	VETS
221.	Wage and Hour Division	WH
222.	White House Military Office	WHMO
	Subtotal	222

BOARDS & COMMISSIONS

	Name	Acronym
1.	American Battle Monuments Commissions	ABMC
2.	Advisory Committee on Nuclear Waste	ACNW
3.	Appalachian Regional Commission	ARC
4.	Benefits Review Board	BRB
5.	Citizen Advisory Board	CAB
6.	Change Board Control	CCB
7.	Consumer Product Safety Commission	CPSC
8.	Chemical Safety Board and Hazard	CSB
9.	Defense Nuclear Facilities Safety Board	DNFSB
10.	Equal Employment Opportunity Commission	EEOC
11.	Environmental Management Advisory Board	EMAB
12.	Federal Accounting Standards Advisory Board	FASAB
13.	Functional Capabilities Board	FCB
14.	Federal Communications Board	FCC
15.	Federal Executive Board	FEB
16.	Federal Election Commission	FEC
17.	Federal Energy Regulatory Commission	FERC
18.	Federal Maritime Commission	FMC
19.	Federal Mine Safety and Health Review Commission	FMSHRC
20.	Federal Reserve Board	FRB
21.	Federal Retirement Thrift Investment Board	FRTIB
22.	Indian Arts and Crafts Board	IACB
23.	International Atomic Energy Commission	IAEA
24.	Interstate Commerce Commission	ICC
25.	International Electrotechnical Commission	IEC
26.	U.S International Trade Commission	ITC
27.	Investment Review Board	IRB
28.	Medicare Payment Advisory Commission	MedPAC
29.	Management Review Board	MRB

30.	Merit Systems Protection Board	MSPB
31.	National Bioethics Advisory Commission	NBAC
32.	National Communications On Libraries and Information Science	NCLIS
33.	National Capital Planning Commission	NCPC
34.	National Historical Publications and Research Commission	NHPRC
35.	National Indian Gaming Commission	NIGC
36.	National Labor Relations Board	NLRB
37.	National Mediation Board	NMB
38.	Nuclear Regulatory Commission	NRC
39.	National Transportation Safety Board	NTSB
40.	National Waste Technical Review Board	NWTRB
41.	Occupational Safety and Health Review Commission	OSHRC
42.	Panama Canal Commission	PCC
43.	Presidents Foreign Intelligence Board	PFIAB
44.	Postal Rate Commission	PRC
45.	Railroad Retirement Board	RRB
46.	Regional Water Quality Control Board	RWQCB
47.	Securities and Exchange Commission	SEC
48.	State Emergency Response Commission	SERC
49.	Site-Specific Advisory Board	SSAB
50.	Selective Service Commission	SSS
51.	Secure Transportation Asset Advisory Board	STAAB
52.	Surface Transportation Board	STB
53.	U.S Commission on Civil Rights	USSCR
54.	U.S Commission on International Religious Freedom	USCIRF
55.	U.S International Trade Commission	USITC
56.	U.S Sentencing Commission	USSC
	Subtotal	56

ACT OF CONGRESS

	Name	Acronym
1.	Americans with Disabilities Act of 1990	ADA
2.	Comprehensive Environmental Response, Compensation, and Liability Act	CERCLA
3.	Continuing Resolution Act	CRA
4.	Emergency Planning and Community Right-to-Know Act	EPCRA
5.	Federal Financial Management Improvement Act	FFMIA
6.	Government Performance and Results Act	GPRA

7.	Health Insurance Portability and Accountability Act	HIPAA
8.	Information Technology Management Reform Act	ITMRA
9.	National Defense Authorization Act	NDAA
10.	National Environmental Policy Act	NEPA
11.	Service Contract Act	SCA
	Subtotal	11

PROGRAMS

	Name	Acronym
1.	Army Acquisition Neck-Down Initiative	AANDI
2.	Program Against Digital Counterfeiting of Currency	ADC
3.	Aid to Families with Dependant Children	AFDC
4.	Air Force Reserve Officer Training Corps	AFROTC
5.	Agricultural Online Access	AGRICOLA
6.	American Housing Survey	AHS
7.	Tautologies Stem Cell Transplantation	AUSCT
8.	Biomonitoring of Environmental Status and Trends	BEST
9.	Business Mission Modernization Program	BMMP
10.	Commercial and Government Entity	CAGE
11.	Cooperative Administrative Support Program	CASU
12.	Correct Coding Initiative	CCI
13.	Chronic Care Improvement Programs	CCIP
14.	Comprehensive Compliance Program	CCP
15.	Comprehensive Epidemiologic Data Resource	CEDR
16.	Child Health Assurance Program	CHAP
17.	HI Enrollment Cards Operation (HECHICN)	CHICN
18.	Combined Health Insurance & Check writing Operations	CHICO
19.	Combined Health Information	CHID
20.	Catastrophic Health Care Program	CHIP
21.	Competitive Incentive Program	CIP
22.	Convent on International Trade in Endangered Species of Wild Fauna and Flora	CITES
23.	Comprehensive Limiting Charge Compliance Program	CLCCP
24.	Capacity Management Process	CMP
25.	Carrier Management Program	CMP
26.	Corporation for National Service	CNS
27.	Consolidated Rail Corporation	Conrail
28.	Cooperative Online Serials	CONSER
29.	Coastal Ocean Program	COP

30.	Common Provider Audit Program	CPAP
31.	Contractor Performance Evaluation Program	CPEP
32.	Cost Report Evaluation Program	CREP
33.	Computer Retrieval of Information on Scientific Projects	CRISP
34.	Conservation Resource Program	CRP
35.	Corporate Storage Management Initiative	CSMI
36.	Customer Service Program	CSP
37.	Cancer Therapy Evaluation Program	CTEP
38.	College and University Affiliations Program	CUAP
39.	Chemical Weapons Convention	CWC
40.	Defense Environmental Restoration Program	DERP
41.	Single Stock Point for Specifications and Standards	DoDSSP
42.	Drug Rebate Initiative	DRI
43.	DoD Standardization Program	DSP
44.	Disabled & Working Initiative	DWI
45.	Emergency Conservation Program	ECP
46.	Electronic Claims Processing	ECP
47.	Electronic Claims Transaction Initiative	ECTI
48.	Electronic Data Gathering, Analysis, and Retrieval	EDGAR
49.	Enterprise Software Initiative	ESI
50.	Faith Based and Community Initiatives	FBCI
51.	Financial Management Modernization Program	FMMP
52.	Government Without Boundaries	GwoB
53.	Hazardous Material Management Program	HMMP
54.	International Information Programs	IIP
55.	Infant Mortality Instructions	IMI
56.	Intra-Governmental Payment and Collection	IPAC
57.	Interagency Placement Assistance Program	IPAP
58.	Internal Quality Control	IQC
59.	Integrated Risk Management Process	IRMP
60.	Intermediary System Testing Plan	ISTP
61.	Logistics Management Program	LMP
62.	Military Assistance Program	MAP
63.	Military Munitions Response Program	MMRP
64.	National Medicare Education Program	NMEP
65.	National Quality Management Program	NQMP
66.	National Resources Conservation Services	NRCS
67.	National Vaccine Program	NVP
68.	National Vital Statistics System	NVSS
69.	Neighborhood Watch Program	NWP

70.	Old-Age and Survivors Insurance and Disability Insurance	OASDI
71.	Operational Support Modernization Program	OSMP
72.	Product Data Management Initiative	PDMI
73.	Performance Management Plan	PMP
74.	Rural Development	RD
75.	Rural Economic and Community Development	RECD
76.	Research, Education, Economics	REE
77.	Rocky Flats Cleanup Agreement	RFCA
78.	Systematic Alien Verification for Entitlement	SAVE
79.	Safe and Drug Free Schools	SDFS
80.	Standard Disbursing Initiative	SDI
81.	Surveillance, Epidemiology, and End Results	SEER
82.	Service members' Group Life Insurance	SGLI
83.	Standard Industrial Classification	SIC
84.	Strategic Resource Decision System Initiative	SRDS
85.	Supplemental Security Income Program	SSI
86.	Temporary Assistance for Needy Families	TANF
87.	Treasury Forfeiture Fund	TFF
88.	Thrift Savings Plan	TSP
89.	U.S Children's Fund	UNICEF
90.	Volunteers in Service to America	VISTA
91.	Waterways Experiment Station	WES
92.	Women, Infants, and Children	WIC
93.	White Sands Missile Range	WSMR
94.	West Valley Demonstration Project	WVDP
95.	Zone Improvement Plan	ZIP
	Subtotal	95

INSTITUTES

	Name	Acronym
1.	National Cancer Institute	NCI
2.	National Eye Institute	NEI
3.	National Human Genome Research Institute	NHGRI
4.	National Highway Institute	NHI
5.	National Heart, Lung, and Blood Institute	NHLBI
6.	National Institute on Aging	NIA
7.	National Institute on Alcohol Abuse and Alcoholism	NIAA
8.	National Institute of Allergy and Infectious Diseases	NIAID

9.	National Institute of Arthritis and Musculoskeletal and Skin Diseases	NIAMS
10.	National Institute of Corrections	NIC
11.	National Institute of Child Health and Human Development	NICHD
12.	National Institute Drug Abuse	NIDA
13.	National Institute Deafness and Other Communication Disorders	NIDCD
14.	National Institute of Dental and Craniofacial Research	NIDCR
15.	National Institute Diabetes and Rehabilitation Research	NIDDK
16.	National Institute Disability and Rehabilitation Research	NIDRR
17.	National Institute Environmental Health Sciences	NIEHS
18.	National Institute for Literacy	NIFL
19.	National Institute General Medical Sciences	NIGMS
20.	National Institute of Health	NIH
21.	National Institute of Justice	NIJ
22.	National Institute Mental Health	NIMH
23.	National Institute Neurological Disorders and Stroke	NINDS
24.	National Institute Nursing research	NINR
25.	National Institute Occupational Safety and Health	NIOSH
26.	National Institute Standards Technology	NIST
27.	National Institute of Standards and Technology Interagency Report	NISTIR
	Subtotal	27

PUBLICATIONS

	Name	Acronym
1.	American Housing Survey	AHS
2.	Commerce Business Daily	CBD
3.	Catalog of Federal Domestic Assistance	CFDA
4.	Code of Federal Regulations	CFR
5.	Consumer Price Index	CPI
6.	Drug Efficacy Study & Implementation	DESI
7.	DoD Index of Specifications and Standards	DoDISS
8.	Denied Persons List	DPL
9.	Environmental Health Perspectives	EHP
10.	Education Resource Organization Directory	EROD
11.	General Agreement on Tariffs and Trade	GATT
12.	Global Change Master Directory	GCMD
13.	Militarily Critical Technologies List	MCTL

14.	Medical Subject Headings	MeSH
15.	Morbidity and Mortality Weekly Report	MMWR
16.	National Program of Cancer Registries	NPCR
17.	National Register of Historic Places	NR
18.	Prisoner of War/ Missing Personnel	POW/MP
19.	Public Use Microdata Samples	PUMS
20.	Toxics Release Inventory	TRI
21.	United States Code	U.S.C
	Subtotal	21

PARTNERSHIPS

	Name	Acronym
1.	National Railroad Passenger Corporation	AMTRAK
2.	Corporation for National Service	CNS
3.	Consolidated Rail Corporation	Conrail
4.	North Atlantic Treaty Organization	NATO
5.	National Endowment of the Arts	NEA
6.	National Endowment of the Humanities	NEH
7.	National Partnership of Reinventing Government	NPR
8.	Saint Lawrence Seaway Development Corporation	SLSDC
9.	United Nations	U.N
10.	Federal Prison Industries	UNICOR
11.	World Treaty Organization	WTO
	Subtotal	11

LABORATORIES

	Name	Acronym
1.	Alternate Crop Systems Laboratory	ACSL
2.	Air Force Research Laboratory	AFRL
3.	Ames Laboratory	AMES
4.	Argonne National Laboratory	ANL
5.	Argonne National Laboratory West	ANLW
6.	Army Research Laboratory	ARL
7.	Building and Fire Research Laboratory	BFRL
8.	Brookhaven National Laboratory	BNL
9.	Environmental Measurement Laboratory	EML
10.	Fermi National Accelerator Laboratory	Fermi lab
11.	Federal Laboratory Center	FLC

12.	Idaho National Laboratory	INL
13.	Jet Propulsion Laboratory	JPL
14.	Knolls Atomic Power laboratory	KAPL
15.	Los Alamos National Laboratory	LANL
16.	Ernest Orlando Lawrence Berkeley National Laboratory	LBL
17.	Laboratory for Energy-Related Health Research	LEHR
18.	Lawrence Livermore National Laboratory	LLNL
19.	New Brunswick Laboratory	NBL
20.	National Energy Technology Laboratory	NETL
21.	National Renewal Energy Laboratory	NREL
22.	Naval Research Laboratory	NRL
23.	National Space Technology Laboratories	NSTL
24.	Oak Ridge National Laboratory	ORNL
25.	Pacific Northwest National Laboratory	PNNL
26.	Sandia National Laboratory	SNL
	Subtotal	26

COMMANDS

	Name	Acronym
1.	Air Combat Command	ACC
2.	Air Education Training Command	AETC
3.	Air Force Reserve Command	AFRC
4.	Air Force Space Command	AFSPC
5.	Air Mobility Command	AMC
6.	U.S Army Criminal Investigation Command	CID
7.	Combatant Command	COCOM
8.	Joint Forces Command	JFCOM
9.	Major Command	MAJCOM
10.	Military Sealift Command	MSC
11.	Naval Air Systems Command	NAVAIR
12.	Naval Facilities Engineering Command	NAVFAC
13.	Naval Sea Systems Command	NAVSEA
14.	Naval Supply Systems Command	NAVSUP
	Subtotal	14

SCHOOLS

	Name	Acronym
1.	Armed Forces College	AFSC

2.	Defense Acquisition University	DAU
3.	Defense Information School	DINFOS
4.	Industrial College of the Armed Forces	ICAF
5.	Institute of Education Sciences	IES
6.	Information Resources Management College	IRMC
7.	Joint Forces Staff College	JFSC
8.	National Defense University	NDU
9.	National Fire Academy	NFA
10.	National War College	NWC
	Subtotal	10

COUNCILS

	Name	Acronym
1.	Advisory Council on Historic Preservation	ACHP
2.	Council of Economic Advisers	CEA
3.	Council on Environmental Equality	CEQ
4.	Chief Financial Officers Council	CFOC
5.	Domestic Policy Council	DPC
6.	Executive Council on Integrity and Efficiency	ECIE
7.	Economic and Social Council	ECOSOC
8.	National Council on Disability	NCD
9.	National Economic Council	NEC
10.	National Security Council	NSC
11.	Overseas Security Advisory Council	OSAC
	Subtotal	11

INTER-AGENCY GROUPS

	Name	Acronym
1.	Accounting and Auditing Policy Committee	AAPC
2.	Federal Open Market Committee	FOMC
3.	Inter-Agency Electronic Grants Committee	IAEGC
4.	Joint Economic Committee	JEC
5.	National Committee on Vital and Health Statistics	NCVHS
6.	Anti-Terrorism Task Force	ATTF
7.	Foreign Terrorist Tracking Task Force	FTTTF
8.	Homeland Security Task Force	HSTF
9.	Joint Terrorism Task Force	JTTF
	Subtotal	9

NETWORKS

	Name	Acronym
1.	Acquisition Reform Network	ARNet
2.	Business Partner Network	BPN
3.	Energy Efficiency and Renewable Energy Network	EREN
4.	Financial Crimes Enforcement Network	FINCEN
5.	Health Alert Network	HAN
6.	InterGovernmental Value-Added Network	IVAN
7.	National Health Information Network	NHIN
8	National Research and Education Network	NREN
9.	Public Health Training Network	PHTN
10.	Telecommunication Management Network	TMN
11.	Trading Partner Network	TPN
12.	Women's Network for Entrepreneurial Training	WNET
	Subtotal	12

BANK

	Name	Acronym
1.	Asian Development Bank	ADB
2.	African Development Bank	AFDB
3.	Community Development Bank	CDBG
4.	Export Import Bank of the U.S.	Ex-Im Bank
5.	Federal Finance Bank	FFB
6.	Federal Housing Financing Bank	FHFB
7.	Overseas Private Investment Corporation	OPIC
	Subtotal	7

SPECIAL TERMS: ACCOUNTING

	Name	Acronym
1.	Audit Clearance Document	ACD
2.	Audit/Civil Monetary Penalties	ACMP
3.	Average Hourly Earnings	AHES
4.	Average Historical Payment	AHP
5.	Adjusted Hourly Salary Equivalency Amount	AHSEA
6.	Audit Intermediary	AI
7.	Annual Loss Expectancy	ALE
8.	Audit Priority Matrix	APM
9.	Average Payment Rate	APR

10.	Billing Cycle Code	BCC
11.	Billing Information Exchange Record	BIER
12.	Bottom Line Unit Cost	BLUC
13.	Bill Summary Records	BSR
14.	Budget Year	BY
15.	Cost Accounting Standards	CAS
16.	Combined Annual Wage Reporting	CAWR
17.	Consolidated Billing	CB
18.	Current Premium Due Amount	CPDA
19.	Cost Plus Incentive Fee	CPIF
20.	Cost Plus Percentage of Cost	CPPC
21.	Cost Per Visit	CPV
22.	Claims Services	CS
23.	Calendar Year	CY
24.	Direct Billing	DB
25.	Direct Billing Integration	DBI
26.	End of Month Operation	ENDOP
27.	End of Month	EOM
28.	End of Year	EOY
29.	Environmental Technologies Cost	ETC
30.	Functional Configuration	FCA
31.	First Credit Month	FCM
32.	Federal Fiscal Year	FFY
33.	Fiscal Year	FY
34.	Government Auditing Standards	GAS
35.	Historical Payment Basis	HPB
36.	Hypothetical Base Year Calculations	HYBC
37.	Initial Billing Date	IBD
38.	Incorrect Bill Notice	IBN
39.	Incurred But Not Reported	IBNR
40.	Initial Bill Process Option	IBPO
41.	Initial Claims Operations	IC
42.	In-house Claim Number	ICN
43.	Inventory Control Number	ICN
44.	Incomplete Claims Reject	ICR
45.	Journal Voucher	JV
46.	Line of Credit	LOC
47.	Limitation on Administrative Expenses	LAE
48.	Low Utilization Payment Adjustment	LUPA
49.	Mandatory Annual Audit Requirement	MAAR

50.	Master Account Title	MAT
51.	Master Control File	MCF
52.	Net Fixed Assets	NFA
53.	Net Impact	NIE
54.	Notice of Deficiencies	NOD
55.	Notice of Program Reimbursement	NOPR
56.	Not Sufficient Funds	NSF
57.	Occupancy Depreciation & Amortization	ODA
58.	On Time Cost	OTC
59.	Priority Audit Memorandum	PAM
60.	Premium Accrual Stop	PAS
61.	Physical Configuration Audit	PCA
62.	Punch Card Accounting Machines	PCAM
63.	Premium Due Amount	PDA
64.	Prior Month Accrual	PMA
65.	Prospective Payment	PP
66.	Processing Payment Cycle	PPC
67.	Potentially Penalty Liable	PPL
68.	Pre Payment Screen	PPS
69.	Present Value	PV
70.	Prior Year	PY
71.	Prior Year Ending	PYE
72.	Quality Control Enforcement Mechanism	QCEM
73.	Return Check Action	REACT
74.	Reduced Expenditure Initiatives	REINS
75.	Routing & Transit Number	RTN
76.	Scheduled Allowance	SA
77.	Statement of Auditing Standards	SAS
78.	Tax Identification Number	TIN
79.	Treatment, Payment, Operations	TPO
80.	Tax Refund Offset	TRO
81.	Uniform Cost Accounting Standards	UCAS
82.	Variable Premium Amount Collectable	VPAC
83.	Year to Date	YTD
	Subtotal	83

SPECIAL TERMS: BUSINESS

	Name	Acronym
1.	American Customer Satisfaction	ACSS

2.	Average Manufacturers Price	AMP
3.	Average Monthly Wage	AMW
4.	Advanced Requirement Management Pilot	ARM
5.	Administrative Services Only	ASO
6.	Average Wholesale Price	AWP
7.	Actual Wholesale Price	AWP
8.	Bid & Proposal	B&P
9.	Business Continuity & Contingency Plan	BCCP
10.	Business Enterprise Area	BEA
11.	Business Impact Analysis	BIA
12.	Buying Eligibility Code	BIEC
13.	Basic Ordering Agreement	BOA
14.	Bill of Materials	BOM
15.	Bargain Purchase Option	BPO
16.	Business Processing Reengineering	BPR
17.	Business Roundtable	BRT
18.	Business Systems Planning	BSP
19.	Business Transformation	BTE
20.	Budget Under Control System	BUCS
21.	Confidential Business Information	CBI
22.	Cost Estimating Relationship	CER
23.	Contractor Furnished Equipment	CFE
24.	Change of Ownership	CHOW
25.	Commercial Item Description	CID
26.	Construction in Progress	CIP
27.	Constructive Key Management	CKM
28.	Contract Management Action	CMA
29.	Change Order	CO
30.	Current Operating Month	COM
31.	Continuous Quality Improvement	CQI
32.	Community Relations Plan	CRP
33.	Change Request Work History	CRWH
34.	Critical Success Factor	CSF
35.	Customer Service Plan	CSP
36.	Common Working File	CWF
37.	Defense Acquisition Management Information Retrieval	DAMIR
38.	Doing Business As	DBA
39.	Defense Business Systems Acquisition Executive	DBSAE
40.	Defense Business Transformation	DBT
41.	Discount Schedule & Marketing Data	DSMD

42.	External Services Providers	ESP
43.	Federal Acquisition	FAC
44.	Federal Acquisition Regulation	FAR
45.	Federal Information Processing Standard	FIPS
46.	Freight on Board	FOB
47.	Functional Quality Assurance	FQA
48.	General & Administrative	G&A
49.	Government Furnished Information	GFI
50.	Government Furnished Material	GFM
51.	Group Purchasing Organization	GPO
52.	Generic Performance Standards	GPS
53.	Growth Target	GT
54.	Hardware Configuration Management	HCM
55.	Human Resources	HR
56.	Invitation for Bids	IFB
57.	Intra-Governmental Transactions	IGT
58.	Initial Review Analysis	IRA
59.	Informal Resolution Conference	IRC
60.	Internal Research & Development	IRD
61.	Information Resources Management	IRM
62.	Job Rehabilitation	JRC
63.	Key Material Identification Number	KMID
64.	Key Result Areas	KRA
65.	Life Cycle Cost	LCC
66.	Letter Charge Proposal	LCP
67.	Local Database Manager	LDBM
68.	Line of Business	LOB
69.	Lead Regional Office	LRO
70.	Labor Relations Staff	LRS
71.	Large Scale Integration	LSI
72.	Management by Objectives	MBO
73.	Maintenance Contractor	MC
74.	Maximum Order Limitation	MOL
75.	Monitored Retrievable Storage	MRS
76.	Name & Address Verification	NAV
77.	National Inventory Control Point	NICP
78.	Office Automation	OA
79.	Office Business Liaison	OBL
80.	Operational Capability Demonstration	OCD
81.	Organizational Conflict of Interest	OCI

82.	Organization for Economic Cooperation and Development	OECD
83.	Operational Emergency Management Team	OEMT
84.	Operational Management Plan	OMP
85.	Organization Structure	OS
86.	On-Scene Coordinator	OSC
87.	Performance Assessment	PA
88.	Project Account Code	PAC
89.	Professional & Administrative Career Examination	PACE
90.	Procurement Cycle	PC
91.	Private Consumer	PCR
92.	Program Decision Package	PDP
93.	Performance Indicator	PI
94.	Project Idea Document	PID
95.	Purchase Order	PO
96.	Principal Official Responsible for Acquisition	PORA
97.	Project Plan	PP
98.	Productivity Per Work Year	PPWY
99.	Priority Value Assessment	PVA
100.	Quality Information Statement	QIS
101.	Quality Management	QM
102.	Qualified Product List	QPL
103.	Quality Support	QST
104.	Quality Assurance Expert System Testbed	QUEST
105.	Reserve Affairs	RA
106.	Rapid Action Development	RAD
107.	Resource-Based Relative Value Use	RBRVS
108.	Report of Benefit Savings	RBS
109.	Rural Business-Cooperative	RBS
110.	Reasonable Charge	RC
111.	Report of Contractor	RCP
112.	Registered Compensatory	RCT
113.	Reason for Assessment	RFA
114.	Request for Contract	RFC
115.	Request for Information	RFI
116.	Request for Quotation	RFQ
117.	Routing Impact Analysis	RIA
118.	Remote Job Entry	RJE
119.	Release Management	RM
120.	Resource Management Plan	RMP
121.	Requirements Management Plan	RMT

122.	Resource Management Unit	RMU
123.	Race & National Origin	RNO
124.	Report of Contact	ROC
125.	Regional Office Contractor Letter	ROCL
126.	Record of Decision	ROD
127.	Report of Eligibility	ROE
128.	Real Property Asset	RPA
129.	Real Property Assets Database	RPAD
130.	Real Property Acceptance Requirements	RPAR
131.	Reasonable Performance List	RPL
132.	Rate Review	RR
133.	Record Status Code	RSC
134.	Record Type	RT
135.	Reports to Congress	RTC
136.	Residual Value	RV
137.	Sampling and Analysis	SAP
138.	Single Award Schedules	SAS
139.	State Buy In	SBI
140.	Small Business Set Aside	SBSA
141.	Strategic Business Unit	SBU
142.	Small & Disadvantaged Business	SDB
143.	System Development Life Cycle	SDLC
144.	Separated Employee File	SEF
145.	Site and Facility Management	SFM
146.	Single Intermediary	SI
147.	Standard Industrial Classification	SIC
148.	Supervision, Inspection, and Overhead	SIOH
149.	Site Management Plan	SMP
150.	Superintendent of Documents	SOD
151.	Solicitation	SOL
152.	Statement of Work	SOW
153.	Sample Persons	SP
154.	Standard Position Description	SPD
155.	Standard Profile Identification Number	SPIN
156.	Standard Solicitation Document	SSD
157.	Standard Unique Employer Identifier	SUEI
158.	Supervisor Call	SVC
159.	Statistically Valid Random Sample	SVRS
160.	Type of Activity Code	TAC
161.	Transfer, Automate, Contractor, Terminator	TACT

162.	Total Location Counter	TLC
163.	Trial Work Period	TWP
164.	United Auto Workers	UAW
165.	United Mine Workers	UMW
166.	Universal Product Number	UPN
167.	Utilization Review Coordinator	URC
168.	Utilization Review Organization	URO
169.	Volume Allocation Manager	VAM
170.	Value Added Reseller	VAR
171.	View Work Area	VWA
172.	Work Breakdown Structure	WBS
173.	Workers Compensation	WC
174.	Women Executive Leadership	WEL
175.	Workgroup	WG
176.	Washington Publishing Company	WPC
177.	Work Year	WY
178.	Expanded Quality Assurance	XQA
179.	Zero Defects	ZD
180.	Zero Overpricing	ZO
	Subtotal	180

SPECIAL TERMS: DEFENSE

	Name	Acronym
1.	Arms, Ammunition, and Explosives	AA&E
2.	Air Force Educational War gaming Toolkit	AFEWT
3.	Acquisition Program Baseline	APB
4.	Defense Agencies Initiatives	DAI
5.	Defense Document	DD
6.	DoD Intelligence Mission Area	DIMA
7.	DoD Enterprise Architecture	DoD EA
8.	DoD Enterprise Electronic Model	DoD EMALL
9.	DoD Activity Address Code	DoDAAC
10.	DoD Architecture	DoDAF
11.	DoD Directive	DoDD
12.	DoD Instruction	DoDI
13.	Defense Transportation Coordination Initiative	DTCI
14.	End State	ES
15.	Formerly used Defense Sites	FUDS
16.	Five Year Defense Plan	FYDP

17.	Headquarters, Air Force	HAF
18.	Integrated Air and Missile Defense	IAMD
19.	Incident Commander	IC
20.	Implementation Conventions	IC
21.	Initial Capabilities Document	ICD
22.	Insensitive Munitions	IM
23.	Intelligence Mission Area	IMA
24.	Initial Operational Capability	IOC
25.	Joint Warfighting Capabilities Assessment	JWCA
26.	Military Assistance Advisory Groups	MAAG
27.	Navy Air Force Interface	NAFI
28.	Navy Facility Assets Data Source	NFADS
29.	Naval Industrial Activities	NIF
30.	Naval Ordnance Disposal Area	NODA
31.	Naval Reactors	NRF
32.	Post Exchange	PX
33.	Quarters of Charge	QC
34.	Unique Identification	UID
35.	Warfighting Mission Area	WMA
36.	Weapons of Mass Destruction	WMD
37.	White Sands Missile Range	WSMR
	Subtotal	37

SPECIAL TERMS: ENGINEERING

	Name	Acronym
1.	Applied Cost Engineering	ACE
2.	Automated Civil Engineer System	ACES
3.	Arithmetic Mean of the Logarithm	AML
4.	Extended Structure Architecture	ESA
5.	Industrial Engineering	IE
6.	Information Engineering Facility	IEF
7.	Infrastructure Reporting	IFI
8.	Inspector General	IG
9.	Knowledge Engineering	KE
10.	Professional Component	PC
11.	Project Engineering Development	PED
12.	Parts Per Million	PPM
13.	Quality Management Certification	QMCE
14.	Structured Development Methodology	SDM

15.	System Design Overview	SDO
16.	Software Engineering Institute Capability	SEIU
17.	Uninterruptible Power Supply	UPS
	Subtotal	17

SPECIAL TERMS: ENVIRONMENTAL

	Name	Acronym
1.	Accelerated Cleanup	AC
2.	Army Environmental	AEBD
3.	Air Emission Inventory	AEI
4.	As Low As Reasonably Achievable	ALARA
5.	Annual Limit on Intake	ALI
6.	Acceptable Quality Level	AQL
7.	Auxiliary Reactor Area	ARA
8.	Burial Ground Complex	BGC
9.	Continuous Air Monitors	CAMS
10.	Central Facilities Area	CFA
11.	Chemical Leaching Pond	CLP
12.	Cask Maintenance Facility	CMF
13.	Convention on Nuclear Safety	CNS
14.	Conceptual Site Treatment Plan	CSTP
15.	Common Vulnerabilities & Exposes	CVE
16.	Disposal Authorization Statement	DAS
17.	Design Basis Accidents	DBAS
18.	Data Base Environment	DBE
19.	Defense Business Sourcing Environment	DBSE
20.	Document Control Number	DCN
21.	Defense Environmental Network and Information Exchange	DENIX
22.	Defense Site Environmental Reportings	DSERTS
23.	Environmental Assessment	EA
24.	Export Administration Regulations	EAR
25.	Exposure Factor	EF
26.	Environmental Justice	EJ
27.	Emergency Protection Coordinators	EPCC
28.	Emergency Planning Zone	EPZ
29.	Environmental Restoration	ER
30.	Emergency Readiness Program	ERAP
31.	Environmental Restoration Disposal Facility	ERDF

32.	Geographic Adjustment Factor	GAF
33.	Geographic Code Book	GCB
34.	Gaseous Diffusion Plant	GDP
35.	Government Furnished Information	GFI
36.	Geographic Information	GIS
37.	Geologic Repository Operations Area	GROA
38.	Highly Enriches	HE
39.	High Efficiency Particulate Attraction	HEPA
40.	High Level Waste	HLW
41.	Hazardous Solid Waste Amendment	HSWA
42.	Hazardous Waste Management Regulations	HWMR
43.	Integrated Water Management Plan	IGWMP
44.	Interim Maintenance Period	IMP
45.	Liquid Effluent Retention Facility	LERF
46.	Low Enriched Uranium	LEU
47.	Long-Term Stewardship	LTS
48.	Low Volume Exemption	LVE
49.	Maximum Contaminant Level	MCL
50.	Naturally Occurring Radioactive Materials	NORM
51.	Notice of Violations	NOV
52.	On Site Disposal Facility	OSDF
53.	Protective Action Guide	PAG
54.	Power Burst Facility	PBF
55.	Positron Emission Tomography	PET
56.	Plutonium Finishing Plant	PFP
57.	Point of Exposure	POE
58.	Remedial Design	RD
59.	Recommended Exposure Limits	REL
60.	Radioactive Material Management Area	RMMA
61.	State Licensed Disposal Area	SDA
62.	Spent Nuclear Fuel	SNF
63.	Spent Nuclear Material	SNM
64.	Savannah River Site	SRS
65.	Short-Term Exposure Limit	STEL
66.	Transport Layer Security	TLS
67.	Threshold Limit Exposure Values	TLV
68.	Test Reactor Area	TRA
69.	Treatment, Storage, and Disposal	TSD
70.	Waste Isolation Pilot Plant	WIPP
71.	Waste Receiving and Processing Facility	WRAP

72.	Waste Reduction Operation Cost	WROC
73.	Waste Water Treatment Facility	WWTF
74.	Extended Development Environment	XDE
	Subtotal	74

SPECIAL TERMS: FINANCE

	Name	Acronym
1.	Accounts Payable	A/P
2.	Adjusted Average Per Capita Cost	AAPCC
3.	Automated Claims Examination	ACE
4.	Annual Compound Rate of Growth	ACRG
5.	Appropriated Funds	APF
6.	Accounts Receivable	AR
7.	Automated Standard Application for Payments	ASAP
8.	Budget Activity	BA
9.	Budget Change Proposal	BCP
10.	Budget & Performance Requirements	BPR
11.	Budget Transfer Request	BTR
12.	Compensation & Pension	C&P
13.	Cost/Benefit Ratio	C/BR
14.	Cost/Burden Reduction	C/BR
15.	Capital Related	CAP-REL
16.	Comprehensive Cost and Requirement	CCAR
17.	Cost or Charge Ratio	CCR
18.	Certificate of Indebtedness	COI
19.	Comprehensive Cost and Requirement	CCAR
20.	Corps of Engineers Financial	CEFMS
21.	Economic Order Quantity	EOQ
22.	Economies of Scale	EOS
23.	Fraud & Abuse	F&A
24.	Fiscal Agent	FA
25.	Federal Financial Management Requirement	FEMR
26.	Federal Financing Accounting and Auditing	FFAA
27.	Federal Financial Participation	FFP
28.	Fiscal Intermediary	FI
29.	Financial Improvement Audit Readiness	FIAR
30.	Fair Market Value	FMV
31.	Financial Operation	FO
32.	Financial Operating Plan	FOP

33.	Fixed Price Incentive	FPI
34.	Fixed Price Level of Effort	FPLF
35.	Five Percent Sample	FPS
36.	Flexible Savings Account	FSA
37.	Federal Tax Information	FTI
38.	Gross Domestic Product	GDP
39.	Information Collection Budget	ICB
40.	Inflation Index Charge	IIC
41.	Market Basket	MB
42.	Military Pay	MilPaY
43.	Comptroller of the Currency	OCC
44.	Overpayment	OP
45.	Overseas Private Investment Corporation	OPIC
46.	Provider Audit List	PAL
47.	Per Capita Payment Rate	PCRP
48.	Personal Earnings & Benefits Statement	PEBS
49.	Private Fee For Service Plan	PFFS
50.	Post Independent Analysis	PIA
51.	Premium Paid Amount	PPA
52.	Planning, Programming, Budgeting	PPB
53.	Ratio of Cost to Charges	RCC
54.	Ratio of Charges to Charges Applied to Costs	RCCAC
55.	Reasonable Compensation Equivalent	RCE
56.	Return on Investment	ROI
57.	Return to Intermediary	RTI
58.	Relative Value Scale	RVS
59.	Supplemental Budget Request	SBR
60.	Separate Cost Entity	SCE
61.	Summary Earnings Record	SER
62.	Standard Form	SF
63.	Statement of Federal Financial Accounting Concepts	SFFAC
64.	Statement of Financial Information	SFI
65.	Security Income Data	SID
66.	Security Income File Type	SIFT
67.	Supplemental Security Income	SSI
68.	State Supplemental Payments	SSP
69.	Supplemental Security Income Record	SSR
70.	Temporary Assistance for Needy Families	TANF
71.	Transaction Back Out	TBO
72.	Total Cost	TC

73.	Transitional Corridor Payments	TCP
74.	Uniform Bill	UB
75.	Unilateral Price Determination	UPD
76.	Upper Payment Limit	UPL
77.	United States Per Capita Cost	USPCC
78.	Wholesale Acquisition Cost	WAC
79.	Workers Compensation	WC
80.	Zero Base Budgeting	ZBB
	Subtotal	80

SPECIAL TERMS: GENERAL

	Name	Acronym
1.	Access Control Table	ACT
2.	After Date of Award Document	ADAD
3.	Alternative Dispute Resolution	ADS
4.	Average Days Work on Hand	ADWOH
5.	Administrative Enhancement	AE
6.	Amount in Controversy	AIC
7.	Auto Liability No Fault	ALNF
8.	Analysis of Variance	ANOVA
9.	All Other Local Screens	AOLS
10.	Arithmetic	ARIMA
11.	Annualized Rate of Occurrence	ARO
12.	Age/ Race/Sex	ARS
13.	Administrative Simplification	AS
14.	Billing Action Code	BAC
15.	Before Outliers	BOR
16.	Baseline Risk Assessment	BRA
17.	Categorical Assistance Code	CAC
18.	Common Access Card	CAC
19.	Change Control Plan	CCP
20.	Closure Description Document	CDD
21.	Core Data Element	CDE
22.	Comprehensive Error	CERT
23.	Cipher Feedback	CFB
24.	Current Logical Model	CLM
25.	Complexity Matrix	CM
26.	Communication Security	COMSEC
27.	Concept of Papers	COP

28.	Change Request	CR
29.	Controlled Rate of Increase	CRI
30.	Clear to Send	CTS
31.	Days After Contractor Award	DACA
32.	Date of Service	DOS
33.	Date of Suspension	DOST
34.	Data Quality Objective	DQO
35.	Design Specification	DSP
36.	Days Work On Hand	DWOH
37.	Employer Identification	EIN
38.	Estimated Test Volume	ETV
39.	Equivalent Work Unit	EWU
40.	Facility File	FF
41.	First In/ First Out	FIFO
42.	Face Identification Mark	FIM
43.	Federal Office Systems Exposition	FOSE
44.	Fixed Standard	FS
45.	Feasibility Study	FS
46.	Group Practice Indicator	GPI
47.	General Records Schedule	GRS
48.	General Schedule	GS
49.	Initial Enrollment Period	IEP
50.	Independent Review Entity	IRE
51.	International Unit	IU
52.	Joint Travel Regulation	JTR
53.	RRB Jurisdiction Change Operation	JURIS
54.	Knocked Down	KD
55.	Key Intelligence Position	KIP
56.	Key Intelligence Question	KIQ
57.	Lowest Charge Level	LCL
58.	Length of Stay	LOS
59.	Last Summary Update	LSU
60.	Location Type	LT
61.	Less Than Effective	LTE
62.	Major Action	MA
63.	Multipurpose Canister	MPC
64.	National Change of Address	NCOA
65.	Not In File	NIF
66.	National Improvement Project	NIP
67.	Notice of Award	NOA

68.	Not Otherwise Classified	NOC
69.	Not on File	NOF
70.	Notice of Rule Making	NRM
71.	National Standardized Amount	NSA
72.	Outside the Continental United States	OCONUS
73.	Operable Unit	OU
74.	Project Assessment	PA
75.	Planning Action Team	PAT
76.	Performance Evaluation	PE
77.	Paducah Gaseous Diffusion Plant	PGDP
78.	Project Initiation	PI
79.	Personal Identification Number	PIN
80.	Premium Inquiry	PINQ
81.	Performance Improvement Plan	PIP
82.	Periodic Interim Reimbursement	PIR
83.	Performance Level	PL
84.	Post Meridiem	PM
85.	Point of Contact	POC
86.	Payment Record Batch	PRB
87.	Prior To Admission	PTA
88.	Public Use Files	PUF
89.	Public Welfare	PW
90.	Performance Work Standard	PWS
91.	Quality Assessment	QA
92.	Quality Assurance Evaluator	QAE
93.	Quality Assurance Representative	QAR
94.	Quality Assurance Standards	QAS
95.	Quality Control Program	QDN
96.	Quality Indicator	QI
97.	Quality Review Studies	QRS
98.	Quick Reference	QW
99.	Risk Assessment	RA
100.	Refugee Cash Assistance	RCA
101.	Report Card Listing	RCL
102.	Remark Line	REM
103.	Regional Office Flag	ROF
104.	Random Search	RS
105.	Standard Analytic File	SAF
106.	Subject Matter Expert	SME
107.	Single Point of Contact	SPOC

108.	Service Request	SR
109.	To Be Provided	TBP
110.	Temporary Duty Travel	TDY
111.	Transmittal Number	TN
112.	Transition Office Contact	TOC
113.	Triple Action Package	TOP
114.	Type of Program	TOPR
115.	Trust Territories	TT
116.	Test Value	TVS
117.	Time Weighted Area	TWA
118.	Universal Control Facility	UCF
119.	Usual, Customary, & Reasonable	UCR
120.	User Etract	UE
121.	United Nations Educational, Scientific, and Cultural Organization	UNESCO
122.	User Request Form	URF
123.	United States Code	USC
124.	United States Conference Mayors	USCM
125.	Unable to Locate	UTL
126.	Volunteers In Police Service	VIPS
127.	Work In Progress	WIP
128.	Executive Control Number	XCN
129.	Cross Memory Services	XMS
	Subtotal	129

SPECIAL TERMS: GOVERNMENT

	Name	Acronym
1.	Agreements in Principle	AIPS
2.	Average Per Diem State Rate	APDSR
3.	Agency Procurement Request	APR
4.	American Samoa	AS
5.	Annual State Evaluation Report/State Assessments	ASER/SA
6.	Annuity & Survivors Master	ASM
7.	Advanced Test Reactor	ATR
8.	Base Realignment and Closure	BRAC
9.	Commercial and Government Entity	CAGE
10.	Claim Account Number	CAN
11.	Carrier Alphabetic State File	CASF
12.	Civil Defense	CD

13.	Code of Federal Regulations	CFR
14.	Continuity of Government	COG
15.	Certificate of Need	CON
16.	Conceptual Site Model	CSM
17.	Commercial Vehicle Safety Alliance	CVSA
18.	Determination & Findings	D&F
19.	Designated Federal Officers	DFO
20.	Federal Travel Regulations	FTR
21.	Government Information Locator Service	GILS
22.	Government Off The Staff	GOTS
23.	Independent Government Cost Estimate	IGCE
24.	Nevada Test Site	NTS
25.	Organization of American States	OAS
26.	Old Age & Survivors Benefits	OASB
27.	Oak Ridge Operations	ORO
28.	State & County	SC
	Subtotal	28

SPECIAL TERMS: HEALTH

	Name	**Acronym**
1.	Advanced Beneficiary Notice	ABN
2.	Average Cost Per Visit	ACPV
3.	Adjusted Community Rate	ACR
4.	Ambulatory Care Sensitive Conditions	ACSC
5.	Adjusted Claim	ADJ
6.	Activities of Daily Living	ADL
7.	Advance Planning Document	ADP
8.	Appropriateness Evaluation Period	AEP
9.	Armed Forces Health Longitudinal Technology Application	AHLTA
10.	Adjusted Historical Payment Basis	AHPB
11.	Advanced Life Support	ALS
12.	Automatic Lump Sum Operation	ALSO
13.	Ambulatory Payment Class	APC
14.	Acute Physiology Score	APS
15.	Aids Related Complex	ARC
16.	Beneficiary Inactive Master File	BIMF
17.	Beneficiary Inquiries Taskforce	BIT
18.	Benefit Period	BP
19.	Base Period Charge	BPC

20.	Community Awareness Emergency Response	CAER
21.	Cost Based Reasoning	CBR
22.	Charge Description Master	CDM
23.	Continuous Home Care	CHC
24.	Center for Hospital & Community Care	CHCC
25.	Continuous Home Health Care	CHHC
26.	Catastrophic Health Insurance	CHI
27.	Critical Health Manpower Shortage Area	CHMSA
28.	Coordination of Benefits	COB
29.	Certificate of Competency	COC
30.	Computerized Patient Record	CPR
31.	Compensation Related Customary Charges	CRCC
32.	Discretionary Adjustment Factor	DAF
33.	Diagnostic Code	DC
34.	Dually Certified	DCF
35.	Developmental Disabilities	DD
36.	Defense Medical Logistics Standard Support	DMLSS
37.	Date of Entitlement	DOE
38.	Draft Standard for Trial Use	DSTU
39.	Eligible But Not Enrolled	EBNE
40.	External Counterpulsation	ECP
41.	Execution Diagnostic Facility	EDF
42.	Exclusions From Coverage	EFC
43.	Employer Group Health Plan	EGHP
44.	Employer Insured Beneficiary	EIB
45.	Electronic Media Claim	EMC
46.	Explanation of Benefits	EOB
47.	Enrollment Period	EP
48.	Expenditure Target	ET
49.	Federal Benefit Rate	FBR
50.	Final Claim	FC
51.	Formula Driven	FDO
52.	Family Health Plan	FHP
53.	Group Health Plan	GHP
54.	Group Premium Payer	GPP
55.	Government Task Monitor	GTM
56.	HI Control Operations	HC
57.	Hieratical Condition Category	HCC
58.	Healthcare Provider Cost Report Information System	HCRIS
59.	HI Enrollment Operations	HE

60.	Health Economic Zone	HEZ
61.	HI General Documentation	HG
62.	Health Insurance Claim Number	HICN
63.	Health Insurance Correction Request	HICR
64.	Health Insurance Flexibility and Accountability	HIFA
65.	Health Insurance Master	HIMA
66.	Health Insurance Master Billing Exception Process	HIMBEX
67.	Health Insurance Master File	HIMF
68.	HI Number	HIN
69.	Health Insurance Plan	HIP
70.	Health Insurance Online Query Response	HIQR
71.	Health Insurance Reinstating Alphabetic Master	HIRAM
72.	Health Insurance Screening & Cross Referencing	HISAC
73.	Health Insurance System Test Module	HISTM
74.	Health Insurance Utilization Master	HIUM
75.	Health Manpower Shortage Areas	HMSA
76.	HCFA On-Line	HOL
77.	Healthcare Open Systems & Trial	HOST
78.	Health Plan Purchasing Cooperative	HPPC
79.	Health Reimbursement Account	HRA
80.	Historical SPAC Amount	HSA
81.	Health Systems International	HSI
82.	Hospital Specific Rate	HSR
83.	Health Underserved Rural Area	HURA
84.	Import Aid	IA
85.	Intermediary Benefit Payment	IBR
86.	Individual Community Care Plan	ICCP
87.	Inter-Contractor Notices	ICN
88.	InterGovernmental Health Policy Project	IHPP
89.	Individual Medical File	IMF
90.	Inspection of Care	IOC
91.	Intraocular Lens	IOL
92.	Local Coverage Determination	LCD
93.	Local Medical Review Policy	LMRP
94.	Logical Record	LRF
95.	Laboratory Roll In	LRI
96.	Life Safety Code	LSC
97.	Long Term Care	LTC
98.	Long Term Care Facility	LTCF
99.	Long Term Care Unit	LTCU

100.	Last Update Month Indicator	LUMI
101.	Left Ventricular Assist Device	LVAD
102.	Living With	LW
103.	Medicare & Medicaid	M&M
104.	Maximum Allowable Actual Charge	MAAC
105.	Major Ambulatory Category	MAC
106.	Major Ambulatory Diagnostic Categories	MADC
107.	Medical Assistance Facility	MAF
108.	Most Accessible Hospital	MAH
109.	Medical Assistance Only	MAO
110.	Medical Assistance Program	MAP
111.	Medicare Advantage Prescription Drug Plans	MA-PD
112.	Medicaid Analytic	MAX
113.	Medicare Beneficiary	MBD
114.	Medicaid Budget & Expenditure	MBE
115.	Master Beneficiary Record	MBR
116.	Mutual Consent Agreement	MCA
117.	Medicare Contractor Administrative Budget	MCAB
118.	Medicare Code Editor	MCE
119.	Managed Care Organization	MCO
120.	Medicare Contractor Systems Information Database	MCSID
121.	Medicare Decision Support	MDS
122.	Medicare Effectiveness	ME
123.	Multiple Electro Conclusive Therapy	MECT
124.	Medicare Exclusion Database	MED
125.	Medicaid Eligibly Terminal	MET
126.	Medicaid Fraud Control Unit	MFCU
127.	Medicare fee Schedule	MFS
128.	Medicaid Grant Awards	MGA
129.	Maximum Hospital Benefit	MHB
130.	Manual Issuance	MI
131.	Medicare Information Request	MIR
132.	Major Service Area	MSA
133.	Medicare Status Notice	MSN
134.	Medicare Social Services	MSS
135.	Medicare Volume Performance Standard	MVPS
136.	National Average Actuarial Value	NAAV
137.	National Alliance for Infusion Therapy	NAIT
138.	National Alliance for the Mentally Ill	NAMI
139.	National Coverage Average	NCA

140.	National Colorectal Cancer Roundtable	NCCR
141.	National Coverage Determination	NCD
142.	National Claims History	NCH
143.	National Contingency Plan	NCP
144.	National Coverage Policy	NCP
145.	National Drug Code	NDC
146.	National Death Repository	NDR
147.	New England Health Assembly	NEHA
148.	Nursing Home	NH
149.	National Health Expenditure	NHE
150.	National Medical Enterprises	NME
151.	Nurse Review Unit	NRU
152.	Old Age Assistance	OAA
153.	Outcome & Assessments Information Set	OASIS
154.	Open Enrollment Period for Institutionalized Individuals	OEPI
155.	Outpatient Feedback	OFB
156.	Opportunity to Improve Care	OIC
157.	Outpatient	OP
158.	Outpatient Rehabilitation Facility	ORF
159.	Outpatient Speech Pathology	OSP
160.	Personal Access Code	PAC
161.	Preadmission Certification	PAC
162.	Pan American Health Organization	PAHO
163.	Premium Billing Code	PBC
164.	Pharmacy Benefit Managers	PBMS
165.	Patient Care Algorithm	PCAS
166.	Primary Care Case Management Provider	PCCMP
167.	Premium Conversion Date	PCD
168.	Personal Care Expenditures	PCE
169.	Provider Claims Processing Requirements	PCPR
170.	Premium Deducted	PD
171.	Phased-Down State Contribution	PDSC
172.	Physician Fee Freeze	PFF
173.	Partial Hospitalization	PH
174.	Prepaid Health Care Plan	PHCP
175.	Post Hospital Emergency Care	PHEC
176.	Personal Health Information	PHI
177.	Primary Insured Amount	PIA
178.	Pro Intermediary Carrier	PIC
179.	Prepaid Inpatient Health Plan	PIHP

180.	Protection for Long Term Assistance Needs	PLAN
181.	Plan of Care	POC
182.	Provider Overpayment Recovery	POR
183.	Plan of Treatment	POT
184.	Pharmaceutical Prime Vendor	PPV
185.	Provider Reimbursement Manual	PRMDA
186.	Prospective Reimbursement Profile	PRP
187.	Payment Reform Policy Development	PRPD
188.	Parameter Release Study	PRS
189.	Physician Sequential	PS
190.	Physician/Supplier Action File	PSAF
191.	Provider Specific File	PSF
192.	Physician Summary Master	PSM
193.	Proposed Site Treatment Plan	PSTP
194.	Provider Update Operation	PUP
195.	Provider Bills	PVB
196.	Persons With Disabilities	PWD
197.	Quality Adjusted Life Year	QALY
198.	Quality Assurance Monitoring	QAM
199.	Quality Medicare Beneficiary	QMB
200.	Quality Utilization Generic Screens	QUGS
201.	Resident Assessment Instrument	RAI
202.	Regional Intermediary	RI
203.	Renal Dialysis Facility	RDF
204.	Regional Education About Choices in Health	REACH
205.	Rural Health Claim	RHC
206.	Re-Bundling of Hospital Payment	RHP
207.	Regional Informational Letter	RIL
208.	Refugee Medical Assistance	RMA
209.	Reasonably Minimally Exposed Individual	RMEI
210.	Return to Provider	RTP
211.	Real-Time Radiography	RTR
212.	RRB Universal RIC	RUNT
213.	Staff Assisted Home Dialysis	SAHD
214.	School Based Clinics	SBC
215.	Sole Community Hospital	SCH
216.	Significant Change In Condition	SCIC
217.	Sole Community Provider	SCP
218.	Specialty Care Transport	SCT
219.	Secondary Diagnostic Category	SDC

220.	Single Drug Price	SDP
221.	Surveillance, Epidemiology, & End Results	SEER
222.	Special Enrollment Period	SEP
223.	Select Health Care	SHC
224.	Supplemental Health Insurance	SHI
225.	State Health Notes	SHN
226.	Single Loss Expectancy	SLE
227.	Specified Low-Income Medicare Beneficiary	SLMB
228.	Standard Med Review Instrument	SMI
229.	Skilled Nursing Care	SNC
230.	Statement of Benefits	SOB
231.	Start of Care	SOC
232.	Seniors Organized to Restore Trust	SORT
233.	Select Provider Program	SPP
234.	Schedule of Providers	SPS
235.	Statistical Report Medicaid Services	SRMC
236.	Social & Rehabilitation Services	SRS
237.	Short Stay Hospital	SSH
238.	Safe Secure Transport	SST
239.	Total Days of Care	TDOC
240.	Transfer Enrollment Period	TEP
241.	Teaching Hospital	TH
242.	Total Parental Nutrition	TPN
243.	Terminate & Stay Resident	TSR
244.	Unbundling of Hospital Payment	UHP
245.	U.S Pharmacopoeia	USP
246.	Ventricular Assist Device	VAD
247.	Voucher Insurance Plan	VIP
248.	Viable Medicare System	VMS
249.	Working Aged	WA
250.	Working Aged Recovery	WAR
251.	Windfall Elimination Provision	WEP
252.	White House Conference on Aging	WHCOA
253.	World Health Organization	WHO
254.	Wound Ostomy Continence Nurses	WOCN
	Subtotal	254

SPECIAL TERMS: INSTRUCTIONAL

	Name	Acronym
1.	ARS Telephone Communications Operating Procedures	ARSTOP
2.	Corrective Action Plan	CAP
3.	Current Good Manufacturing Practicing	CGMP
4.	Corrective Measures Implementation	CMI
5.	Corrective Measures Studies	CMS
6.	Change of Address	COA
7.	Contractor Performance Evaluation	CPE
8.	Data Administration Plan	DAP
9.	DB Rules Processors	DBRP
10.	Data Conversion Plan	DCP
11.	Defense Planning Guidance	DPG
12.	Disaster Recovery Assessment	DRA
13.	Disaster Recovery Plan	DRP
14.	Early Complaint Resolution Process	ECRD
15.	Engineering Requirements	ERQ
16.	Functional Requirements Document	FRD
17.	Hispanic Agenda for Action	HAA
18.	Instrumental Activities of Daily Living	IADL
19.	Informal Dispute Resolution	ICPR
20.	Implementation Guidance Document	IGD
21.	Interim Remedial Action	IRA
22.	Live Test Demonstration	LTD
23.	Memorandum	MAA
24.	Management Control Plan	MCP
25.	Method of Evaluation	MOE
26.	Memorandum of Understanding	MOU
27.	On the Job Training	OJT
28.	Organization Purpose	OP
29.	Operation Policy Letter	OPL
30.	Output Performance Standards	OPS
31.	Proposed Action Memorandum	PAM
32.	Proposal Evaluation Plan	PEP
33.	Program Evaluation & Review Technique	PERT
34.	Program Memoranda	PM
35.	Project Management Plan	PMP
36.	Plan of Expenditures	POE
37.	Place of Service	POS

38.	Program Requirement	PR
39.	Protocol for Regional Office Monitoring	PROM
40.	Proposal Submission Requirements	PSR
41.	Quality Improvement Plan	QIP
42.	Requirements Gathering Techniques	RGT
43.	Reduced Instruction Service Center	RISC
44.	Remote Procedure Call	RPC
45.	Remote Procedure Generator	RPG
46.	State Agency Evaluation Plan	SAEP
47.	Significant Change in Status Assessment	SCSA
48.	Systems Issues, Policies, & Procedures	SIPP
49.	Strategic National Implementation Process	SNIP
50.	Standard Operating Procedure	SOP
51.	Status Operating Procedure	SOP
52.	Task Management Plan	TMP
53.	Task Order	TO
54.	Uniform Cost Report Demonstration	UCRD
55.	Work Plan Objective Code	WOC
56.	Transmit	XMT
	Subtotal	56

SPECIAL TERMS: LEGAL

	Name	Acronym
1.	Background Investigation	BI
2.	Claim In Process	CIP
3.	Civil Monetary Penalty	CMP
4.	Civil Monetary Penalty Law	CMPL
5.	Civil Monetary Penalty Tracking System	CMPTS
6.	Cross Service Agreement	CSA
7.	Environmental Conservation Law	ECL
8.	Final Settlement	FS
9.	Government Purpose License Rights	GPCI
10.	Government Wide Acquisition Contract	GWAC
11.	Interim Agreement	IA
12.	Interim Measures	IM
13.	Joint Agreement Statement	JAS
14.	Ledger Account File	LAF
15.	Last Action Processed	LAP
16.	Laws, Regulations, and Policies	LRP

17.	Legal Weight Truck	LWT
18.	Mutual Assistance Agreement	MAA
19.	Mutual Legal Assistance Treaty	MLAT
20.	National Criminal Justice	NCJRS
21.	Post Entitlement	PE
22.	Settlement	SA
23.	Special Action Code	SAC
24.	Service Level Agreements	SLA
25.	Successful Offer	SO
26.	Statement of Intent	SOI
27.	Submitting Office Number	SON
28.	Third Party	TP
29.	Tri-Party Agreement	TPA
30.	Third Party File	TPF
31.	Third Party Liability	TPL
32.	Third Party Member	TPM
33.	Third Party Record	TPR
34.	Third Party Rules Processor	TPRP
35.	Unfair Labor Practice	ULP
36.	Voluntary Data Sharing Agreement	VDSA
	Subtotal	36

SPECIAL TERMS: SYSTEM

	Name	Acronym
1.	Advanced Distributed Learning System	ADLS
2.	Automated Disbursing System	ADS
3.	Air Education and Training Support System	ADSS
4.	Air Force Restoration Info Management System	AFRIMS
5.	Air Force Recruiting Information Support System	AFRISS
6.	Air Facility Sub- System	AFS
7.	Air Force Safety Automated System	AFSAS
8.	Aerometric Information Retrieval System	AIRC
9.	Aviation Resource Management System	ARMS
10.	Air National Guard Reserve Order Writing Systems	AROWS
11.	Bill Processing System Test	BPST
12.	Behavioral Risk Factor Surveillance System	BRFSS
13.	Carrier Access Billing System	CABS
14.	Carrier Access Billing System	CABS

15.	Contractor Administrative Budget & Cost Reporting System	CABS
16.	Conventional Ammunition Management System	CAIMS
17.	Cadet Administrative Management Information System	CAMIS
18.	Claims Automated Processing System	CAPS
19.	Contractors Analysis & Reporting System	CARES
20.	Consolidated Acquisition Reporting System	CARS
21.	Carrier Alpha State Microfilm/Microfiche System	CAST
22.	Customer Billing Services System	CBSS
23.	Contract Cost Data Reporting System	CCDRS
24.	Contract Control System	CCS
25.	Correspondence Database System	CDB
26.	Central Distribution System	CDS
27.	Chain Directory System	CDS
28.	Cost Effectiveness Measurement System	CEMS
29.	Comprehensive Environmental Response, Competency, Liability Information System	CERCLIS
30.	Cost Estimating System	CES
31.	Case Folder Control System	CF
32.	Common Food Management System	CFMS
33.	Change of Address System	CHAFF
34.	Chain Provider Director System	CHAIN
35.	Charge Distribution System	CHDS
36.	Case Investigation Management System	CIMS
37.	Claims Only Entry System	CLOE
38.	Civil Monitory Penalty Tracking System	CMPTS
39.	Community Options Program Entry System	COPES
40.	Calculations of Overpayment Recovery Timeliness System	CORTS
41.	Contractors Performance Assessment Reporting System	CPARS
42.	Classified Position System	CPS
43.	Carrier Quality Assurance System	CQAS
44.	Congressional Reporting System	CRS
45.	Cuff Records Tracking System	CRTS
46.	Civil Service Retirement System	CSRS
47.	Contractor Workload System	CWS
48.	Direct Billing Integration System	DBIS
49.	Direct Billing System	DBS
50.	Debt Collection System	DCS
51.	Direct Deposit System	DDS
52.	Distributed Database System	DDS

53.	Defense Enterprise Accounting and Management System	DEAMS
54.	Dollar Equivalency System	DES
55.	Defense Logistics Agency Publishing System	DLAPS
56.	Defense Logistics Management System	DLMS
57.	Defense Medical Human Resources System	DMHRS
58.	Disk Management System	DMS
59.	Dynamic Object Oriented Requirements System	DOORS
60.	Distribution Planning Management System	DPMS
61.	Defense Property System	DPS
62.	Dictionary/Repository Access Facility Tools System	DRAFT
63.	Data Program System	DRS
64.	Defense Security Assistance Management System	DSAMS
65.	Development & Support Management System	DSMS
66.	Depot Support System	DSS
67.	Decision Support System	DSS
68.	Defense Travel System	DTS
69.	Daily Update Control System	DUCS
70.	Daily Update Data Exchange System	DUDEX
71.	Data Universal Numbering System	DUNS
72.	Enterprise Business System	EBS
73.	Export Control Automated Support System	ECASS
74.	Electronic Correspondence Referral System	ECRS
75.	Electronic Certification System	ECS
76.	Expeditionary Control Automated Support System	ECSS
77.	ESRD Data Entry & Editing System	EDEES
78.	Electronic Funds Transfer System	EFTS
79.	Executive Information System	EIS
80.	Electronic Key Management System	EKMS
81.	Electronic military Personnel Records System	EMPRS
82.	Emergency Medical Service System	EMSS
83.	Engineering and Base Operations support System	ENBOSS
84.	Enrollment Online Inquiry System	EOIS
85.	Excluded Parties List System	EPLS
86.	Experimental Reimbursement System	ERS
87.	Enrollment Statistical Tabulation System	ESTS
88.	Enumeration Verification System	EVS
89.	Federal Agencies Centralized Trial-balance System	FACTS
90.	Federal Logistics Information System	FLIS
91.	Financial Management System	FMS
92.	Global Air Transportation Execution System	GATES

93.	Global Combat Support System	GCSS
94.	General Fund Enterprise Business System	GFEBS
95.	Hazardous Material Information Resource System	HMIRS
96.	Hazardous Substance Management System	HSMS
97.	Industrial Base Information System	IBIS
98.	Integrated Booking System	IBS
99.	Information Center Management System	ICMS
100.	Information Data Management System	IDMS
101.	Integrated General Ledger Accounting System	IGLAS
102.	International Logistics Communication System	ILCS
103.	Intervening Medical Care Analysis System	IMACS
104.	Incident Management System	IMS
105.	Interim Payment System	IPS
106.	Information Resource Depository System	IRDS
107.	Interim & Resident Information System	IRIS
108.	International Trade Data System	ITDS
109.	Inspection Tracking System	ITS
110.	Knowledge-Based Corporate Reporting System	KBCRS
111.	Major Automated Information System	MAIS
112.	Marine Corps Total Force System	MCTFS
113.	Military Standards System	MILS
114.	Management Information System	MIS
115.	Movement Tracking System	MTS
116.	National Claims History System	NCHS
117.	National Communications System	NCS
118.	National Disaster Medical System	NDMS
119.	National Drug Pricing System	NDPS
120.	National Data Reporting System	NDRR
121.	National Electronic Disease Surveillance System	NEDSS
122.	National Integrated Medicaid Management System	NIMMS
123.	National Law Enforcement Telecommunications Systems	NLETS
124.	Network Monitoring System	NMS
125.	National Polar-orbiting Operation Environmental Satellite System	NPOESS
126.	National Respiratory and Enteric Virus Surveillance System	NREVSS
127.	National Security Personnel System	NSPS
128.	Navy Tactical Command Support System	NTCSS
129.	Patient Accounting System	PAS
130.	Past Performance Information Retrieval System	PPIRS
131.	Patient Safety Reporting System	PSR

132.	Automated Voucher System	RAVC
133.	Reserve Component Automation System	RCAS
134.	Recertified Check System	RCR
135.	Regional Economic Information System	REIS
136.	Rental Facilities Management Information System	RFMIS
137.	Standard Automated Material Management System	SAMMS
138.	Safe Drinking Water Information System	SDWIS
139.	Standard Procurement System	SPS
140.	Systems Requirements Definitions	SRD
141.	Student Registration and Record System	SRRS
142.	Systems Security Assessment	SSA
143.	Standard System Maintainers	SSM
144.	Scientific and Technology Enterprise System	STES
145.	Terrorism Information and Preventive Systems	TIPS
146.	Transportation Operational Personal Property Standard System	TOPS
147.	Technical Training Management System	TTM
148.	Viable Information Processing Systems	VIPS
149.	Web-Based Injury Statistics Query and Reporting System	WISQARS
150.	Weapon System Life Cycle Management	WSLM
151.	Weapon System Life Cycle Management Entity	WSLMSE
152.	Wounded Warrior Accountability System	WWAS
153.	Xerox Network System	XNS
	Subtotal	153

SPECIAL TERMS: SCIENCE & TECHNOLOGY

	Name	Acronym
1.	Applications Alarms Infrastructure	AAI
2.	Abnormal Ending	ABEND
3.	Automated Change Control	ACC
4.	Automatic Calling Unit	ACU
5.	Arithmetic Coefficient of Variation	ACV
6.	Application Development System Online	ADSB
7.	Accumulation File number	AFN
8.	Automated Insertion Machine	AIM
9.	American National Standard	ANS
10.	Application Owning Region	AOR
11.	Award Processing	AP
12.	Application Portability Profile	APP

13.	Advanced Program to Program Communication	APPC
14.	Automated Response Unit	ARU
15.	Audio Response Unit	ARU
16.	American Standard Code for Information Interchange	ASCII
17.	Application Software Configuration Management	ASCM
18.	Application Specific Integrated Circuit	ASIC
19.	Assembler H Software	ASMH
20.	All Trunks Busy	ATB
21.	Asynchronous Transfer Mode	ATM
22.	Baltimore Computer Conference & Exposition	BCCE
23.	Binary Coded Decimal	BCD
24.	Border Gateway	BGP
25.	Business Software Alliance	BSA
26.	Binary Synchronomous Communications	BSC
27.	Composite Analysis	CA
28.	Computer Aided Logistics Report	CALS
29.	Computer Based Training	CBT
30.	Change Control Coordination	CCC
31.	Challenge Handshake Authentication Program	CHAP
32.	Commitment Information Number	CIN
33.	Count Key Data	CKD
34.	Call Level Interface	CLI
35.	Chain of Trust	COT
36.	Cyclic Redundancy	CRC
37.	Common Supplier Engagement	CSE
38.	Data Acquisition	DA
39.	Data Analysis	DA
40.	Defense Automatic Addressing	DAAS
41.	Discretionary Access Control	DAC
42.	Data Entity	DAE
43.	Database Management	DBM
44.	Data Control Block	DCB
45.	Data Carrier Direct	DCD
46.	Direct Data Exchange	DDE
47.	Data Description Language	DDL
48.	Dual Entitlement Code	DEC
49.	Data Encryption Standard	DES
50.	Data Flow Diagram	DFP
51.	Duplication In, Duplication Out	DIDO
52.	Defense Information Infrastructure	DII

53.	Dual In-Line Package	DIP
54.	Data Language	DL
55.	Data Model	DM
56.	Data Model Diagram	DMD
57.	Data Management Language	DML
58.	Data Management	DMSS
59.	Developmental Office Minicomputer	DOM
60.	Data Set Name	DSN
61.	Deployed Theatre	DTAS
62.	Data Terminal Equipment	DTE
63.	Data Use Agreement	DUA
64.	Evaluation Assurance Level	EAL
65.	Evaluation Criterion	EC
66.	Event Cycle	EC
67.	Electronic Code Book	ECB
68.	Extended Count Key Data	ECKD
69.	Electronic Counter Measures	ECM
70.	Enterprise Database	EDB
71.	Electronic Data Interchange	EDI
72.	Electronic Data Processing	EDP
73.	Electronic Data Warehouse	EDW
74.	Extremely Low Frequency	ELF
75.	Enrollment Module	EM
76.	Enquiry Control	ENQ
77.	Electronic Network Services	ENS
78.	Electronic Postmark	EPM
79.	Entity Relationship	ER
80.	Entity Relationship Diagram	ERD
81.	Electronic Remittance Notice	ERN
82.	Entity Relationship Verification	ERV
83.	Enterprise System Architecture	ESA
84.	End of Block	ETB
85.	Extended Terminal Multiplexer	ETM
86.	File Control Table	FCT
87.	Federal Enterprise Architecture	FEA
88.	Federal Systems Integration Management	FEDSIM
89.	Federal Standard	FED-STD
90.	Federal Information Processing Resources	FIPR
91.	Federal Information Processing Standard	FIPS
92.	Future Logical Model	FLM

93.	Federal Software Exchange	FSE
94.	General Systems Design	GSD
95.	Hierarchical Input Processing & Output	HIPO
96.	High Level Qualifier	HLQ
97.	Higher Monitoring Authority	HMA
98.	Information Access	IA
99.	Innovative Access Method	IAM
100.	Information Control Area	ICA
101.	Integrated Computer Aided Manufacturing	ICAM
102.	Interface Control Document	ICD
103.	Internet Control Message Protocol	ICMP
104.	Implementation Data	ID
105.	Institutional Controls	IDC
106.	Investigational Device Exemptions	IDE
107.	Improved Data Record Capability	IDRC
108.	Integrated Data Dictionary	IDS
109.	Information Exchange	IE
110.	Internet Protocol	IP
111.	Initial Program Load	IPL
112.	Integrated Planning Process	IPP
113.	Internal Quality Control	IQC
114.	Initial Review Unit	IRU
115.	Intersystem Communication	ISC
116.	Integrated Services Digital Network	ISDN
117.	Information Systems Management	ISM
118.	Interconnection System Operation	ISO
119.	Intelligence, Surveillance, & Reconnaissance	ISR
120.	Information Systems Security Plan	ISSP
121.	Information Technology	IT
122.	Joint Aviation Technical Data Integration	JATDI
123.	Joint Control Language	JCL
124.	Job Entry Subsystem	JES
125.	Knowledged Based Intelligence Tracking	KBIT
126.	Knowledged Based Software Assistant	KBSA
127.	Local Area Network	LAN
128.	Lightweight Directory Access Protocol	LDAP
129.	Logical Database Design	LDD
130.	Logical Data Model	LDM
131.	Local Shared Resource	LSR
132.	Machine-Readable Cataloging	MARC

133.	Multistation Access Unit	MAU
134.	Management Information System	MIS
135.	Multiply Occurring	MO
136.	Master Processing	MP
137.	Network Data Mover	NDM
138.	Netware Directory Services	NDS
139.	National Information Infrastructure	NII
140.	National Internal Telecommunications	NIT
141.	Network Performance Analyzer	NPA
142.	Narrative Provider Plan	NPP
143.	National Spatial Data Infrastructure	NSDI
144.	National Standard Electronic Format	NSEF
145.	New Technology	NT
146.	Outcome Based Quality Monitoring	OBQM
147.	Optical Character Recognition	OCR
148.	Original Equipment Manufacturer	OEM
149.	Optional Form	OF
150.	Only Handle Information Once	OHIO
151.	On-Line Analytical Process	OLAP
152.	Online Mapping	OLM
153.	Online Query	OLQ
154.	Online Transaction Processing	OLTP
155.	Out of Service Area	OSA
156.	Open Software Evaluation	OSE
157.	Program Data Vector	PDV
158.	Practical Quantization Limit	PQL
159.	Procurement Request Info	PRI
160.	Problem Statement Analysis	PSA
161.	Problem Source of Identification	PSI
162.	Processing Time	PT
163.	Performance Test Platform	PTP
164.	Query By Example	QBE
165.	Quality Call Monitoring	QCM
166.	Radio Detection & Ranging	RADAR
167.	Redundant Array of Independent Disk	RAID
168.	Ready Assessment Packages	RAP
169.	Remote Access Trojan	RAT
170.	Role-Based Access Control	RBAC
171.	Research Demonstration & Evaluation	RD&E
172.	Restructured Extended Executor Language	REXX

173.	Software Asset Management	SAM
174.	Service Computation	SCD
175.	System Design Activity	SDA
176.	Standards Enforcement Software	SES
177.	Secure Hash Algorithm	SHA
178.	Secure Hyper Text Transfer Protocol	SHTIP
179.	Special Indicator Code	SIC
180.	Society for Information Management	SIM
181.	System Internal Specifications	SIS
182.	System Manager	SM
183.	Systems Measurement Facility	SMF
184.	Structure of Management Information	SMI
185.	System Network Interface	SNI
186.	Synchronous Optical Network	SONET
187.	System of Record	SOR
188.	Systems of Records	SORS
189.	Sequential Processing Facility	SPF
190.	Structured Query Language	SQL
191.	Technology Assessment	TA
192.	Technical Component	TC
193.	Technical Evaluation Criteria	TEC
194.	Transport Layer Security	TLS
195.	Technical Reference Model	TRM
196.	Technical Strategy	TS
197.	Telecommunication Services and Enterprise Acquisition Services	TSEAS
198.	Technical Support Facility	TSF
199.	Testing Phase	TST
200.	Text Telephones	TTY
201.	Unit Analysis	UA
202.	User Acceptance Testing	UAT
203.	Utilization Control	UC
204.	Utilization Database	UDB
205.	User Defined Exit	UDE
206.	Users Group Management Terminal	UGMT
207.	User Language	UL
208.	Uniform Resource Locator	URL
209.	User Requirements	URQ
210.	Utilization Status Query	USQ
211.	Voice Added Exchange	VAX

212.	Visual Basic Architecture	VBA
213.	Value Code	VC
214.	Very Large Scale Integration	VLSI
215.	Web Based Training	WBT
216.	Cross Reference Account Code	XAC
217.	Extended Data Processing	XDP
218.	Extended Data Representation	XDR
219.	Exchange Identifier	XID
220.	Excelerator	XL
	Subtotal	220

Additional acronyms can be found at the following websites:

- http://www.dtic.mil/doctrine/dod_dictionary/
- http://gov.onvia.com/Government-acronyms/
- http://members.cox.net/govdocs/govspeak.
- http://www.all-acronyms.com/ - searchable by acronym, not name.

Chapter 25

Government Writing Exercises

This chapter provides instructions on how to write documents unique to the government's decision-making and communication processes. The sample base program document (BPD) is the *only* additional resource document to be used for the various writing exercises (the BPD can be found at the end of this chapter). The BPD discusses issues relevant to the political environment, along with additional information required to develop the issues, background, analysis and recommendations to complete the respective exercises. In summary, the BPD is the government's *institutional memory* for the addressed issue and comprises of the following:

- The historic position or positions the agency or department has taken, inclusive of analyses and decision criteria generated in the past;
- The agency's or department's current position on the issue;
- The up-to-date data and analysis associated with the issue;
- The political and policy position of the agency or department head, which may or may not differ dramatically from the institutional position; and
- The position taken by the major stakeholders involved in the issue, both those who support the agency's institutional and political positions and those who oppose them.

The flow of written instruments that facilitates the government's decision-making process is reflected in the following order:

1. **Biography** – To facilitate establishing good working relationships between Internal/External government stakeholders;
2. **Issue Paper** – To facilitate provision of an objective education on the specific and narrow issues your management identifies;
3. **Decision Paper** – To facilitate conducting a credible and professional analysis of decision alternatives your management requests;
4. **Appeals Document** – To facilitate provision of an analysis targeted to identify potential flaws in management decisions;
5. **Briefing Memoranda** – To facilitate an understanding of the decisions made and their rationale as written for internal Executive Branch consumption;
6. **Regulation** – To provide a detailed and precise interpretation of regulation required to ensure that the Congress' intent is achieved;
7. **Congressional Budget Justification** – To facilitate conducting the level-of-effort analysis associated with human, dollar, and extramural resources required to meet the Administration's performance objectives;
8. **Guidance Directive** – To facilitate in providing specific instructions for implementing a program that does not have the enforcement component found in regulations;
9. **Congressional Testimony** – To facilitate the articulation of Administration's position and the key reasons for it;
10. **Advocacy Document** – To facilitate advocacy for the Administration's position among stakeholders on issues, proposals, and solutions reached within the Executive Branch;
11. **Correspondence** – To facilitate preparation of clear responses to questions raised   by the public; and
12. **Press Release** – To facilitate the public announcement and explanation of the government's initiatives and rationale.

Instructions and Formatting

For all writing exercises, please:

- Write no more than two and a half (2 ½) pages in length when it is type written (Times New Roman, font size 12) and double-spaced.
- If you do not type the assignment, please print neatly in block letters.
- Include your name, position, and Department/Agency in the left hand corner of your written exercise paper.
- Read, comprehend, and utilize the BPD on the California condor as your primary resource to complete written exercise assignments.
- Only information included within the BPD is to be used to determine how to apply your leadership goals and your position on the condor issue.
- Choose a position to support and explain why you decided to support that position.

- Remember, as you prepare your assignment; apply strategic thinking, external awareness, decisiveness, financial and human capital management, problem solving methods and political savvy, as appropriate to your perspective.

Exercises

1. BIOGRAPHY

This exercise combines unique government-oriented rules with standard rules for preparing a biography. A biography introduces you to the stakeholders involved in the decision-making process, both internal and external to the government. The objective is to provide concise information required to establish your creditability, your personality, and also a personal side to facilitate the development of a solid working relationship.

The following distinctive information is recommended:

- Name. Include any honorific title in the initial reference; optional after that;
- Birthplace & where you grew up;
- Current position and ***brief resume*** of experience expressed by discussing accomplishments in professional life;
- An interesting personal factoid which articulates a personal attribute or trait; and
- Family related item, e.g. my family and I climbed Mount Everest.

Key stylistic rules to follow include:

- Write in third person view;
- Use plain English;
- Be concise and punctual; and
- Avoid using acronyms.

Exercises Requiring Use of the BPD

1. BENCH MARK WRITING EXERCISE: BPD POSITION STATEMENT

To begin, please prepare the following written exercise.

Objectives

The objectives and concepts associated with preparation of this exercise assignment include:

- Demonstrating why effective government writing is critical to achieving government leadership objectives;

- Stating your position on one of the alternatives discussed in the condor Base Program Document (BPD) from a career government leadership perspective, as well as a reflection of your understanding of the chosen issue;
- Demonstrating the strengths of your current writing skills and approaches; and
- Your capability to apply the Plain Language in Government Writing Initiative[1] to clearly, transparently, and concisely articulate your position.

Exercise Philosophy

The Office of Personnel Management (OPM) has identified five executive core qualifications (ECQs) to guide career leaders. Consequently, career Senior Executives apply them to further advancement within the career civil service. The five ECQs are Leading Change, Leading People, Results Driven, Business Acumen, and Building Coalitions. Your written product should apply these criteria, as appropriate, to the exercise assignment.

In addition to applying the guidance found in the ECQs, the following specific guidance is provided to assist you with the writing exercise:

- Assume you will advance to become a senior leader in one of the following governmental disciplines: HQ Policy/Program/Field Operations Manager, Budget/Finance Officer, Science/Technical Lead Investigator, or External Affairs Manager.
- Your written product will be evaluated using the following criteria: effectiveness in communicating your position and rationale, skill in writing clearly, and demonstrating your leadership potential.

This guidance is provided to assist you to think through an appropriate flow for your writing assignment, including: leadership perspective, background information influencing your position, integrating facts and figures from the BPD to make your rationale persuasive. You are not precluded from applying budgetary impacts or political implications in the writing exercise.

2. ISSUE PAPER

The primary purpose of an issue paper is to examine an issue and discuss approaches associated with addressing that issue. This instrument is designed to educate government executives on the alternatives for addressing an issue. An effective issue paper provides an expert comparison of alternatives in a concise and accurate manner. The target audience is comprised of those who can influence policy.

---

[1] *http://www.gpo.gov/fdsys/pkg/FR-1998-06-10/pdf/98-15700.pdf - (FR Doc. 98-15700, Federal Register, v.63, no.111, June 10, 1998).*

The issue paper exercise is to be responsive to the issue your manager is seeking to understand. The paper must be written in plain English and be concise, objective and informative, while remaining respectful of opposing viewpoints.

Issue papers are not decision papers; they are used solely to explain viable alternatives and educate managers. Recommendations should not to be made at this stage of the process.

The following steps should be employed to prepare the issue paper:

- Develop a narrow question that succinctly but clearly states the issue;
- Develop several bullets that provide a factual, transparent and clear background that would allow management to comprehend each of the alternatives delineated;
- Include why management is addressing the issue; and
- Develop three alternatives that address the policy and political context and principle the alternative represents.

The alternatives should be categorized in the following order and based on the assumptions presented:

- The political executive's position articulated in a strong and clear manner;
- The government's current position or the change career experts believe are required due to recent findings or documented experience; and
- The most credible opposition position presented in an objective manner to management.
- The analysis of the alternatives should include bullets which provide:

  o Supporting facts;
  o Optimal operational considerations;
  o Potential impacts inclusive of what facts are relevant versus information that could be considered extraneous to management;
  o The pros and cons of each alternative presented objectively; and
  o Next steps that outline any additional requirements for analysis.

Remember, decisions within the Executive Branch are based on objective, uniform and succinct analyses presented in a professional format. Too little information collected, analyzed and presented can be detrimental to the process. Too much information can also be detrimental and can result in confusion, delays and needless controversy.

3. DECISION PAPER

The decision paper articulates the decision(s) required prior to taking a specific action. It describes the background, logic, reasoning, and impact associated with the options from which a decision should be chosen. This decision document is an internal instrument related to the budget, regulations, management, or policy issues. While it should be prepared in a manner similar to the issue paper, specific decision criteria should be addressed in the background section and a recommendation must be provided. The recommendation is always option number two: the institutional choice.

The decision document is developed at the conclusion of the pre-decision phase. The pre-decision phase accomplishes several objectives, it:

- Identifies problems that warrant deferral action;
- Clearly communicates the scope of the problems;
- Defines the objectives of a federal response; and
- Chooses the appropriate responses needed to achieve these objectives.

After these objectives are determined the decision document can be constructed. The first step in writing the document is to clearly identify the problem and explain why federal action is needed. In order to define the problem the writer must use sufficient detail to explain why this problem raises an issue for the federal government. It is important that the problem be defined in a way that is not open for interpretation and is not biased.

After the problem has been identified the document should include a background section that will outline the facts collected regarding the issue. This should include reports and data collected on the issue by credible sources.

The next step is to determine what options the agency has to come to a recommendation. Typically there are three options:

1. What is the political perspective incumbent in the decision to be made?
2. What is the institution's balanced and expert perspective inherent in the decision to be made?
3. What is the opposition's most credible perspective that is different from the political and institution's known position explicitly reflected for consideration?

After analyzing these options, the agencies have a recommended a course of action on the issue. The recommendation is based on the objective conclusion acquired through the process discussed in the instrument.

After articulating the options, a brief but concise analysis of these options must drive the decision-maker to the most effective decision. In order to determine which option best resolves the issue. Based on the analysis the decision document will conclude with the agency's recommendation. This clearly states which option the agency chose to address the problem and it identified based on the facts and objective analysis that was conducted.

4. APPEAL DOCUMENT

Appeals Papers provide the information that a political executive requires for a comprehensive understanding of the impacts of their decisions. They also present the factual and objective information explaining why a program manager is seeking reconsideration of a decision or a change in existing policy.

Appeals Papers should:

- Develop a narrow question that articulates the issue being appealed.
- Develop a background section that presents the flaws in facts and changes in circumstances that support the change the program manager is seeking.
- Present the three options to frame the decision-making process:

  o The political official's decision adjusted to minimize the potential negative impacts associated with its implementation.
  o The bureaucracy's option that demonstrates, to the extent possible, how the objective associated with the political official's original decision can be achieved.
  o The opposition's option that is neither supported by the political official nor the bureaucracy.

5. BRIEFING MEMORANDA

This instrument is used to share information between the government and other government stakeholders on program, policy, or operational decisions being implemented. Also, the use of charts and graphs can be included to illustrate expected performance and results.

A briefing document should consist of three parts:

- Purpose - state clearly the purpose of the document including the decision made by the agency and advises readers on important dates pertaining to the decision.
- Summary - gives objective facts about the institution's decision and discusses how it came to the decision that it made.
- Discussion - discuss the decision and include additional information about where relevant data, studies, and reports on the subject can be found.

This is a tool used to inform a government stakeholder of a policy, regulatory or operational decision that has been made. The premise is to ensure that all government stakeholders understand the uniform and final government perspective. The first section of the memo should clearly state who the memo is to and who is it from. It should also include the date and a subject line.

The opening statement should address the context of the issue, the particular action or non-action the government will implement, and the purpose of the memo.

After addressing the issue the memo should include a discussion of the subject. The writer should explain the basis for the decision that has been made and what changes will occur as a result. It should also outline any requirements that the audience will need to follow. This discussion should be clear, concise, and address all the key points of the issue.

The writer should then include a description of what the writing agency expects from its audience upon receipt of the memo. It will suggest courses of actions and new requirements. It will advise the audience as to where to find additional information and contact information for questions relating to the subject.

6. REGULATION

There are numerous written documents associated with the development and promulgation of regulations. For the purposes of these writing exercises, please draft only the Notice of Intent.

Regulatory Analysis

As per Executive Orders 13563 and 12866, all agencies' budget officers must provide to the public and to OMB a careful and transparent regulatory impact analysis (RIA) of the anticipated impacts of economically significant regulatory actions. This analysis includes an assessment, quantification and monetization of benefits and costs anticipated to result from the proposed action and from alternative regulatory actions.

An "economically significant" rule is defined as:

1. Having an annual effect on the economy of $100 million or more or adversely affect in a material way the economy, a sector of the economy, productivity, competition, jobs, the environment, public health or safety, or State, local, or tribal governments or communities;
2. Creating a serious inconsistency or otherwise interfere with an action taken or planned by another agency;
3. Materially altering the budgetary impact of entitlements, grants, user fees, or loan programs or the rights and obligations of recipients thereof; or
4. Raising novel legal or policy issues arising out of legal mandates, the President's priorities, or the principles set forth in this Executive order.

The purpose of the RIA is to inform agency decisions in advance of regulatory actions and to ensure that regulatory choices are made after appropriate consideration of the anticipated consequences.

Goals of RIA include[2] (1) establishing whether federal regulation is necessary and justified to achieve a social goal and (2) to clarify how to design regulations in the most efficient, least burdensome, and most cost-effective manner.

---

[2] OMB Circular A-4.

An RIA should include the following three basic elements:

- A statement of the need for the regulatory action;
- A clear identification of a range of regulatory approaches; and
- An estimate of the benefits and costs—both quantitative and qualitative—of the proposed regulatory action and its alternatives.

In addition, the benefit cost analysis should:

- Describe the need for the regulatory action;
- Define the baseline;
- Specify a timeframe of analysis;
- Identify a range of regulatory alternatives;
- Identify the consequences of regulatory alternatives;
- Quantify and monetize the benefits and costs;
- Discount future benefits and costs;
- Evaluate non-quantified and non-monetized benefits and costs; and
- Characterize uncertainties in benefits, costs, and net benefits.

The Rule Making Process

Congress created the framework under which rulemaking is conducted in 1946 when it enacted the Administrative Procedure Act (APA). The APA, though affected by statutes and executive orders throughout the past 60 years, remains the basic legislative standard. Of those executive orders, perhaps the most influential is Executive Order 12866, which mandates presidential review of significant rules through the Office of Information and Regulatory Affairs at the Office of Management and Budget. The elements of the rulemaking process are as follows.

Pre-Rule Phase

Some agencies, such as the Federal Communications Commission, begin with a Notice of Intent for the purpose of gathering information on a subject or generating new ideas.

Following the Notice of Intent (NOI), if employed, the agency prepares publication of an Advance Notice of Proposed Rulemaking (ANPRM), or Pre-rule, in which an agency publicly announces plans to propose certain requirements. According to the APA, the ANPRM must contain:

- A statement of the time, place, and nature of public rulemaking proceedings;
- A reference to the legal authority under which the rule is proposed; and
- Either the terms or substance of the proposed rule or a description of the subjects and issues involved.[37]

---

[3] *Federal Rulemaking: Procedural and Analytical Requirements at OSHA and Other Agencies*, GAO-01-852T, June, 2001, <http://www.gao.gov/new.items/d01852t.pdf> accessed June, 2010.

Proposed Rule Phase

Following the ANPRM, the agency will issue the proposed rule. Interested parties must then be given an opportunity to comment. The APA does not specify the length of this comment period, but agencies commonly allow at least 30 days. The rule will remain in this phase until a Final Rule is published in the Federal Register, which can sometimes be months or even years after publication of the NPRM.[4] The format and required sections of a proposed rule include:

- **Preamble**: Background and intent are described.
- **Proposed Rule**: Specific proposed requirements are spelled out in similar detail to how it would be published in the final rule.
- **Listing of Acts and Regulations Affected**: All acts and regulations to be modified are listed.
  - **Proposed Timetable**: Specific timetable for comment period and for proposed implementation is provided.

Final Rule Phase

After considering the public comments, the agency may then publish the final rule in the *Federal Register*. In general, according to the APA, a final rule cannot become effective until at least 30 days after its publication.[5]

The format of a final rule includes the following:

- **Preamble**: Background and intent are described;
- **Response to Comments**: All comments on the proposed rule are addressed and responded to;
- **Final Rule**: Specific requirements are spelled out in detail in CFR format and as they would appear in the final regulation published in the CFR;
- **Listing of Acts and Regulations Affected**: All acts and regulations to be modified are listed along with how they are modified; and
- **Implementation Timetable**: Specific timetable with effective date.

1. CONGRESSIONAL BUDGET JUSTIFICATION

Budget justifications explain the program logic associated with budgetary requests, the pricing methodology and the relationship of performance metrics to the anticipated results. Within these documents are materials that include data relied upon during the formulation, presentation, and execution phases of the annual budget process. Members and staff, some with little knowledge of the subject at issue, will have to be sufficiently influenced by the data and objective strength demonstrated by the narrative in order to gain the desired outcomes.

---

[4] Ibid.
[5] Ibid.

Using short declaratory sentences and limiting the use of technical terms and jargon assists Members and staff to evaluate the issue and its resource requirements. The structure for a budget justification is as follows:

Introduction and reasoning:

- State precisely the problem that will be solved.
- Explain how solving this problem will help the United States.
- Show how the solution will benefit national objectives. Tie the program to Presidential priorities and the goals and objectives in the department's strategic plan.
- State how the program will make or is making a unique contribution to solving a problem that would not be achieved otherwise.
- Extrapolate on the duration of a new program or the increased/decreased level of effort being proposed.
- Identify other agencies, foreign governments, state or local governments, or the private sector that will be participants in the program. Discuss stakeholders such as program beneficiaries, service providers, and the bill payers (taxpayers).

Budgeting and finance:

- Discuss the budget years cost and include a projection of future resource demands to carry out program;
- Align budget accounts and program activity lines; including the broad policies and strategies proposed and the total amounts of discretionary and mandatory budgetary resources requested;
- Justification for an increase requires an example of the incremental benefits to be gained;
- Justification should summarize the impacts if the budget remained at the guidance level or a decreased level and, reasons why such a budget request would not be appropriate;
- Use tables, charts, and graphs in lieu of or to supplement text; and
- Include a discussion of the risks associated with the program and how the department plans to address those risks.

Benefit/Cost analysis:

- A comparison of total program benefits and total program costs, using quantitative, objective data to the maximum extent possible, as well as qualitative or judgmental material;
- A comparison of the marginal benefits and the marginal costs associated with the additional funds or reduced funding proposed; and
- Supporting information that takes into consideration agency and outside program evaluations and related analytic studies, whether or not they agree with the proposed policy.

2. GUIDANCE DIRECTIVE

"Each agency shall avoid regulations that are inconsistent, incompatible, or duplicative with its other regulations or those of other Federal agencies."*Executive Order 12866 – Regulatory Planning and Review.*

When Executive Order 12866 was issued in 1993, the goal was to reduce the duplication and sometimes-contradictory regulation being issued by the Federal government. However, with hundreds of thousands of regulations covering every sector of the government, it is almost impossible to avoid repeating, confusing and sometimes even conflicting directives. Further, with the pace of technology moving forward continuously and at an ever increasing rate, regulations need to be updated and clarified constantly and in real-time. Finally, language in Acts and Regulation can be construed in different ways by various stakeholders, with each side vying for an alternative outcome; thus leading to confusion as what can and cannot be permitted by law. Guidance directives are sometimes needed when these issues require clarification.

Three questions must be answered by the guidance directive clarifying "gray areas."

1. What is the purpose of this guidance?
2. Who must comply with this guidance?
3. Why is this guidance being written?

Thus, when writing a guidance directive, it is important to incorporate the following:

- Clearly delineate what the issue is;
- Cite the appropriate law or regulation that the guidance is clarifying;
- Include a discussion of both sides of the issue; and
- Conclude with clear and concise guidelines that cannot be misinterpreted.

3. CONGRESSIONAL TESTIMONY

Congressional testimonial documents will provide the administration's position to members of Congress at formal committee hearings. It will include a written statement from which an oral statement is presented. The document should be written as a speech, and flow logically from beginning to end. The objective is to have the hearing committee fully understand the Administration's position and why it is necessary for the agency's program to be implemented. The written statements represent the only written documentation of the Administration's formal position on an issue. When developing a congressional testimony it is important to include the following information:

- Introduce yourself and acknowledge the committee hearing the testimony.
- Introduce the specific topic that will be discussed.
- Explanation of why the issue is important to the hearing.
- Discuss what has been done in the past to address the issue.
- Address what formal studies have been conducted and their conclusions.

- Present the agency's goals and objectives and how they plan on achieving them.
- Outline alternative states of action regarding the topic indicating the agency's preferred choice and why.
- Discussion of relevant budgetary elements, e.g. previous funding and future funding that will be needed.
- Delineate how the funding will be distributed and how it will be used.
- Select and explain the agency's preferred choice of action.

4. ADVOCACY DOCUMENT

There are many occasions in which the Government must advocate its policies to private sector stakeholders that follow government programs. These stakeholders manage resources and commodities that rely on government policies and program operations. State and local Governments, as well as some of the federal departments, have economic development agencies that work with outside stakeholders, e.g. non-profit organizations, academic institutions etc. to establish operations in their locale. Thus, the Government's success is dependent on coordination with stakeholders as well as the mutual understanding with how government policies and operations impact stakeholders.

Before drafting an advocacy document, it is necessary to determine the specific message and associated policies to be advanced in the document. Advocacy documents bring government operations to life. For acceptance, they must clearly state the program or policy associated with the government's campaign and provide substantive support that is more persuasive to stakeholders than other documents that seek to change the government's direction.

Key considerations to consider when preparing an advocacy document for private sector are:

- Identification of a strategic objective that meets the Government's and stakeholders communal goal or goals;
- Identify your audience and show an understanding of their current position on the issue;
- Present the alternatives and the reasons why the decision was made;
- Provide substantive support for your position;
- Emphasize the positive and, where possible, tie your proposed strategy to how it will benefit and positively impact all involved;
- Be conscious of the stakeholder's interests and present solutions or proposals to address them;
- Provide enough information to educate and persuade your audience. It can be a mistake to assume that the stakeholder already agrees with you or comprehends the information you are conveying; and
- Summarize your message briefly by outlining the issue, resolution, and the reasons for the chosen resolution.

5. CORRESPONDENCE

The purpose of correspondence documents is to answer all stakeholder inquiries (e.g. Congressional committees, trade associations, NGO, etc.) regarding government policies and programs. There are four types of correspondence:

- Interim correspondence – acknowledges receipt of a letter and informs the sender that the letter has been received and work on the issue has begun.
- Procedural correspondence – responds to inquiries that raise questions or issues concerning the manner.
- Policy correspondence – used when the writer is addressing an issue within a letter they received and the requested information is now known.
- FOIA requests – federal agencies are required to make information available to anyone who properly requests it. Proper requests have two specifications:

  o The request must reasonably describe the records being sought; and
  o The request must be made in accordance with the agency's published FIOA regulations.

Common writing techniques when developing a correspondence document include; logical organization and mindfulness of the audience, and using active language with short concise sentences and paragraphs. The writer should use common everyday words and avoid using technical jargon to assist the reader in understanding the content.

In order for a correspondence to be effective it is important to first identify your audience and provide them with information about why they are receiving a correspondence document and how it is related to them. It may be new information to the reader and explanation of why they are receiving it might be warranted. The document should be easy to follow and quick to read. This document does not necessitate long explanations, but rather short concise paragraphs that do not require the reader to re-read any of the material. Using an active voice leaves the reader with concrete instructions and clear expectations.

6. PRESS RELEASES

Writing a press release will disseminate the facts about a policy, program, or decision. There is an expectation that the media will find the subject newsworthy.

Press releases should address all the questions the general public will find informational. The press release must address which agency is taking action.
It should identify:

- The course of action it will be taking.
- When the proposed action or program will take place and the duration of time it will take to implement.

- The affected people and geographical locations that will be impacted in addition to outlining why the agency is taking the action they are and its expected impact on society.
- Include a discussion of the actual implementation process and describe how the new program or policy will come into effect.

Provide contact information for public inquiries.

SAMPLE CALIFORNIA CONDOR BASE PROGRAM DOCUMENT

The *BASE PROGRAM DOCUMENT* (BPD) is a dynamic *work in progress*, whose purpose is to assist a leader in preparing high quality issue papers, decision memoranda, testimony, budget justifications, regulatory and associated analytics and other time sensitive government written instruments. This document will be added to and altered as necessary, as facts and circumstances change. The BPD should be consistently relied upon to generate other documents and correspondence throughout the life of the project. Obviously, government leaders must insure that the BPD is accurate and comprehensive in scope; thus statutory, regulatory, budgetary, managerial, and operational considerations must be addressed.

The **four bright lines** of government writing are evident within the BPD. Leadership competencies rely on effective writing, including application of political savvy in order to validate the role of an **institutional politician**. The BPD should emphasize the most important aspect of a program's history, otherwise known as **institutional memory**. In writing the BPD, you should be objective and not reflect any institutional bias; thus reflecting **neutral competence**. Finally, within the justification of an Administration's decisions and the subsequent interface with stakeholders, you should incorporate the appropriate emphasis or **spin**.

I.   BACKGROUND

The Condor Has:

- The largest wingspan, 9.8 feet, of any North America bird and weighs up to 26 pounds, making it equal to the Trumpeter Swan.
- A life span of up to 60 years of in the wild.
- A scavenger classification and eats large amounts of carrion.
- Black coloring with patches of white on the underside of the wings and a bald head, exposing its skin to the sterilizing effects of dehydration and solar ultraviolet light at high altitudes.

The condor is a rare bird and as such is on the federal endangered species list. Their critical habitat has been validated through numerous scientific studies.

Breeding Habits:

- Condors are monogamous.
- Mated females are expected to lay one bluish-white egg every other year as early as January to as late as April. Recent studies are documenting 30% fewer eggs laid in the wild and 25% less in captivity.
- Condor eggs weigh about 10 ounces and measure from 3 to 5 inches in length and 2.5 inches in width.
- The eggs hatch after 53 to 60 days of incubation by both parents.

- Some experts believe condors pair for life in the wild and captivity.

Habitat:

- In Pleistocene times, condors ranged from Canada to Mexico, from the Pacific to the Atlantic Oceans. From evidence of bones, feathers, and eggshells found in caves, the condors used the Grand Canyon as a preferred nesting area.
- Condors live in rocky scrubland, coniferous forests, and oak savannas, near cliffs or large trees, which are used as nesting sites.
- Individual condors have been known to travel up to 150 miles in search of their preferred pick of cattle, pigs and carrion.

Current Fish and Wildlife Service Condor Concerns:

- Current Population: 410
- Captive: 180
- Wild: 230
- California: 350
- Baja California, Mexico: 10
- Arizona/Utah: 50
- Based on biological studies required by the Endangered Species Act (ESA) the condor population is declining at an increasingly alarming rate.
- The debate between Republicans, Democrats and Independents is targeted to recovery of the condors to its historical numbers of approximately 1,500 birds.

Population Decline:

- A dramatic range reduction occurred about 10,000 years ago, coinciding with the late Pleistocene extinction of large mammals that condors fed on.
- By the time Europeans arrived in western North America, condors had retreated to a stronghold along the Pacific coast from British Columbia to Baja California.
- By 1900, the condor population plummeted due to many factors including loss of habitat, a low reproductive rate, poisoning, and shooting. The condor was limited to southern California.
- The condors maintained a strong population in southern California until hunting, predatory eggs encroachment, poisoning by cyanide traps set for coyotes, collisions with power lines, wind farm operations, general habitat degradation, and lead poisoning began to take a heavy toll on the population.

Threats to the Condor:

- Increased development of energy operations, including wind farms.
- Increased human encroachment into condor habitats and the resulting degradation of that habitat.
- Increased development of human infrastructure including power distribution lines which the condor will collide with.
- Eating carrion poisoned by lead bullet fragments from hunters.

- Eating carrion poisoned by lead bullet fragments used by the U.S. Military for target practice.
- Eating carrion poisoned by cyanide traps set for coyotes.
- Food chain disruption caused by the decline in population of large game animals throughout their habitat.
- Mating rituals that limit the condor from finding another mate if their first mate has been killed.
- Breeding patterns that limit the condor to breed once every two years, producing only one egg.
- The thin-shelled eggs are susceptible to pesticides and other manmade chemicals.
- An increase in the raven population, which are the main predatory threat to the condor egg.

The aforementioned factors are the basis for the national interest associated with ensuring it is protected from extinction.

Papers and other documentation:

- Rehfus, Ruth. *California Condor (*Gymnogyps Californianus); *the Literature since 1900.* Washington, DC: U.S. Department of the Interior, 2005.
- *California Condor Recovery Plan;* Prepared by the California Condor Recovery Team and Sanford R. Wilbur.
- Wilbur, Sanford R. *The California Condor, 1966 -76: A look at its Past.* Washington, DC: U.S. Department of the Interior, 1978.
- Brower, David Ross and David Phillips and Hugh Nash. *The Condor Question, Captive or Forever Free?* San Francisco, CA: Friends of the Earth, 2012.
- Darlington, David. *In Condor Country.* Boston, MA: Houghton Mifflin, 2000.
- Caras, Roger A. *Source of the Thunder; the Biography of a California Condor.* Boston, MA: Little Brown, 1970.

II.   RECOVERY OPTIONS

The three options to recover the condor population and the subsequent budget justifications for doing so are centered on the following principles:

- Condor Breeding in Captivity to Recover Condor Population;
- Breeding in the Wild; and
- Command and Control to Manage the Condor Population.

Within the budget justifications, there are four sub-elements of each of the above principles. These sub-elements remain the same in each principle:

1. Candidate Conservation (CCP) - The key role of the CCP is to provide technical assistance and work with numerous partners on proactive conservation to remove or reduce threats so that listing species may be unnecessary. This begins with a rigorous assessment using the best scientific information available to determine whether a species faces threats such that it is a candidate for listing and should remain listed under the ESA. This entails close co-operation with states and other appropriate parties. This information is used to target conservation at specific known threats that may make listing unnecessary.

2. Listing & Critical Habitat Program (LCHP) - The LCHP provides protection under the ESA for foreign and domestic plants and animals when a species is determined to be threatened or endangered on the basis of the best available scientific information concerning threats. This determination includes information crucial for recovery planning and implementation, and helps to identify and address the conservation needs of the species, including the designation of critical habitat. Without the legal protections afforded under Section 9 of the ESA that become effective upon listing, many species would continue to decline and become extinct.

3. Consultation & Habitat Conservation Plans (CHCPP) - The CHCPP leads a collaborative process between the Fish and Wildlife Service (FWS) and other federal agencies to identify opportunities to conserve listed species. Working in partnership with other agencies and organizations is foundational for the Endangered Species program, because the conservation of the Nation's biological heritage cannot be achieved by any single agency or organization. Essential partners include other federal agencies, states, tribes, non-governmental organizations, industry, academia, private landowners, and other FWS programs or partners. Other federal agencies consult with the Service to balance adverse impacts of their development actions with conservation actions that contribute toward species survival and also often to their recovery.

4. Recovery - The Recovery Program implements actions for species near delisting or reclassification from endangered to threatened, and actions that are urgently needed for critically endangered species. The Endangered Species Program will participate in this Cooperative Recovery Initiative by combining our resources with those of the National Wildlife Refuge System, the Partners for Fish and Wildlife Program, the Fisheries Program, the Science Program and the Migratory Bird Program through a national, proposal-driven process to identify and implement the highest priority projects.

Each of these aforementioned programs is within the authority of the United States Fish and Wildlife Service (FWS). The program overview and base description of these sub-elements will not vary, however, the funding level and narrative for the various programs will change due to the different needs and requirements depending on the desired outcome.

The U.S. Fish and Wildlife Service's Endangered Species program implements the Endangered Species Act of 1973 (ESA), in coordination with numerous partners. The program provides expertise to accomplish key purposes of the ESA, which are to provide a means for conserving the ecosystems upon which endangered and threatened species depend and to provide a program for the conservation of such species.[6]

The program's strategic framework is based on two over-arching goals to achieve the ESA's purposes: 1) recovery of endangered or threatened (federally listed) species, and 2) conservation of species-at-risk, so that listing them may be unnecessary. The program achieves these goals through the minimization or abatement of threats that are the basis for listing a species.

The ESA categorizes threats into the following five factors:

1. The present or threatened destruction, modification, or curtailment of a listed species' habitat or range;
2. Overutilization for commercial, recreational, scientific, or educational purposes;
3. Disease or predation;
4. The inadequacy of existing regulatory mechanisms; and
5. Other natural or manmade factors affecting a species' continued existence.

The key factor identified for many species is related to habitat alteration. The scope and severity of habitat-based threats and the number of species involved increases substantially with the complexity of threats. Minimizing or removing threats, which may include supporting species' capacity to respond adequately or increase their resilience to changing conditions, may conserve a species, eliminating the need for protection under the ESA.

The California condor flourished along the Pacific coast for many years and then in large part to habitat loss, illegal shootings, and lead poisoning. By 1985, the entire wild population had been reduced to just 9 birds, which was when a decision was made to bring all of the remaining wild birds into captivity, thus preserving the species through captive breeding and eventual reintroduction. The goal of the California Condor Recovery Plan was to establish two geographically separate populations, two in California and one in Arizona, each with 150 birds and at least 15 breeding pairs. As the Recovery Program works toward this goal the number of release sites has grown. There are three active release sites in California, one in Arizona and one in Baja California, Mexico. The recovery program for the California condor was showing success, and the birds were expanding their range and reoccupying portions of their historic range, which includes areas of existing and proposed wind energy development. However, significant increases in fatalities to the condor over recent

---

[6] FY 2014 Budget Justification: United States Department of the Interior.

years have resulted in the total number of condors reducing dramatically. Thus, it is recommended that the implementation of the California condor captive breeding program be placed into operation without delay.

I. <u>Condor Breeding in Captivity to Recover Condor Populations</u>

In response to the significantly diminished condor population, the Condor Breeding in Captivity Recovery Program's strategy focuses on:

- Increasing reproduction in captivity;
- The release of condors to the wild;
- Minimizing condor death factors;
- Maintaining habitat for condor recovery; and
- Implementing condor information and education programs.

A primary objective of the recovery program is to take the condor species off of the endangered species list and work to downgrade it to a threatened species.

- The goal is to have 3 separate populations of 150 birds, which sets a safety net for the birds. Estimated time for achieving this goal is 2020.
- To achieve that goal, the plan is to establish two geographically separate populations, two in California and one in Arizona, each with 150 birds and at least 15 breeding pairs.
- As progress is made the number of release sites will grow.
- The San Diego Wild Animal Park and Los Angeles Zoo will lead the captive breeding program.

Breeding Techniques

- Utilizing the bird's ability to double clutch, biologists will implement an unique captive breeding technique by removing the first egg from the nest which should result in the condor producing a second and sometimes a third egg.
- The extra eggs will be incubated and caretakers using a hand puppet shaped like a condor head will raise the chicks.

Historical Budget for the California Condor Recovery Program:

- In 1978, the estimated annual budget for this recovery effort was approximately $1 million. This number has increased annually.

Recovery Program Stakeholders Include:

- U.S. Fish and Wildlife Service
- Conservation and Research for Endangered Species
- San Diego Wild Animal Park
- Los Angeles Zoo
- The Peregrine Fund
- California Department of Fish and Game
- Arizona Game and Fish
- Bureau of Land Management
- Oregon Zoo
- Santa Barbara Zoo
- Ventana Wildlife Society

BUDGET JUSTIFICATION FOR CONDOR BREEDING IN CAPTIVITY TO RECOVER CONDOR POPULATION ACTIVITY:

- SUMMARY TABLE

				FY 2014		
	2012 Actual	2013 Enacted	Fixed Costs & Related Changes (+/-)	Program Changes (+/-)	Budget Request	Change from 2012 Enacted (+/-)
Candidate ($)	$2,345,678	$2,567,890	+$1,123,456	+$1,962,975	$5,654,321	+$3,086,431
Conservation (FTE)	13	17	+14	+3	34	+17
Listing & Critical Habitat ($)	$2,345,678	$2,123,456	$0	$0	$2,123,456	$0
(FTE)	23	26	0	0	26	0
Consultation & Habitat ($)	$9,876,543	$9,999,999	$0	-$1,111,111	$8,888,888	-$1,111,111
Conservation Plans (FTE)	28	30	0	-7	23	-7
Recovery ($)	$3,456,789	$4,567,890	+$1,000,000	+$7,000,000	$12,567,890	+$8,000,000
(FTE)	21	26	+24	0	50	+24
California Condor ($)	$18,024,688	$19,259,235	$2,123,456	$7,851,864	$29,234,555	$9,975,320
(FTE)	85	99	38	-4	133	34

- **Principle: Breeding in Captivity**
  Sub-Element: Candidate Conservation

	2012 Actual	2013 Enacted	FY 2014			
			Fixed Costs & Related Changes (+/-)	Program Changes (+/-)	Budget Request	Change from 2013 Enacted (+/-)
Candidate ($)	$2,345,678	$2,567,890	+$1,123,456	+$1,962,975	$5,654,321	+$3,086,431
Conservation (FTE)	13	17	+14	+3	34	+17

Justification for Program Changes for Candidate Conservation Program

The FY 2014 budget request for Candidate Conservation Program (CCP) is $5,654,321 and 34 FTE, a net program change of +$3,086,431 and +17 FTE.

Total numbers for the California condor have decreased from 410 in 2010 to 383 in 2012, a staggering 6.6% decrease. This is inclusive of the 38 condor chicks that hatched in that time, meaning that the condor population has been decimated by the totally unacceptable number of 65 in just a two-year period. Should the numbers continue to decline at such an alarming rate, the California condor could be extinct within 10 years. There are three main reasons for the sharp decline:

- Condors are being killed by newly constructed wind farms;
- Condors are being killed by lead poisoning from hunting ammunition; and
- Pesticide poisoning is killing condors.

In conjunction with other stakeholders, including the Department of Agriculture, Department of Energy, State and Local governments, and the NRA, the CCP will continue to conduct rigorous evaluations of potential hazards and threats to determine the most amenable outcome for all parties involved. CCP is also currently undertaking a number of studies of zoos, both nationally and internationally, that have the capability to accommodate a breeding pair of California condors. The overall FY 2014 program funding and Full-Time Equivalent Employees (FTE) increase reflects the increased cost and workload associated with these studies. Each study is expected to use an additional 2.5 FTE per year over a three-year period. The fixed cost increase reflects the cost for renovation of the San Diego Old Tram Warehouse which will be used to headquarter the newly formed California Condor Operation, as authorized in the *FY 2013 Urgent Situation Supplemental Act* (P.L. 007). The FTE increase reflects the 14 staffers required to operate the office.

- PRINCIPLE: BREEDING IN CAPTIVITY
  SUB-ELEMENT: LISTING AND CRITICAL HABITAT

			FY 2014			
	2012 Actual	2013 Enacted	Fixed Costs & Related Changes (+/-)	Program Changes (+/-)	Budget Request	Change from 2012 Enacted (+/-)
Listing & Critical ($)	$2,345,678	$2,123,456	$0	$0	$2,123,456	$0
Habitat (FTE)	23	26	0	0	26	0

Justification for Program Changes for Listing and Critical Habitat Program

The FY 2014 budget request for the LCHP is $2,123,456 and 26 FTE, a net program change of $0 and 0 FTE.

As described, the California condor situation is critical. A compilation of studies undertaken by the LCHP recommends that for the California condor species to survive, the implementation of a captive breeding program, similar to the program undertaken for the prairie chicken in the 1980s, be initiated urgently. At the time of writing, 19 zoos throughout the continental United States have been identified as being appropriate for immediate transfer of a breeding condor pair. Further studies are currently underway to identify additional suitable locations. With funding already provided for these studies in FY 2012, the FY 2014 budget request remains at the same level as FY 2013, with FTEs also remaining constant.

- PRINCIPLE: BREEDING IN CAPTIVITY
  SUB-ELEMENT: CONSULTATION AND HABITAT CONSERVATION PLANS

			FY 2014			
	2012 Actual	2013 Enacted	Fixed Costs & Related Changes (+/-)	Program Changes (+/-)	Budget Request	Change from 2012 Enacted (+/-)
Consultation & Habitat ($)	$9,876,543	$9,999,999	$0	-$1,111,111	$8,888,888	-$1,111,111
Conservation Plans (FTE)	28	30	0	-7	23	-7

Justification for Program Changes for Consultation and Habitat Conservation Plans

The FY 2014 budget request for Consultation and Habitat Conservation Plan Program (CHCPP) is $8,888,888 and 23 FTE, a net program change of -$1,111,111 and -7 FTE.

Funding for CHCPP for FY 2014 is reduced as the condor captive breeding program takes effect. The breeding program will result in a smaller area of federal and private land to be monitored, thus resulting in a reduction of 7 FTEs. These FTEs will be transferred to the recovery program where they will appear as new FTEs for program budgeting and accounting purposes.

- **PRINCIPLE: BREEDING IN CAPTIVITY
  SUB-ELEMENT: RECOVERY**

			FY 2014			
	2012 Actual	**2013 Enacted**	**Fixed Costs & Related Changes (+/-)**	**Program Changes (+/-)**	**Budget Request**	**Change from 2012 Enacted (+/-)**
Recovery ($)	$3,456,789	$4,567,890	+$1,000,000	+$7,000,000	$12,567,890	+$8,000,000
(FTE)	21	26	+24	0	50	+24

Justification for Program Changes for Recovery

The FY 2014 budget request for Recovery is $12,567,890 and 50 FTE, a net program change of + $8,000,000 and + 24 FTE.

The significant budget request increase for FY 2014 will provide funding to relocate 19 breeding pairs of the California condor to various zoos across the country. It is expected that this funding will continue to increase in program out-years as more zoos, both nationally and internationally, are identified to accommodate the captive breeding program. It is hoped that this immediate relocation will result in the steady increase of numbers of the California condor, similar to the increases seen in the 1990s and early 2000s. Additionally, the funding will be used to facilitate the renovation of 16 existing aviaries to ensure they meet the requirements of the federally enforced National Keeping Big Wild Birds in a Zoo code (321 USC 123), and 12 new planned aviaries, still to be constructed. Funding for design and planning was appropriated for these activities in the last fiscal year.

The additional 24 FTEs are required to administer and oversee the planned relocation. These additional FTEs will also be used to train and tutor current ornithologists on best practices for the continued upkeep of the California condor while being bred in captivity. Recovery specialists will complete the training of 42 zoo staff per year. The fixed cost increase is in relation to the new salaries required for the additional FTEs.

II. **Breeding in Wild:**

- Conservationists believe the condor will adapt well in the wild due to the condor's familiarity with the natural surroundings.
- The costs associated with capturing condors will be significant.
- The costs associated with housing and taking care of the condors will be significant due to their long life span, of 60 years.
- Studies show death is common during capture due to the stress induced by the process of securing the bird.
- Capturing condors disrupts the natural order of life.
- Condors have difficulty breeding in captivity due to feeling "forced" to do so. Breeding rates for captive birds are lower than that of naturally occurring pairs.
- The breeding rates for captive condors are negatively affected by the trauma and stress of the new habitat.
- The male and female take turns incubating the egg, once it hatches. For up to a year, they feed the offspring until it learns to find its own food.
- In general, condors are social animals and being captive in a zoo promotes isolation
- Surveyed residents and subsequently the current overall feeling of the US citizens prefer an anti-capturing campaign and support natural breeding policies.
- Strong lobby for wild and free breeding (Friends of California Condors Wild & Free, Hopper Mountain National Wildlife Refuge Complex and other organizations).
- The pairs prefer to nest in caves or on cliff clefts, especially ones with nearby roosting trees and open spaces for landing due to their large wingspan.
- Since the young are able to fly after five to six months, but continue to roost and forage with their parents until they are in their second year, they need open and safe environments to grow.
- Condors roost in large groups and communicate with a combination of hisses, growls, and grunts as well as a system of body language.

Risk Assessment of the Effects of Wind Energy on the Wild California Condor:

- Wind energy is an important component of the renewable energy portfolio for the State of California.
- The California Condor Wind Energy Work Group is to be assembled as a subgroup of the California Condor Recovery Team and appointed by the FWS per the ESA.
- The purpose of the work team is to assist the FWS recovery efforts through assessment and risk mitigation associated with wind energy activities within the range of this federally and state endangered bird.

- Wind energy has the potential to conflict with the recovery of the condor unless projects are properly sited and measures are taken to minimize risks to condors.
- The FWS believes it is imperative to use the best scientific and technical guidance available to ensure that wind energy development proceed without compromising California condor recovery.
- This analysis will examine current habitat patterns to identify the probability that California condors will expand and occupy particular areas of their historic range. This information will aid in identifying potential areas of conflict between wind energy and long-term conservation of the California condor.
- Results from the analyses also will provide the tools to develop assessment criteria for future wind resource development within the range of the California condor.
- The Work Group will also be working with counties and special interest groups to gather additional information that will be valuable in understanding the issues.

Agencies and Entities Participating in Program:

- *U.S Fish and Wildlife Service* **(FWS) - field research and conservation**
- *U.S. Forest Service* **(USFS) - habitat managers**
- *California Department of Fish and Game* **(CDFG) - support**
- *California Public Utilities Commission* **(CPUC) – wind energy development analysis**
- *California Fish and Game Commission* **(CFGC) - field research and conservation**
- *Bureau of Land Management* **(BLM) - habitat managers**
- *National Audubon Society* **(NAS) - field research and conservation**

BUDGET JUSTIFICATION FOR CONDOR BREEDING IN THE WILD:

- **SUMMARY TABLE**

	2012 Actual	2013 Enacted	FY 2014			
			Fixed Costs & Related Changes (+/-)	Program Changes (+/-)	Budget Request	Change from 2012 Enacted (+/-)
Candidate ($)	$778,952	$812,953	+20,000	+119,414	$952,367	+139,414
Conservation (FTE)	45	47	0	+14	61	+14

Listing & Critical ($)	$1,123,456	$1,123,456	$0	+111,111	$1,234,567	+$111,111
Habitat (FTE)	34	34	0	+11	45	+11
Consultation & Habitat ($)	$1,234,567	$1,234,567	$0	-$111,111	$1,123,456	-$111,111
Conservation Plans (FTE)	23	23	0	-5	18	-5
Recovery ($)	$987,654	$999,999	$0	+ $112,346	$1,112,345	+ $112,346
(FTE)	5	6	0	+6	12	+6
California Condor ($)	**$4,124,629**	**$4,170,905**	**+ $20,000**	**+ $231,760**	**$4,422,735**	**+ $251,760**
(FTE)	**107**	**110**	**0**	**+ 23**	**133**	**+ 23**

- PRINCIPLE: BREEDING IN THE WILD
  SUB-ELEMENT: CANDIDATE CONSERVATION

			FY 2014			
	2012 Actual	2013 Enacted	Fixed Costs & Related Changes (+/-)	Program Changes (+/-)	Budget Request	Change from 2013Enacted (+/-)
Candidate ($)	$1,778,952	$1,812,953	+$20,000	+$119,414	$1,952,367	+$139,414
Conservation (FTE)	45	47	0	+14	61	+14

Justification for Program Changes for Candidate Conservation Program

The FY 2014 budget request for Candidate Conservation Program (CCP) is $1,952,367 and 51 Full-Time Equivalent Employees (FTE), a net program change of + $139,414 and + 4 FTE from the previous year.

In 2014, the CCP will continue to provide technical assistance and facilitate efforts by landowners, states, Tribes, territories, federal agencies and other strategic partners for conservation programs for species at risk including the California condor. The funding increase will support the planning and associated costs of completing a number of studies detailing the effects of wind farms on the nesting and flight patterns of the

California condor. Increased applications for the planning and the actual construction of numerous wind farm sites in California, Nevada and Arizona have led to the deaths of 3 and injuries to 7 California condors as well as numerous reports of injuries and deaths to other indigenous species such as the short-winged New Mexico fruit bat and the long-eared mid-western parakeet. It is expected that these studies, in conjunction with the Department of Energy, will require 14 new FTEs to complete in accordance with the National Environmental Protection Act (NEPA). The fixed cost increase represents rental costs associated with renewal of various building leases through GSA.

- **PRINCIPLE: BREEDING IN THE WILD**
  SUB-ELEMENT: LISTING AND CRITICAL HABITAT

			FY 2014			
	2012 Actual	2013 Enacted	Fixed Costs & Related Changes (+/-)	Program Changes (+/-)	Budget Request	Change from 2012 Enacted (+/-)
Listing & Critical ($)	$1,123,456	$1,123,456	$0	+111,111	$1,234,567	+$111,111
Habitat (FTE)	34	34	0	+11	45	+11

Justification for Program Changes for Listing and Critical Habitat Program

The FY 2014 budget request for the Listing and Critical Habitat Program (LCHP) is $1,345,678 and 45 FTE, a net program change of + $111,111 and + 11 FTE from the previous year.

The budget request increase is necessary to continue funding for the work associated with California condor for the species to continue its recovery following the increase from just 9 birds in 1985 to over 300 presently, including 15 breeding pairs. In keeping with the Administration's position on the continuous recovery of endangered species, 11 new FTEs are required to disseminate and expedite recommendations from the numerous reports and studies undertaken during the California condor program period for use in other essential recovery programs. This work could not be completed as requested in FY 2013 as no new hires were authorized because the funding levels remained at FY 2012 levels due to the various Continuing Resolutions enacted during that time period.

- **PRINCIPLE: BREEDING IN THE WILD**
  SUB-ELEMENT: CONSULTATION AND HABITAT CONSERVATION PLANS

	2012 Actual	2013 Enacted	FY 2014			
			Fixed Costs & Related Changes (+/-)	Program Changes (+/-)	Budget Request	Change from 2012 Enacted (+/-)
Consultation & Habitat ($)	$1,234,567	$1,234,567	$0	-$111,111	$1,123,456	-$111,111
Conservation Plans (FTE)	23	23	0	-5	18	-5

Justification for Program Changes for Consultation and Habitat Conservation Plans

The FY 2014 budget request for Consultation and Habitat Conservation Plan Program (CHCPP) is $1,123,456 and 18 FTE, a net program change of - $111,111 and - 5 FTE from the previous year.

The cuts in the program, while regrettable, are due to three reasons: 1) as per guidance in the President's Memorandum from January of this year; *M-13-99 – Budgetary Guidance for the Upcoming Fiscal Year,* any increases in other programs must be offset by at least 30% by cuts to other programs; 2) the recent sequester limits the amount of budgetary resources allowable for the program as a whole; and 3) while the work conducted by the CHCCP is necessary during the critical onset of a newly endangered species program, as the species becomes more naturally sustainable, the less involved the CHCPP will become. Thus, it is expected that budget requests in future budget out-years will continue to decrease as the California condor population continues its steady rise. The cuts in this program are expected to be budget neutral as these decreases in funding from this program are anticipated to be requested as increases in other California condor and Endangered Species programs.

- PRINCIPLE: BREEDING IN THE WILD
  SUB-ELEMENT: RECOVERY

	2012 Actual	2013 Enacted	FY 2014			
			Fixed Costs & Related Changes (+/-)	Program Changes (+/-)	Budget Request	Change from 2012 Enacted (+/-)
Recovery ($)	$987,654	$999,999	$0	+ $112,346	$1,112,345	+ $112,346
(FTE)	5	6	0	+6	12	+6

Justification for Program Changes for Recovery

The FY 2014 budget request for Recovery is $1,112,345 and 9 FTE, a net program change of + $112,346 and + 3 FTE.

The funding increase request is necessary for the California condor program as the species is expected to be reclassified to the threatened level due to the population increase and the achievement of many of the recovery goals, including the identification and protection of all lands, water and air necessary to recover the species. The increase in funding is due to the fact that all funding for the reclassification will be requested through this program, with transfers being made to supporting agencies and stakeholders.

The addition of 6 new FTEs is required for the training and monitoring of staff at the San Diego zoo as a pair of breeding California condors are to be transferred there from the wild for safety reasons stemming from the construction of a new wind farm in Eastern Nevada.

III. <u>Command and Control Methodology</u>

The California condor should be managed by a traditional command and control methodology.

- Condors are under attack by the encroachment of windmill farms into their habitat.
- Condors are dying from lead poisoning from bullets used by hunters after the condor eats the poisoned the carrion.
- Condors are dying from eating poisoned coyotes that have died from ingesting cyanide traps.
- Humans have begun using poison to control vermin and other wildlife deemed untenable.
- Condor habitat is being encroached upon by development activity and the impact of climate.
- The only way to ensure the survival of the California condor is to enact and promulgate statutes and associated regulations which prohibit use of lead based ammunition and poison traps as well as specific conditions limiting construction and use of wind energy facilities and operations in condor habitat.

Acts and Other Regulatory Efforts:

California Lead Poisoning Act:

- Since lead poisoning is the leading cause of mortality among the condor population this act protects condors from lead poisoning by requirement the use of non-lead ammunition for hunting big game within the condor's current and historic range.

- As carrion feeders, condors often find lead shot or fragments of lead rifle bullets in gut piles left by hunters and in the remains of sick or injured domestic animals and "varmints" dispatched by ranchers.
- Lead rifle bullets tend to leave about 15-30% of their mass behind in the carcass when the bullet passes through (sometimes over 200 fragments from one bullet).
- Copper and other forms of non-lead ammunition are less toxic and most importantly, they do not fragment.
- Scientists started putting transmitters on condors and learned that there was collateral damage caused by lead ammunition.
- The major drawbacks to switching over are the effort of identifying the right ammunition type and mandating that all suppliers purchase it, at a slightly higher cost to suppliers and ultimately consumers.
- The secondary push back will come from the hunters that will have to go to a shooting range to accustom oneself to how the new ammunition works in one's old gun.
- The Arizona Game & Fish Department (AZGFD) will be requested to make it easy for hunters to find the right non-lead alternative for their guns; the list is under the "Non-lead ammunition" link at www.azgfd.gov/condor.

Condor Protection Act:

- Due to condors being injured and killed by windmills, the act will limit the number, location and home of the condor population.
- The Act will develop strict policy outlawing hunting or killing vermin, game or shooting any gun within the condor's habitat.
- The Act will outlaw the use of cyanide pills to kill vermin or other scavenger animals.

Endangered Species Act:

- Provides conservation of ecosystems upon which threatened and endangered species of fish, wildlife, and plants depend on.
- Authorizes the determination and listing of species as endangered and threatened.
- Prohibits unauthorized taking, possession, sale, and transport of endangered species.
- Provides authority to acquire land for the conservation of listed species, using land and water conservation funds.
- Authorizes establishment of cooperative agreements and grants-in-aid to States that establish and maintain active and adequate programs for endangered and threatened wildlife and plants.
- Authorizes the assessment of civil and criminal penalties for violating the Act or regulations.

- Authorizes the payment of rewards to anyone furnishing information leading to arrest and conviction for any violation of the Act or any regulation issued there under.

Regulations:

- 42 CFR 1.8008
    - o No windmill will be constructed within a 30-mile radius of any condor breeding area.
    - o Enforcement - $2 million fine plus one year in prison.

- 42 CFR 2.8002
    - o No hunter will be allowed to shoot to lead bullets at either game or vermin within 50 miles of any condor breeding area.
    - o Enforcement - $500 fine plus 30 days in jail.

- 42 CFR 3.803
    - o Cyanide or any other man made toxins used to kill vermin or scavengers is restricted from use within 75 miles of a condor's breeding area.
    - o Enforcement - $2000 fine plus 60 days in jail.

BUDGET JUSTIFICATION FOR CALIFORNIA CONDOR "COMMAND & CONTROL" PROGRAM

- **SUMMARY TABLE**

	2012 Actual	2013 Enacted	FY 2014			
			Fixed Costs & Related Changes (+/-)	Program Changes (+/-)	Budget Request	Change from 2012 Enacted (+/-)
Candidate ($)	$15,001,100	$15,555,420	+$2,000,000	+$2,321,123	$19,876,543	+$4,321,123
Conservation (FTE)	38	40	+10	+9	59	+19
Listing & Critical ($)	$16,989,545	$17,381,826	0	+$3,852,741	$21,234,567	+$3,852,741
Habitat (FTE)	88	86	0	+13	99	+13
Consultation & Habitat ($)	$37,123,987	$56,147,528	-$5,000,000	-$12,987,654	$38,159,874	-$17,987,654
Conservation Plans (FTE)	36	38	0	0	38	0

Recovery ($)	$75,635,852	$84,036,147	+115,963,852	0	$199,999,999	$+115,963,852
(FTE)	52	66	+47	0	113	+47
California Condor ($)	$144,750,484	$112,120,921	$112,963,852	-$6,813,790	$279,273,983	$106,150,062
(FTE)	214	230	57	22	309	79

- **PRINCIPLE: COMMAND AND CONTROL PROGRAM**
  SUB-ELEMENT: CANDIDATE CONSERVATION

			FY 2014			
	2012 Actual	2013 Enacted	Fixed Costs & Related Changes (+/-)	Program Changes (+/-)	Budget Request	Change from 2013Enacted (+/-)
Candidate ($)	$15,001,100	$15,555,420	+$2,000,000	+$2,321,123	$19,876,543	+$4,321,123
Conservation (FTE)	38	40	+10	+9	59	+19

Justification for Program Changes for Candidate Conservation Program

The FY 2014 budget request for Candidate Conservation Program (CCP) is $19,876,543 and 59 FTE, a net program change of +$4,321,123 and +19 FTE over the previous year.

Total numbers for the California condor have decreased from 410 in 2010 to 383 in 2012, a staggering 6.6% decrease. This is inclusive of the 38 condor chicks that hatched in that time, meaning that the condor population has been decimated by the totally unacceptable number of 65 in just a two-year period. Should the numbers continue to decline at such an alarming rate, the California condor could be extinct within 10 years. There are three main reasons for the sharp decline:

- Condors are being killed flying through newly constructed wind farms;
- Condors are being killed by lead poisoning from hunting ammunition; and
- Pesticide poisoning is killing condors.

The FY 2014 budget request is $4,321,123 more than the FY 2013 total. The increase is due to the escalating costs associated with the adoption and monitoring of new regulations and program guidance associated with the command and control program. In addition, 19 new FTEs are requested to conduct R&D efforts, and perform biological and habitat studies in conjunction with the USDA, with the resulting data used to ensure the successful growth of the condor population. The fixed costs changes increase according to the increased salary demands.

- PRINCIPLE: COMMAND AND CONTROL PROGRAM
  SUB-ELEMENT: LISTING AND CRITICAL HABITAT

	2012 Actual	2013 Enacted	FY 2014			
			Fixed Costs & Related Changes (+/-)	Program Changes (+/-)	Budget Request	Change from 2012 Enacted (+/-)
Listing & Critical ($)	$16,989,545	$17,381,826	0	+$3,852,741	$21,234,567	+$3,852,741
Habitat (FTE)	88	86	0	+13	99	+13

Justification for Program Changes for Listing and Critical Habitat Program

The FY 2014 budget request for the Listing and Critical Habitat Program (LCHP) is $21,234,567 and 99 FTE, a net program change of +$3,852,741 and +13 FTE.

The LCHP will work with Congress, the USDA, the DOE, and the NRA to oversee the command and control program, which will achieve the following outcomes:

- New statutory authority under the *National Keeping Big Wild Birds in a Zoo Act* (S. 9654) (the "Act") to;
- Enforce a captive breeding program;
- Prohibit hunters and farmers using lead ammunition when hunting big game in California, Nevada, Arizona, Oregon, and New Mexico;
- Expand the range of the protected area by an additional 15 miles in all directions;
- Direct DOE to conduct additional studies before approval of any new wind farm construction;
- Ban the use of harmful pesticides currently being used on vegetable and fruit farms in the condor's habitat; and
- Place 19 pairs of breeding condors in zoos across the country by the end of 2014.

The FY 2014 budget request is $21,234,567, an increase of $3,852,741 from the FY 2012 amount, with an addition of 13 new FTEs. The increase in the budget level is attributable to the costs related to moving the breeding condor pairs to zoos across the Unites States. The designation of these zoos as critical habitat and the alteration of enclosures and related surrounding areas is a one-off cost, and the program is expected to recoup much of the costs through ticket receipts from patrons of the zoos. As per statutory authority in the Act, these receipts will be placed in a revolving fund designated the "California Condor Trust Fund."

- **PRINCIPLE: COMMAND AND CONTROL PROGRAM**
  SUB-ELEMENT: CONSULTATION AND HABITAT CONSERVATION PLANS

			FY 2014			
	2012 Actual	2013 Enacted	Fixed Costs & Related Changes (+/-)	Program Changes (+/-)	Budget Request	Change from 2012 Enacted (+/-)
Consultation & Habitat ($)	$37,123,987	$56,147,528	-$5,000,000	-$12,987,654	$38,159,874	-$17,987,654
Conservation Plans (FTE)	36	38	0	0	38	0

Justification for Program Changes for Consultation and Habitat Conservation Plans

The FY 2014 budget request for Consultation and Habitat Conservation Plan Program (CHCPP) is $38,159,874 and 38 FTE, a net program change of -$17,987,654 and 0 FTE.

The FY 2014 budget request is $17,987,654 less than the FY 2012 amount. The reduction is a result of the completion of the studies associated with transferring the breeding condor pairs to the 19 zoos selected for the program, for which the increase in funding was requested in FY 2013. The reduction of $5,000,000 from the fixed costs budget is due to the transfer of the FWS building in Santa Fe to the USDA. FTE numbers will remain the same.

- **PRINCIPLE: COMMAND AND CONTROL PROGRAM**
  SUB-ELEMENT: RECOVERY

			FY 2014			
	2012 Actual	2013 Enacted	Fixed Costs & Related Changes (+/-)	Program Changes (+/-)	Budget Request	Change from 2012 Enacted (+/-)
Recovery ($)	$75,635,852	$84,036,147	+15,963,852	0	$199,999,999	$+115,963,852
(FTE)	52	66	+47	0	113	+47

Justification for Program Changes for Recovery

The FY 2014 budget request for Recovery is $199,999,999 and 113 FTE, a net program change of +$115,963,852 and + 47 FTE above the FY 2012 level.

As per the "Act", $100,000,000 has been authorized for the purchase of two helicopters from the Department of Defense at a discounted price. These helicopters will patrol the condor conservation area. 24 additional FTEs are required to administer and oversee the planned relocation. These additional FTEs will also be used to train and tutor current ornithologists on best practices for the continued upkeep of the California condor while being bred in captivity. Recovery specialists will complete the training of 42 zoo staff per year. In addition, 23 new FTEs will be hired by the Park Service to monitor and control the new ammunition laws for hunting in the region, as well as working in tandem with USDA inspectors for the new pesticide regulations. Fixed cost increases are in relation to the new salaries required for the additional FTEs.

SAMPLES OF WRITTEN INSTRUMENTS

1. BIOGRAPHY

- EXAMPLE – GOOD BIOGRAPHY

John Smith was born in Detroit, Michigan and lived there until he completed his undergraduate studies in Economics at Drake University. While an undergraduate, he interned for Iowa's Governor, Ray R. Raymond.

Upon graduation, Mr. Smith served on the Governor's immediate staff before being appointed State Model Cites Coordinator in 1971. In 1972, the Governor named Mr. Smith as Director of State Community Development and Associate State Planner. In 1974, he became a consultant to the Governor of Vermont, with responsibilities for conducting national land use studies and representing Vermont on the Council of State Community Affairs Agencies.

In 1975, Mr. Smith completed his graduate education in Public Administration and Economics at Harvard University Kennedy School of Public Administration where he also served as Teaching Assistant for two years. After graduation from Harvard, Mr. Smith served as Director of Environment Programs for the National Association of Counties.

From 1976 to 1980 Mr. Smith was an Examiner in the White House Office of Management and Budget, where he worked primarily on environmental issues. In 1980, Mr. Smith went to the Department of the Interior's (DOI) Office of Budget, advising the Secretary on budgetary issues involving the National Park Service, Fish and Wildlife Service programs, and particularly DOI programs in Alaska. He also directed the development of the Department's Hazardous Waste program and Superfund efforts. In 1984, Mr. Smith was reassigned as Director of Budget and Finance for the Bureau of Indian Affairs at DOI. During his tenure, he improved the $1.3 billion trust investment program and streamlined the entire Bureau's Animal Development Program operation.

In 1985, Mr. Smith accepted an executive assignment with the Export-Import Bank of the U.S. to improve the Bank's program of direct credits, financial guarantees, and overseas sales of U.S. chemical processing industry equipment. He was instrumental in negotiations with the Office of Community Economic Development in developing both

U.S. and international policies for mixed credits. He also developed an engineering/operations and maintenance direct credit program later adopted by the Bank's Board of Directors.

In 1986, Mr. Smith became Senior Executive Assistant and Controller to the Assistant Secretary for Fish and Wildlife Service and Parks at DOI, providing budget, legislative and administrative oversight for the National Park Service, the Fish and Wildlife Service, and the Superfund Program.

Mr. Smith is also a board member of the Statue of Liberty-Ellis Island Foundation, Inc., the Jefferson National Expansion Memorial Commission, the Wolf Trap Foundation, and the Pennsylvania Avenue Development Corporation.

In March 1992, Mr. Smith founded the ABC Group and ABC Foundation (501C3) in Washington, D.C.

- **EXAMPLE – POOR BIOGRAPHY**

Originally from Louisiana, I worked at the Department of the Interior for eleven years. Prior to working for Interior, I worked in other Government Agencies and as a consultant in New York on a number of different issues. During this time, I received numerous accolades and awards for my outstanding work in my field. I have a B.A. from New York University and furthered my studies in Washington. I am a member of the XYZ Foundation and married with three children. I have season tickets to the Jets and like baseball.

CRITIQUE –

The example above is insufficient for the following reasons:

- It does not include the writer's full name and title, or where he was born and raised.
- It is written in 1st person.
- It includes that the writer worked at a consulting firm and at a government agency; however, there is no way to tell what field the author worked in or what issues they worked on.
- The interesting fact and discussion of family is short and not informational and it does not add to the value of the biography.

Even though a reader can gather basic information from this biography it is obvious that we as readers do not gain any knowledge about whom or what this person writing the biography does or how he could be helpful to an organization.

2. **ISSUE PAPERS**

- **EXAMPLE – GOOD ISSUE PAPER**

Statement of Issue

Should the California condor continue to breed in the wild?

Background

- The condor population has declined to levels resulting in various stakeholder requests that the government focus on whether the existing recovery strategy is best to prevent further decline and possible extinction.
- Experts believe that hazards in the wild such as increased contact with power lines and wind farm energy operations, human encroachment, ingestion of poisons, and hunting are the major contributors to the decline.
- Authorities point out that the 180 condors in zoos are breeding. However, the breeding pattern of the remaining 230 condors in the wild is being disrupted by an increase in natural predators and a loss of prime habitat.

Alternatives

1. Continue condor breeding in the wild;
2. Rely on captive breeding; or
3. Enhance breeding by removing hazards in the wild through command and control.

Issue Analysis

The conservation community asserts that the improvement of the current natural habitat breeding program estimated at approximately $4.4 million will result in increased population due to several factors, including:

- Studies show death is common during capture due to the stress induced by the process of securing the bird.
- Condors have had difficulty breeding in captivity due to feeling "forced" to do so.
- Historically, breeding rates for captive birds are lower than that of naturally occurring pairs.
- The breeding rates for captive condors are negatively affected by the trauma and stress of the new habitat.
- Scientific experts assert that the most beneficial and efficient solution is the support that a controlled breeding environment such as a zoo offers. The budget estimate for this program is approximately $29 million. The most significant facts supporting this assertion are:

  o The captive breeding program involves 19 zoos throughout the continental United States, all of which have been identified as being appropriate for immediate transfer of a breeding condor pair.
  o Utilizing the bird's ability to double clutch can result in the condor

producing a second and sometimes a third egg. Chelation treatment, an expensive and sometimes fatal treatment to remove lead and copper from the bird's blood system will no longer be required as the threat of poisoning from toxic lead ammunition will be removed.

- o Funding for the program will result in the construction of 12 new aviaries and the renovation of 16 existing aviaries.

A regulatory solution is estimated to cost $279 million; a staggering increase over both of the other options without evidence that it would succeed. The methodology behind this potential solution includes:

- Enact and promulgate statutes and regulations which prohibit the use of lead based ammunition and poison traps in California, Nevada, Arizona, Oregon and New Mexico.
- Limit the construction and use of wind energy facilities in the existing and planned condor habitats.
- Ban the use of harmful pesticides currently being used on vegetable and fruit farms in the condor's habitat.
- Expand the range of the protected area by an additional 15 miles in all directions.
- Prominent stakeholders on both sides of the debate agree that subjecting the U.S. Public to increased regulation and restrictions is not as advantageous as either breeding in the wild or captivity.

Next Steps

- Conduct various studies including:

  - o The effects of wind farms on the nesting and flight patterns of the California condor.
  - o The effects of hunting, predatory eggs encroachment, poisoning by cyanide traps set for coyotes, general habitat degradation, and lead poisoning.
  - o Biological and habitat analyses in conjunction with the USDA and other partners.

- Continued work with stakeholders to hold a symposium to discuss the proposal of the U.S. Fish and Wildlife Service's Listing and Critical Habitat program; the implementation of a captive breeding program, similar to the program undertaken for the prairie chicken in the 1980s.
- Compare and analyze the cost benefits with the relevant appropriations committees to determine the efficacy of the alternatives.
- The California Condor Wind Energy Work Group is to be assembled as a subgroup of the California Condor Recovery Team and appointed by the U.S. Fish and Wildlife Service (FWS) per the Endangered Species Act. The purpose of the work team is to assist the U.S. FWS recovery efforts through

assessment and risk mitigation associated with wind energy activities within the range of this federally and state endangered bird.

- Work in conjunction with other stakeholders, including the Department of Agriculture, Department of Energy, State and Local governments, and the NRA, to continue to conduct rigorous evaluations of potential hazards and threats to determine the most amenable outcome for all parties involved.

- **EXAMPLE – POOR ISSUE PAPER**

Statement of the Issue - Do you think the U.S. government would be wise to spend federal funds in trying to save California condor from extinction or should the government just allow the bird to take nature's course?

Background - The California condor is a big issue for the U.S. Fish & Wildlife Service. There are not many California condors left in existence and we do not think that there are enough to sustain the population if left in the wild. There is a lot of controversy between the two political parties over whether spending federal money to ship the condor to the zoo is a good use of federal dollars.

Statement of Alternatives -

- Leave the condor in the wild.
- Capture all the condors in the wild and put them in a recovery and reintroduction program.
- Initiate a command and control program.

Analysis of Alternatives -

- The goal of the California Condor Recovery Plan was to establish two geographically separate populations, two in California and one in Arizona, each with 150 birds and at least 15 breeding pairs. As the Recovery Program works toward this goal, the number of release sites has grown. There are three active release sites in California, one in Arizona and one in Baja California, Mexico.
- A compilation of studies undertaken by the Listing and Critical Habitat Program recommends that for the California condor species to survive, the implementation of a captive breeding program, similar to the program undertaken for the prairie chicken in the 1980s, be initiated urgently. At the time of writing, 19 zoos throughout the continental United States have been identified as being appropriate for immediate transfer of a breeding condor pair.
- The Department of Interior will work with Congress, the USDA, the DOE, and the NRA to oversee the command and control program which will achieve the following outcomes:
- New statutory authority under the *National Keeping Big Wild Birds in a Zoo Act* (S. 9654) (the "Act") to

- o Enforce a captive breeding program;
- o Prohibit hunters and farmers using lead ammunition when hunting big game in California, Nevada, Arizona, Oregon, and New Mexico;
- o Expand the range of the protected area by an additional 15 miles in all directions; and
- o Direct DOE to conduct additional studies before approval of any new wind farm construction.

Next Steps

Adopt option 1 immediately.

CRITIQUE

The issue paper above is not a good example of a well written document for the following reasons:

- The statement of issue is not narrowly defined and leaves the issue up for interpretation.
- The statement of issue is posed as a question and presents the manager with alternatives to analyze.
- The background section provides little information that does not clearly communicate the facts of the issue to management.
- There is no indication as to why management is addressing this issue at hand, or why their office is involved.
- Three distinct alternatives were provided but their analysis was inadequate.
- Analysis should include bullets that provide management with:

  - o Supporting facts about the issue;
  - o Optimal operation considerations;
  - o Potential impacts inclusive of what facts are relevant versus information that could be considered extraneous to management;
  - o The pros and cons of each alternative presented objectively; and
  - o Next steps which outline any additional requirements for analysis.

- The *Next Steps* section statement is incomplete and does not offer instructions on how to move forward on this issue. Due to weak analysis, a manager would not have the necessary information needed to move forward towards a decision.
- Recommendations should not be made within the *Next Steps* section. The purpose is to educate the manager as to what alternatives are available to resolve the issue.

3. DECISION PAPER

   - EXAMPLE – GOOD DECISION PAPER

Issue

The California condor population is currently at near-extinction levels. Current studies have indicated that the population has decreased from 410 in 2010 to 383 in 2012. Should this decline in population be allowed to continue, experts estimate that the species will become extinct within 10 years.

Background

The California condor once flourished along the Pacific coast. However, in large part due to habitat loss, illegal shootings, and lead poisoning, the entire wild known population had been reduced to just 9 birds. At that time, a decision was made to bring all of the remaining wild birds into captivity to preserve the species through captive breeding and eventual reintroduction. In 1992, 2 captive-reared juveniles were released into the wild along with two juvenile Andean condors. By 2006, the California condor population had risen to its highest number yet. However, recent constructions of wind farms, loss of habitat and fatalities due to hunting and poisoning have resulted in a steady decrease in population numbers. Increased federal action is required to negate the decline of this truly majestic species.

Options

Continued Breeding in the Wild - The conservation community asserts that habitat improvement estimated at approximately $4.4 million will result in increased breeding due to:

- Studies show death is common during capture due to the stress induced by the process of securing the bird.
- Condors have had difficulty breeding in captivity due to feeling "forced" to do so. Breeding rates for captive birds are lower than that of naturally occurring pairs.
- The breeding rates for captive condors are negatively affected by the trauma and stress of the new habitat.

Captive Breeding – Scientific experts assert that the most providing and efficient solution is the support that a controlled breeding environment such as a zoo offers. The budget estimate for this program is approximately $29 million. Significant facts supporting this assertion are:

- Goal is to have 3 separate populations of 150 birds, which sets a safety net for the birds. Estimated time for achieving this goal is 2020.
- At the time of writing, 19 zoos throughout the continental United States have been identified as being appropriate for immediate transfer of a breeding condor pair.

- Breeding in the wild only offers a continuation of current practice which is detrimental to the condor as this method historically results in population decline.

Command and Control - A regulatory solution is estimated to cost $279 million; a staggering increase over the captive breeding estimate of $29 million.

- Other prominent stakeholders in the debate agree that subjecting the U.S. public to increased regulation and restrictions are not as advantageous as either breeding in the wild or captivity.

Political and Operational Analysis

Political and operational arguments in support of leaving the California condor in the wild include:

- Costs of capturing, transporting, housing, and feeding the condor for a captive breeding program are substantially higher than the wild breeding program;
- Studies show death is common during capture due to increased trauma and stress of a new habitat;
- Surveyed local residents and subsequently the current overall feeling of the US citizens (according to a 2011 Pew Study) support an anti-capturing campaign and instead prefer natural breeding policies; and
- Strong lobby for wild and free breeding (Friends of California Condors Wild & Free, the Hopper Mountain National Wildlife Refuge Complex, and other nonprofit organizations).

Conservationists believe that with the intervention of the government, the condor population will flourish in the wild due to the condor's familiarity with the natural surroundings and that capturing condors disrupts the natural order of life.

The latest FWS study provides distinct evidence that the condor pairs prefer to nest in caves or on cliff clefts, especially ones with nearby roosting trees and open spaces for landing due to their large wing span. The continuation of the wild breeding program is the best choice to meet the aforementioned conditions.

Agency Recommendation

It is imperative that the federal government initiate a multi-agency effort to support the continuation of the natural habitat breeding program.

- **EXAMPLE – POOR DECISION PAPER**

Statement of the Issue- Should the U.S. Fish and Wildlife Service recommend that the condor be left in its natural habitat or do what the Administration wants which is to capture, breed, and reintroduce the bird back to the wild after a successful population increase?

Background- This recovery and release plan is too expensive and politically untenable. It would be much easier just to let conservation groups pay for the condor if they want to save it from extinction. Fish and Wildlife knows this and you should too.

Options

1. Leave the condor in the wild.
2. Capture the condors still in the wild and make them breed and live in the zoo forever.
3. Make it a felony to shoot a California condor.

Analysis of Options

1. This option will allow for private conservation groups to fund the recovery process.
2. This is a very pricey option and would be bad to consider this even though this is what the loyal opposition has suggested would work best.
3. Statistics show that imposing heavy jail times and fines limit illegal poaching.

Recommendation- Leave the birds in the wild if you don't mind the media harping on the foolish spending and the negative impact on the budget or make it a felony to kill condors in the wild or capture and reintroduce the condor.

CRITIQUE

The purpose of the decision document is to clearly identify the problem and explain why the federal government needs to become involved. The following outlines why the example above does not suffice as a decision document.

- The statement issue is represented as a question and includes confusing options within it. It should be short and concise while communicating what decision needs to be made.
- The background section does not contain data or cite any reports or studies done to provide information on the topic. It does not supply the information needed for decision making. It lists no credible sources on the subject or discusses previous action taken, if any.
- The options for resolution are not presented politically, institutionally, or as an oppositional approach; this leaves the decision maker with limited information to make clear decisive decisions.
- The option analysis does not offer the necessary information and lacks:

  o Supporting objective data to inform the manager of each option available;
  o Clarity to distinguish between the pros and cons of each option; and

      o   Evidence of previous actions taken on the issue and the outcomes of those actions.

- The recommendation does not clearly state the direction the agency plans to move forward in. It is vague and mentions all three options presented. It needs to clearly state which option the agency chose to address the problem, and it should outline the facts from the objective analysis that was used to make this recommendation. The example above makes no recommendation, and does not explain why the statement given.

4. APPEAL PAPER

- **EXAMPLE – GOOD APPEAL PAPER**

Statement of the Issue

Should the California condor continue to breed in the wild?

Background

Current evidence demonstrates captive breeding is contributing more to the increase in the condor population than breeding in the wild.

- Scientific studies conclude that for the California condor species to survive, the implementation of a captive breeding program, similar to the program undertaken for the prairie chicken in the 1980s, be initiated urgently.
- 19 zoos throughout the continental United States have been identified as being appropriate for immediate transfer of a breeding condor pair.
- Funding has already been appropriated for further studies to identify additional suitable locations for the captive breeding program. Failure to implement this program would result in the loss of millions of dollars of taxpayers' money.
- The total program cost for the upcoming fiscal year is $29 million, approximately one-tenth the cost of the command and control option.
- Breeding in the wild only offers a continuation of current practice which is detrimental to the condor as this method historically results in population decline.
- Should the numbers continue to decline at such an alarming rate, the California condor could be extinct within 10 years.

Options

1. Continue condor breeding in the wild;
2. Rely on captive breeding; or
3. Enhance breeding by removing hazards in the wild through command and control.

Appeal analysis

A primary objective of the recovery program is to take the condor species off of the endangered species list and work to downgrade it to a threatened species.

- The wild breeding recovery program for the California condor was showing success, and the birds were expanding their range and reoccupying portions of their historic range, which includes areas of existing and proposed wind energy development. However, significant increases in fatalities to the condor over recent years have resulted in the total number of condors reducing dramatically.
- The captivity program will assist in minimizing and removing threats, which include supporting a species' capacity to respond adequately or increase their resilience to changing conditions, a species may be conserved, eliminating the need for protection under the Endangered Species Act.
- The goal is to have three separate populations of 150 birds, which sets a safety net for the birds. Estimated time for achieving this goal is 2020.
- To achieve that goal, the plan is to establish two geographically separate populations, two in California and one in Arizona, each with 150 birds and at least 15 breeding pairs.
- Stakeholders supporting this program financially include the U.S. Fish and Wildlife Service, The Conservation and Research for Endangered Species, the San Diego Wild Animal Park, the Los Angeles Zoo, The Peregrine Fund, the California Department of Fish and Game, the Arizona Game and Fish, Bureau of Land Management, the Salem Zoo, the Santa Barbara Zoo, and the Ventana Wildlife Society.

Recommendation

The most prudent course of action would be to implement a captive breeding program with immediate relocation in order to increase the California condors overall numbers, similar to the increases seen in the 1990s and early 2000s.

- **EXAMPLE – POOR APPEAL PAPER**

Statement of the Issue

The best decision to treat the declining condor population is captive breeding, but others say other options might work as well, what is the best option?

Background

Over time it has been said it would be a very expensive conservation technique to capture and breed the condor and then reintroduce them to their natural habitat so the choice was to keep them in the wild.

Options

1. Leave the condor in the wild.
2. Capture all the condors in the wild and put them in a recovery and reintroduction program.
3. Capture the condors still in the wild and make them breed and live in the zoo forever.

Analysis of Options

1. Option one is politically sensitive and should not be considered under any circumstance.
2. This option is the best policy decision, thus it should be chosen.
3. This does not have Congressional support so should not be chosen.

Recommendation

The staff thinks you should try to save the condor. The staff thinks you should allow conservation groups to help fund the recovery of the condor.

CRITIQUE

The aforementioned appeals document would not allow a decision maker to accurately differentiate between the available choice options. It fails to meet the following standards:

- A narrowly defined question that clearly articulates the issue being appealed;
- A well developed background section presenting areas of misinterpreted facts or changes in circumstances that support the change the manager is seeking;
- Well defined alternative options each supporting the political decision, the bureaucratic decision, and the opposition's decision.

The analysis section of this document does not offer clear objective evidence. It shows opinions from the writer with now supporting data. There is no discussion of pros and cons, or flaws in previously stated facts.

The recommendation is a subjective "suggestion" that that leaves out an explanation of action or justification for its recommendation. The recommendation does not indicate how the agency will save or recover the condor population but only that is should do something. It defers the workload away from the agency and places the burden elsewhere.

5. **BRIEFING MEMORANDUM**

   - **EXAMPLE – GOOD BRIEFING MEMORANDUM**

MEMORANDUM

TO: Mary Beeler, U.S. Fish and Wildlife Service (FWS) Migratory Bird
        Management Office Chief, Pacific Southwest Region
FROM: David Davidson, U.S. Fish and Wildlife Service Migratory Bird Program
Chief
RE: Wind Farm Development in Protected Condor Habitat

This memo is in regard to the federal government's decision to proceed with wind farm development and the potential conflict this creates with the FWS mandate under the Endangered Species Act (ESA).

The California condor once flourished along the Pacific coast. However, by 1985, in large part to habitat loss, illegal shootings, and lead poisoning, the entire wild known population had been reduced to just 9 birds. At that time, a decision was made to bring all of the remaining wild birds into captivity to preserve the species through captive breeding and eventual reintroduction. In 1992, two captive-reared juveniles were released into the wild along with two juvenile Andean condors. As of 2012, the California condor population had risen to 125.

The production, development, and delivery of renewable energy, including wind energy is one of the Department of Interior's highest priorities, and an important component of the renewable energy portfolio for the State of California. The recovery program for the California condor is showing success, and the birds are expanding their range and reoccupying portions of their historic range, which includes areas of existing and proposed wind energy development. The FWS believes it is imperative to use the best scientific and technical guidance available to ensure that wind energy development proceed without compromising California condor recovery.

In January 2013, the State of California issued five licenses for the development of wind farms in the condor region.

The FWS is a federal designee for the protection of threatened and endangered species. The purpose of the Endangered Species Act is to protect and recover imperiled species and the ecosystems upon which they depend.

It is the position of the FWS that the ESA must be enforced. You are directed to explore the range of options to appeal the legality of the wind farm licenses granted by the State of California. We are currently in the process of setting up a meeting between the FWS General Counsel and officials from the Department of Justice to explore the issues involved in the potential upcoming case. Please inform your legal team to make themselves available for these upcoming meetings.

I have enclosed the Department of Energy's full report of projected wind energy developments for the State of California. In addition I have enclosed the FWS's report of migratory flight patterns common to the condor.

All questions regarding this issue should be directed to:

David Davidson
U.S. Fish and Wildlife Service
Migratory Bird Program Chief
(555) 123 - 4567

- **EXAMPLE – POOR BRIEFING MEMORANDUM**

<u>MEMORANDUM</u>

TO: Mary Beeler, Migratory Bird Management Office Chief, Pacific Southwest Region, FWS
FROM: David Swinborne, U.S. FWS Migratory Bird Program Chief
RE: Condor Recovery Program

This memo is the first step in introducing the new recovery program to try our best to capture the condors still living, even though we believe that will be nearly impossible, and then reintroduce the condor so that it is able to thrive.

Since the recovery program is likely to be the costliest conservation program ever conducted in the U.S.; the political sensitivity of the issue is very high but is still the best option.

The history of trying to capture endangered species, breed them, and them reintroduce them is very limited and hard to quantify but is the best policy option.

CRITIQUE

There are a number of reasons as to why the example above would not be useful to a program manager.

- The message being addressed is unclear.
- The memo does not advise the recipient as to why they are receiving the memo and the expected action upon recipient.
- The memo did not inform the recipient of the actions recommended in the decision process.
- Changes that have occurred since the decision and how the agency plans to move forward have not been addressed.
- The memo does not include any reference to facts, reports, or studies.
- The memo fails to offer any insight into where the recipient can obtain additional information on the present issue and who to contact with their questions.

6. **RIA/ NOTICE OF INTENT**

- **EXAMPLE – GOOD NOTICE OF INTENT**

Notice

Preparation of an Environmental Impact Statement for Issuance of a wind farm permit associated with a Habitat Conservation Plan (HCP) for the federally endangered California condor.

A notice by the **Fish and Wildlife Service** on **01/01/2013**

Action

Notice of Intent

Summary

Pursuant to the National Environmental Policy Act (NEPA), the U.S. Fish and Wildlife Service (FWS) advises the public that we intend to gather information necessary to prepare an Environmental Impact Statement (EIS) on the proposed HCP for the federally endangered California condor (*Gymnogyps californianus*).

Windy Farm Inc., located in Los Angeles County, California, intends to request a permit for the construction of a new 45 megawatt (MW) wind farm which would require conducting a HCP for the endangered California condor. This HCP is required under Section 99 of the *Endangered Species Act* (ESA), as amended.

We provide this notice to:

1. Describe the proposed action and possible alternatives;
2. Advise other Federal and State agencies, affected Tribes, and the public of our intent to prepare an EIS;
3. Announce the initiation of a 30-day public scoping period; and
4. Obtain suggestions and information on the scope of issues and alternatives to be included in the EIS.

Table of Contents

1. Dates
2. Addresses
3. For Further Information Contact
4. Supplementary Information
5. Reasonable Accommodation
6. Background
7. Endangered Species Program - California condor
8. Habitat Conservation Plan
9. Environmental Impact Statement

Dates:

Public meetings will be held on: Tuesday, January 31, 2013, from 3 p.m. to 5 p.m. and 7 p.m. to 9 p.m. Written comments should be received on or before February 26, 2013.

Addresses:

The public meetings will be held at Condor Hall, 999 Condor Place, Condor Park, Los Angeles, CA. Information, written comments, or questions related to the preparation of the EIS and the NEPA process should be submitted to Connie Condorson, U.S. Fish and Wildlife Service, 2493 Condor Road, Suite B, Condor Park, Los Angeles, California, 33333; conniecondorson@fws.gov or fax (987) 654-3210.

For Further Information Contact:

Connie Condorson at the above address, or at (987) 123-4567

Supplementary Information

Reasonable Accommodation:

Persons needing reasonable accommodations in order to attend and participate in the public meeting should contact Dick Dickerson of Fish and Wildlife Office at (987) 987-6543 as soon as possible. In order to allow sufficient time to process requests, please call no later than 1 week before the public meeting. Information regarding this proposed action is available in alternative formats upon request.

Background:

Section 99 of the *Endangered Species Act*, as amended (Act) (123 USC *et seq.*) and Federal regulations prohibit the issuance of a construction permit in the area that may affect a fish or wildlife species listed as endangered or threatened. Under the Act, the following activities are defined as "affect": harass, harm, pursue, hunt, shoot, wound, kill, trap, capture or collect listed animal species, or attempt to engage in such conduct. However, under section 456 (a, b and c) of the Act, we may issue permits following completion and approval of a HCP for the listed species.

Endangered Species Program - California condor:

The FWS Endangered Species program has been studying the population decline of the California condor in coordination with numerous partners for a number of years. FWS provides the expertise to accomplish important population objectives for many species, including the California condor, as a means for conserving the ecosystems upon which endangered and threatened species depend and to provide a program for the conservation of such species[7].

The program's strategic framework is based on two over-arching goals to achieve the ESA's purposes: 1) recovery of federally endangered or threatened species, and 2) management and conservation of species-at-risk, to avoid triggering expensive listing and related activities. The program achieves these goals through the minimization or abatement of threats that are the basis for listing a species. The ESA categorizes threats into the following five factors:

- The present or threatened destruction, modification, or curtailment of a listed species' habitat or range;
- Overutilization for commercial, recreational, scientific, or educational purposes;
- Disease or predation;
- The inadequacy of existing regulatory mechanisms; and
- Other natural or manmade factors affecting a species' continued existence.

Habitat Conservation Plan:

The proposed Windy Farm HCP will include all lands within the boundaries of the Windy Farm Ranch that are owned by the Windy Farm Inc., or its affiliates that lies inside the Condor Valley, and encompasses approximately 340 square miles. The Windy Farm HCP is designed principally to avoid affecting the California condor; however, it includes provisions to minimize and mitigate the impacts of any take that may occur.

Activities covered by the proposed Windy Farm Condor HCP (Covered Activities) include construction activities, such as construction and maintenance of all underground utilities including any oil, gas, water, or other pipelines and fiber optic cables; construction of windmills and associated infrastructure; and recreational activities such as fishing, fishing-related construction, equestrian activities, bicycling events, boating, sailing, swimming, camping, hiking, four-wheel driving, bird watching, and other nature-based activities.

The Windy Farm HCP describes how the effects of the farm's activities on the California condor will be minimized and mitigated through the implementation of avoidance, minimization, mitigation, and monitoring measures. Under the proposed HCP, development of the area over the 50-year permit term will occur in areas that are rarely used by the California condors, and the development will be designed to maintain the value of areas used by California condors.

---

[7] FY 2014 Budget Justification: United States Department of the Interior.

Windy Farm Inc. and the FWS have selected ABC Associates, Inc. to prepare the EIS. The document will be prepared in compliance with the *National Environmental Policy Act* (42 U.S.C. 4321, *et seq.*). ABC Associates, Inc. will prepare the EIS under the supervision of the FWS, who is responsible for the scope and content of the document.

The EIS will consider the proposed action, the issuance of a construction permit under the Act, and a reasonable range of alternatives. A detailed description of the impacts of the proposed action and each alternative will be included in the EIS. Several alternatives will be considered and analyzed, representing varying levels of conservation, impacts, and permit area configurations. A No Action alternative will be included in the analysis of the alternatives considered. The No Action alternative means that the FWS would not issue a permit.

The EIS will also identify potentially significant direct, indirect, and cumulative impacts on biological resources, land use, air quality, water quality, water resources, economics, and other environmental issues that could occur with the implementation of the proposed actions and alternatives. For all potentially significant impacts, the EIS will identify avoidance, minimization, and mitigation measures to reduce these impacts, where feasible, to a level below significance.

- **EXAMPLE – POOR NOTICE OF INTENT**

Notice

Proposal of a rule to enforce the law requiring an Environmental Impact Statement for Issuance of a wind farm permit associated with a Habitat Conservation Plan (HCP) for the federally endangered California condor.

Summary

The U. S. Fish and Wildlife Service (FWS) is proposing a rule to make it illegal for private landowners in any kind of partnership from not completing a Habitat Conservation Plan as outlined by law.

Comment Period

The FWS is not accepting public comment on this topic as it is a legal matter. The usual comment period will be waived.

Background

Over the past couple of years, certain landowners have tried to "get around" having to complete a HCP when constructing on their land due to cost and time factors. As this is already deemed illegal, the FWS is seeking to reiterate this law by proposing a rule that ensures that this law is followed to the letter.

CRITIQUE

- The notice is duplicative and repetitive as it is proposing a rule that already exists in a different format.
- A rule making a law illegal does not make any sense.
- No comment period is allowed; the guidelines clearly state a comment period must occur, whether you or your team agrees with it or not.
- The background is inadequate, as it does not offer any kind of history or timeline of the "issue."

7. CONGRESSIONAL BUDGET JUSTIFICATION

- EXAMPLE – GOOD CONGRESSIONAL BUDGET JUSTIFICATION

CALIFORNIA CONDOR CAPTIVE BREEDING PROGRAM
FUNDING PROFILE BY SUBPROGRAM AND ACTIVITY

				FY 2014		
	2012 Actual	2013 Enacted	Fixed Costs & Related Changes (+/-)	Program Changes (+/-)	Budget Request	Change from 2012 Enacted (+/-)
Candidate Conservation ($)	$2,345,678	$2,567,890	+$1,123,456	+$1,962,975	$5,654,321	+$3,086,431
(FTE)	13	17	+14	+3	34	+17
Listing & Critical Habitat ($)	$2,345,678	$2,123,456	$0	$0	$2,123,456	$0
(FTE)	23	26	0	0	26	0
Consultation & Habitat Conservation Plans ($)	$9,876,543	$9,999,999	$0	-$1,111,111	$8,888,888	-$1,111,111
(FTE)	28	30	0	-7	23	-7
Recovery ($)	$3,456,789	$4,567,890	+$1,000,000	+$7,000,000	$12,567,890	+$8,000,000
(FTE)	21	26	+24	0	50	+24
California Condor ($)	$18,024,688	$19,259,235	$2,123,456	$7,851,864	$29,234,555	$9,975,320
(FTE)	85	99	38	-4	133	34

The out-year numbers for the California condor breeding program do not reflect programmatic requirements. Rather, they are an extrapolation of the FY 2014 request based on the spending inflation rate assumed in the Budget Control Act of 2011. The Administration will develop out-year funding levels based on actual programmatic requirements at a later date. Major out-year priorities and assumptions will be delineated in that update.

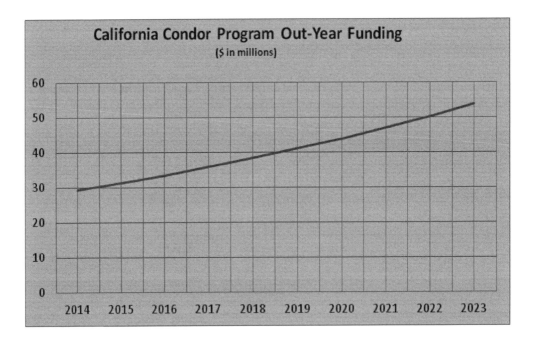

PUBLIC LAW AUTHORIZATIONS

Endangered Species Act of 1973
Urgent Situation Supplemental Act of 2013 (P.L. 007)
National Keeping Big Wild Birds in a Zoo Act (321 USC 123)

OVERVIEW

The U.S. Fish and Wildlife Service's Endangered Species program implements the Endangered Species Act of 1973 (ESA), in coordination with numerous partners. The program provides expertise to accomplish key purposes of the Act, which are to provide a means for conserving the ecosystems upon which endangered and threatened species depend and to provide a program for the conservation of such species.[8]

---

[8] FY 2014 Budget Justification: United States Department of the Interior.

"For more than three decades, the Endangered Species Act has successfully protected our nation's most threatened wildlife, and we should be looking for ways to improve it -- not weaken it. Throughout our history, there's been a tension between those who've sought to conserve our natural resources for the benefit of future generations, and those who have sought to profit from these resources. But I'm here to tell you this is a false choice. With smart, sustainable policies, we can grow our economy today and preserve the environment for ourselves, our children, and our grandchildren.[9]"

The program's strategic framework is based on two over-arching goals to achieve the ESA's purposes: 1) recovery of endangered or threatened (federally-listed) species, and 2) conservation of species-at-risk, so that listing them may be unnecessary. The program achieves these goals through the minimization or abatement of threats that are the basis for listing a species. The ESA categorizes threats into the following five factors:

1. The present or threatened destruction, modification, or curtailment of a listed species' habitat or range;
2. Overutilization for commercial, recreational, scientific, or educational purposes;
3. Disease or predation;
4. The inadequacy of existing regulatory mechanisms; and
5. Other natural or manmade factors affecting a species' continued existence.

The key factor identified for many species is related to habitat alteration. The scope and severity of habitat-based threats and the number of species involved increases substantially with the complexity of threats. By minimizing or removing threats, which may include supporting species' capacity to respond adequately or increase their resilience to changing conditions, a species may be conserved, eliminating the need for protection under the ESA.

The California condor flourished along the Pacific coast for many years and then in large part to habitat loss, illegal shootings, and lead poisoning. By 1985 the entire wild known population had been reduced to just 9 birds, which was when a decision was made to bring all of the remaining wild birds into captivity to preserve the species through captive breeding and eventual reintroduction. The goal of the California Condor Recovery Plan was to establish two geographically separate populations, two in California and one in Arizona, each with 150 birds and at least 15 breeding pairs. As the Recovery Program works toward this goal the number of release sites has grown. There are three active release sites in California, one in Arizona and one in Baja California, Mexico. The recovery program for the California condor was showing success, and the birds were expanding their range and reoccupying portions of their historic range, which includes areas of existing and proposed wind energy development. However, significant increases in fatalities to the condor over recent

---

[9] Any form of "to be" (am, are, is, were, was, been, being, be). President Barack Obama, Remarks By The President To Commemorate The 160th Anniversary of The Department of the Interior, Washington, D.C. March 3, 2009.

years have resulted in the total number of condors reducing dramatically. Thus, it is recommended that the implementation of the California condor captive breeding program be placed into operation without delay.

PROGRAM ACCOMPLISHMENTS AND MILESTONES

In FY 2013, the California condor program accomplished significant milestones in program development. These accomplishments include:

- Identification of 19 zoos throughout the continental United States suitable for the captive breeding program;
- Training of 73 zoo staff on the handling and continued upkeep of the condor;
- Completion of studies in conjunction with the Department of Energy to analyze the effects of wind farms on the condor habitat; and
- Renovation began at the San Diego Old Tram Warehouse. This site will headquarter operations for the program.

EXPLANATION OF CHANGES

The FY 2014 request for the Captive Breeding Program is a fifty one percent increase over the enacted FY 2012 level. This increase will provide for the following:

- Studies to determine the capability of a number of zoos, nationally and internationally, to accommodate a pair of breeding condors;
- Continuation of zoo staff training with an additional 42 staff completing training per year;
- Relocation of 19 breeding condor pairs to various zoos around the country; and
- Renovation of sixteen existing aviaries to bring them up to code.

STRATEGIC MANAGEMENT

From the President's "21ˢᵗ Century Strategy for America's Great Outdoors" initiative, the FWS Division Chief has established the following key goals:

- Reconnect Americans, especially children, with the variety of wildlife, flora and fauna in this vast country, especially species under threat of extinction;
- Promote community-based recreation and conservation, including zoos, wildlife reserves and national parks;
- Use science based management practices to restore and protect our lands, waters and species for future generations; and
- Build upon state, local, private and tribal priorities for the conservation of the condor, and determine how the federal government can best advance these priorities through the use of public/private partnerships and locally supported conservation strategies.

The FY 2014 request for the captive breeding initiative will support a strategy based on readiness to help the California condor program achieve the stated goals.

PRINCIPLE: CALIFORNIA CONDOR

SUB-ELEMENT: CANDIDATE CONSERVATION

			FY 2014			
	2012 Actual	2013 Enacted	Fixed Costs & Related Changes (+/-)	Program Changes (+/-)	Budget Request	Change from 2013Enacted (+/-)
Candidate ($)	$2,345,678	$2,567,890	+$1,123,456	+$1,962,975	$5,654,321	+$3,086,431
Conservation (FTE)	13	17	+14	+3	34	+17

Justification for Program Changes for Candidate Conservation Program

The FY 2014 budget request for Candidate Conservation Program (CCP) is $5,654,321 and 34 FTE, a net program change of + $3,086,431 and + 17 FTE.

The key role of the CCP is to provide technical assistance and work with numerous partners on proactive conservation to remove or reduce threats so that listing species may be unnecessary. This begins with a rigorous assessment using the best scientific information available to determine whether a species faces threats such that it is a candidate for listing and should remain listed under the ESA. This entails close co-operation with states and other appropriate parties. This information is used to target conservation at specific known threats that may make listing unnecessary.

Total numbers for the California condor have decreased from 410 in 2010 to 383 in 2012, a staggering 6.6% decrease. This is inclusive of the 38 condor chicks that hatched in that time, meaning that the condor population has been decimated by the totally unacceptable number of 65 in just a two year period. Should the numbers continue to decline at such an alarming rate, the California condor could be extinct within 10 years. There are three main reasons for the sharp decline:

- Condors are being killed by newly constructed wind farms;
- Condors are being killed by lead poisoning from hunting ammunition; and
- Condors are being killed by pesticide poisoning.

In conjunction with other stakeholders, including the Department of Agriculture, Department of Energy, State and Local governments, and the NRA, the CCP will continue to conduct rigorous evaluations of potential hazards and threats to determine the most amenable outcome for all parties involved. CCP is also currently undertaking a number of studies of zoos, both nationally and internationally, that have the capability to accommodate a breeding pair of California condors. The overall FY 2014 program funding and FTE increase reflects the increased cost and workload associated with these studies. Each study is expected to use an additional 2.5 FTE per year over a three year period. The fixed cost increase reflects the cost for renovation of the San Diego Old Tram Warehouse which will be used to headquarter the newly formed California Condor Operation, as authorized in the *FY 2013 Urgent Situation Supplemental Act* (P.L. 007). The FTE increase reflects the 14 staffers required to operate the office.

PRINCIPLE: CALIFORNIA CONDOR

SUB-ELEMENT: LISTING AND CRITICAL HABITAT

			FY 2014			
	2012 Actual	2013 Enacted	Fixed Costs & Related Changes (+/-)	Program Changes (+/-)	Budget Request	Change from 2012 Enacted (+/-)
Listing & Critical ($)	$2,345,678	$2,123,456	$0	$0	$2,123,456	$0
Habitat (FTE)	23	26	0	0	26	0

Justification for Program Changes for Listing and Critical Habitat Program

The FY 2014 budget request for the Listing and Critical Habitat Program (LCHP) is $2,123,456 and 26 FTE, a net program change of $0 and 0 FTE.

The LCHP provides protection under the ESA for foreign and domestic plants and animals when a species is determined to be threatened or endangered on the basis of the best available scientific information concerning threats. This determination includes information crucial for recovery planning and implementation, and helps to identify and address the conservation needs of the species, including the designation of critical habitat. Without the legal protections afforded under Section 9 of the ESA that become effective upon listing, many species would continue to decline and become extinct.

As described, the California condor situation is critical. A compilation of studies undertaken by the LCHP recommends that for the California condor species to survive, the implementation of a captive breeding program, similar to the program undertaken for the prairie chicken in the 1980s, be urgently initiated. At the time of writing, 19 zoos throughout the continental United States have been identified as being appropriate for immediate transfer of a breeding condor pair. Further studies are currently underway to identify additional suitable locations. With funding already provided for these studies in FY 2012, the FY 2014 budget request remains at the same level as FY 2013, with FTEs also remaining constant.

PRINCIPLE: CALIFORNIA CONDOR

SUB-ELEMENT: CONSULTATION AND HABITAT CONSERVATION PLANS

	2012 Actual	2013 Enacted	FY 2014			
			Fixed Costs & Related Changes (+/-)	Program Changes (+/-)	Budget Request	Change from 2012 Enacted (+/-)
Consultation & Habitat ($)	$9,876,543	$9,999,999	$0	-$1,111,111	$8,888,888	-$1,111,111
Conservation Plans (FTE)	28	30	0	-7	23	-7

Justification for Program Changes for Consultation and Habitat Conservation Plans

The FY 2014 budget request for Consultation and Habitat Conservation Plan Program (CHCPP) is $8,888,888 and 23 FTE, a net program change of -$1,111,111 and -7 FTE.

The CHCPP leads a collaborative process between the Fish and Wildlife Service and other federal agencies to identify opportunities to conserve listed species. Working in partnership with other agencies and organizations is foundational for the Endangered Species program, because the conservation of the Nation's biological heritage cannot be achieved by any single agency or organization. Essential partners include other federal agencies, states, tribes, non-governmental organizations, industry, academia, private landowners, and other Service programs or partners. Other federal agencies consult with the Service to balance adverse impacts of their development actions with conservation actions that contribute toward species survival and also often to their recovery.

Funding for CHCPP for FY 2014 is reduced as the condor captive breeding program takes effect. The breeding program will result in a smaller area of federal and private land to be monitored, thus resulting in a reduction of 7 FTEs. These FTEs will be transferred to the recovery program where they will appear as new FTEs for program budgeting and accounting purposes.

PRINCIPLE: CALIFORNIA CONDOR

SUB-ELEMENT: RECOVERY

	2012 Actual	2013 Enacted	FY 2014			
			Fixed Costs & Related Changes (+/-)	Program Changes (+/-)	Budget Request	Change from 2012 Enacted (+/-)
Recovery ($)	$3,456,789	$4,567,890	+$1,000,000	+$7,000,000	$12,567,890	+$8,000,000
(FTE)	21	26	+24	0	50	+24

Justification for Program Changes for Recovery

The FY 2014 budget request for Recovery is $12,567,890 and 50 FTE, a net program change of +$8,000,000 and +24 FTE.

The Recovery Program implements actions for species near delisting or reclassification from endangered to threatened and actions that are urgently needed for critically endangered species. The Endangered Species Program will participate in this Cooperative Recovery Initiative by combining our resources with those of the National Wildlife Refuge System, the Partners for Fish and Wildlife Program, the Fisheries Program, the Science Program and the Migratory Bird Program through a national, proposal-driven process to identify and implement the highest priority projects.

The significant budget request increase for FY 2014 will provide funding to relocate 19 breeding pairs of the California condor to various zoos across the country. It is expected that this funding will continue to increase in program out-years as more zoos, both nationally and internationally, are identified to accommodate the captive breeding program. It is hoped that this immediate relocation will result in the steady increase of numbers of the California condor, similar to the increases seen in the 1990s and early 2000s. Additionally, the funding will be used to facilitate the renovation of 16 existing aviaries to ensure they meet the requirements of the federally enforced National Keeping Big Wild Birds in a Zoo code (321 USC 123), and 12 new planned aviaries, still to be constructed. Funding for design and planning was appropriated for these activities in the last fiscal year.

Although the funding level for the Recovery program has increased from FY 2013, the number is offset by savings from a significant reduction in the number of birds that will require chelation treatment. This treatment, which removes high levels of lead and copper from the bird's blood system, will no longer be necessary following the relocation of the breeding pairs to the specified facilities, as the condors will not face the threat of poisoning from toxic lead ammunition.

An additional 24 FTEs are required to administer and oversee the planned relocation. These additional FTEs will also be used to train and tutor current ornithologists on best practices for the continued upkeep of the California condor while being bred in captivity. Recovery specialists will complete the training of 42 zoo staff per year. Fixed cost increase in relation to the new salaries required for the additional FTEs.

- EXAMPLE – POOR CONGRESSIONAL JUSTIFICATION

BUDGET JUSTIFICATION FOR CALIFORNIA CONDOR "COMMAND & CONTROL" PROGRAM

PROGRAM ELEMENT: CANDIDATE CONSERVATION

The FY 2014 budget request is $4,321,123 more than the FY 2013 total. The increase is due to the escalating costs associated with the adoption and monitoring of new regulations and program guidance associated with the command and control program. In addition, 19 new Full Time Equivalents (FTEs) are requested to conduct R&D efforts, and perform biological and habitat studies in conjunction with the USDA, with the resulting data used to ensure the successful growth of the condor population. The fixed costs changes increase according to the increased salary demands.

PROGRAM ELEMENT: LISTING AND CRITICAL HABITAT

The FY 2014 budget request is $21,234,567, an increase of $3,852,741 from the FY 2013 amount, with an addition of 13 new FTEs. The increase in the budget level is attributable to the costs related to moving the breeding condor pairs to zoos across the United States. The designation of these zoos as critical habitat and the alteration of enclosures and related surrounding areas is a one-off cost, and the program is expected to recoup much of the costs through ticket receipts from patrons of the zoos. As per statutory authority in the Act, these receipts will be placed in a revolving fund designated the "California Condor Trust Fund."

PROGRAM ELEMENT: CONSULTATION AND HABITAT CONSERVATION PLANS

The FY 2014 budget request is $17,987,654 less than the FY 2013 amount. The reduction is a result of the completion of the studies associated with transferring the breeding condor pairs to the 19 zoos selected for the program, for which the increase in funding was requested in FY 2013. The reduction of $5,000,000 from the fixed costs budget is due to the transfer of the Fish and Wildlife building in Santa Fe to the USDA. FTE numbers will remain the same.

SUB-ACTIVITY: CALIFORNIA CONDOR
PROGRAM ELEMENT: RECOVERY

As per the "Act", $100,000,000 has been authorized for the purchase of two Apache attack helicopters from the Department of Defense at a discounted price. These helicopters will patrol the condor conservation area and eliminate the breeding grounds of the nefarious prairie chicken, which feeds on the eggs and newly hatched condor chicks. One of the top priorities for the Administration and the U.S. Fish and Wildlife service is to eradicate this invasive vermin species by the end of 2015.

It is requested that there be 24 additional FTEs to administer and oversee the planned relocation. These additional FTEs will also be used to train and tutor current ornithologists on best practices for the continued upkeep of the California condor while being bred in captivity. Recovery specialists will complete the training of 42 zoo staff per year. In addition, 23 new FTEs will be hired by the Park Service to monitor and control the new ammunition laws for hunting in the region, as well as working in tandem with USDA inspectors for the new pesticide regulations. Fixed cost increases are in relation to the new salaries required for the additional FTEs.

CRITIQUE

The ultimate goal of a congressional budget testimony is to convince a committee that the issue being presented will benefit the United States, and that it is necessary for federal action to take place. The example above falls short in a variety of areas that could result in their program not being funded.

- The problem that is being solved is not precisely outlined in the beginning. There should be a discussion of the issue and how solving the issue will help the United States.
- The document fails to address how the program fits in with national objectives and ignores areas that establish adherence to Presidential priorities and the agency's goals and objectives.
- The example lacks a thorough justification for increased spending requests. Although, it outlines the different elements of the program and what the increases are, the writer fails to explain why the increase will benefit the U.S., beyond the means of just needing the additional funds and employees.
- Most importantly, the example fails short in the analysis section. A cost benefit analysis should always be conducted in order to illustrate what benefits the program will result in after receiving this additional funding. The analysis should include:
- A comparison of total program benefits and total program costs, using quantitative, objective data to the maximum extent possible, as well as qualitative or judgmental material;
- A comparison of the marginal benefits and the marginal costs associated with the additional funds or reduced funding proposed; and
- Supporting information that takes into consideration agency and outside program evaluations and related analytic studies, whether or not they agree with the proposed policy.

8. GUIDANCE DIRECTIVE

- EXAMPLE – GOOD GUIDANCE DIRECTIVE

MEMORANDUM

To: Regional Directors, Regions 1, 2, 3, 4, 5, 6

From: Deputy Director, Fish and Wildlife Service
Subject: Relationship of Energy Construction Permitting and Habitat Conservation Planning Efforts in relation to the California condor

In recent years, the Habitat Conservation Plan (HCP) program under section 123(abc) of the Endangered Species Act has grown rapidly. When Congress enacted the HCP provisions, it stressed the need for developing "creative partnerships" between the public and private sector in resolving endangered species issues, especially on private lands. These partnerships, although very effective, raise several important questions regarding the relationship between new construction and HCP efforts.

One of the main questions raised is the acquisition of land by the government and private stakeholders though co-operative grants and loan guarantees in HCP planning areas for energy related activities. Stakeholders now claim that such partnerships, in effect, absolve private land developers of their obligations to mitigate the impacts of their activities on listed species. This misconception can be clarified by ensuring that the establishment of a partnership with the government does not obviate the habitat mitigation requirements. Under section 9999 of the Act, the landowner must mitigate regardless of what is required of or carried out by other entities within the HCP, to the extent deemed appropriate, as defined in an approved HCP.

The following simple guidelines are provided for determining appropriate courses of action in cases involving establishment and management of HCPs:

1. Mitigation measures must be included for all HCPs, regardless of ownership.
2. All elements of an Environmental Impact Assessment must be followed as per statute, regardless of ownership.
3. For HCP purposes, all public/private partnerships are to be treated the same as solely private organizations.

Additional guidance and examples can be found in the FWS' Habitat Conservation Planning Handbook.

- **EXAMPLE – POOR GUIDANCE DIRECTIVE**

MEMORANDUM

To: All Department of Interior Employees
From: Fish and Wildlife Service
Subject: Transportation of the California Condor to Other Habitats

When moving the California condor to another habitat or zoo, there is a specific method of transportation outlined by the FWS. We recommend that the moving company use government licensed equipment and trained personnel. However, with the ever-increasing costs of transportation, we also allow some leeway with these methods.

For further clarification, consult with your immediate supervisor.

Critique:

The memo above lacks sufficient information that could be used to help guide a program manager on specific actions related to a new program. The writer has wrongly assumed that the recipient understands fully the new program and its dimensions. It fails to address:

- The purpose;
- To who it applies to; and
- Why the guidance was written.

It is imperative that when a guidance document is created that it incorporates these aspects:

- Clearly states issue and its importance;
- A citation of relevant laws or regulations that the guidance is clarifying;
- A conclusion with clear and concise guidelines that cannot be misinterpreted.

9. CONGRESSIONAL TESTIMONY

    - EXAMPLE – GOOD CONGRESSIONAL TESTIMONY

Statement of Dr. Robert R. Robertson, Deputy Director, U.S. Fish and Wildlife Service – Endangered Species program, before the Senate Interior and Environment Appropriations Subcommittee

Senator Black and Senator White; Members of the Committee. Thank you for the opportunity to testify about the Administration's plan and activities associated with increasing the California condor population in the United States.

The California condor is truly a majestic species. This spectacular bird, with the largest wingspan of any North American bird, has an average lifespan of up to 60 years. Sadly, it is currently under threat of extinction from a variety of sources, including:

- The construction of wind farms on the nesting and flight pattern areas of the California condor;
- Increased contact with power lines, antennas and cell-phone towers; and
- The effects of hunting, predatory egg encroachment, poisoning and general habitat degradation.

The California condor population has decreased from 410 in 2010 to 383 in 2012, a staggering 6.6% decrease. This is inclusive of the 38 condor chicks that hatched in captivity in that time, meaning that the condor population has been decimated by the totally unacceptable number of 65 in the wild in just a two year period. Should the numbers continue to decline at such an alarming rate, the California condor could be extinct within 10 years.

The U.S. Fish and Wildlife Service's (FWS) Endangered Species program has been studying this phenomenon in coordination with numerous partners for years. FWS provides the expertise to accomplish important population objectives for many species as a means for conserving the ecosystems upon which endangered and threatened species depend and to provide a program for the conservation of such species.[10]

The program's strategic framework is based on two over-arching goals to achieve the ESA's purposes: 1) recovery of federally endangered or threatened species, and 2) management and conservation of species-at-risk, to avoid triggering expensive listing and related activities. The program achieves these goals through the minimization or abatement of threats that are the basis for listing a species. The ESA categorizes threats into the following five factors:

1. The present or threatened destruction, modification, or curtailment of a listed species' habitat or range;
2. Overutilization for commercial, recreational, scientific, or educational purposes;
3. Disease or predation;
4. The inadequacy of existing regulatory mechanisms; and
5. Other natural or manmade factors affecting a species' continued existence.

Based on studies undertaken by the FWS, one of the key factors identified for many species is related to habitat alteration. The scope and severity of habitat-based threats and the number of species involved increases substantially with the complexity of threats. By minimizing or removing threats, which may include supporting species' capacity to respond adequately or increase their resilience to changing conditions, a species may be conserved, eliminating the need for protection under the ESA.

The California condor flourished along the Pacific coast for many years and then in large part to habitat loss, illegal shootings, and lead poisoning. By 1985 the entire wild known population had been reduced to just 9 birds, which was when a decision was made to bring all of the remaining wild birds into captivity to preserve the species through captive breeding and eventual reintroduction. The goal of the California Condor Recovery Plan was to establish two geographically separate populations, one in California and one in Arizona, each with 150 birds and at least 15 breeding pairs. As the Recovery Program works toward this goal the number of release sites has grown. There are three active release sites in California, one in Arizona and one in Baja California, Mexico.

The recovery program for the California condor was showing success, and the birds were expanding their range and reoccupying portions of their historic habitat, which

---

[10] FY 2014 Budget Justification: United States Department of the Interior.

includes areas of existing and proposed wind energy development. However, significant increases in fatalities to the condor over recent years have resulted in the total number of condors reducing dramatically. Thus, the Administration has commenced a California condor captive breeding program.

The support began with FY 2013 funding. The FY 2014 budget request for the captive breeding program is $29.2 million, broken into the following four sub-categories:

- Candidate Conservation - $5.6 million
- Listing and Critical Habitat - $2.1 million
- Consultation and Habitat Conservation Plans - $8.9 million
- Recovery - $12.6 million

The request will fund a number of projects including the relocation of 19 breeding condor pairs to an assortment of various zoos and wildlife reserves identified as being the most promising sites to host the breeding program. In addition, the outlay will reflect the costs associated with the renovation of the San Diego Old Tram Warehouse which will be used to headquarter the newly formed California Condor Operation, as mandated in the *FY 2013 Urgent Situation Supplemental Act* (P.L. 007). Additionally, the funding will be used to facilitate the renovation of 16 existing aviaries to ensure they meet the requirements of the federally enforced *National Keeping Big Wild Birds in a Zoo code* (321 USC 123), and 12 new planned aviaries, still to be constructed. Funding for design and planning was appropriated for these activities in the last fiscal year.

Two other options have also been put forward to this committee in recent weeks; continue condor breeding in the wild; and, enhance breeding by removing hazards in the wild through command and control. While these programs do have their merits, it must be noted that although the budget for continued breeding in the wild is only $4.4 million, and may seem like the best option given the current fiscal situation, breeding in the wild only offers a continuation of current practice which is detrimental to the condor as this method historically results in population decline. A regulatory solution is estimated to cost $279 million; a staggering increase over both of the other options without evidence that it would succeed. Other prominent stakeholders in the debate agree that subjecting the U.S. public to increased regulation and restrictions are not as advantageous as either breeding in the wild or captivity.

Thus, the most prudent course of action would be to implement a captive breeding program with immediate relocation in order to increase the California condors overall numbers, similar to the increases seen in the 1990s and early 2000s. As our studies have shown, by utilizing the bird's ability to double clutch, biologists will implement an unique captive breeding technique by removing the first egg from the nest which should result in the condor producing a second and sometimes a third egg. This captive breeding process will result in the increase in numbers within 10 years to levels that will result in removing the California condor from the Endangered Species list.

I thank you for your time and will be happy to answer any questions you may have.

- ### EXAMPLE – POOR CONGRESSIONAL TESTIMONY

Statement of Dr. Robert R. Robertson, Deputy Director, U. S. Fish and Wildlife Service – Endangered Species program, before the Senate Interior and Environment Appropriations Subcommittee

Good morning committee members, I am here to discuss my outrage in the declining populations of California's most majestic bird, the *Gymnogyps californianus*. Some folks from the Fish and Wildlife Service told me this issue needs to be talked about, and this is the committee that gets to hear my point of view on the subject.

I have heard of some people that have been working on increasing the population of these birds but they need more help because they are running out of money. I know that the people working with these birds want the birds to be healthy and hatch more baby condors.

There might have been previous programs like this before but they are not important right now because the issue is still causing alarm. Everything that has been done previously has shown to be inadequate and should be forgotten about. We should only focus on the here and now and how to increase the bird's population.

The way that the condors can be saved is by appropriating $50 million to the Fish and Wildlife Service. They will know what needs to be done and I know that they will get it done. There shouldn't be much of an impact to anyone except to the growth of the population of the birds. I am sure that the FWS will take the necessary steps to ensure the bird's survival. They will know how to spend the money effectively and responsibly.

Ultimately the FWS needs money for this program, and seeing as this committee appropriates money for programs such as this our office feels that they should receive the funds they need and they be allowed to spend it in a way they feel will help the birds the most.

CRITIQUE

Flaws with the speech outlined above include:

- The use of the scientific name for the condor – no-one is going to know what is being referred to.
- Personal feelings should not be included – testimony reflects the Agency or Departmental position, not your own!
- All points referenced are hearsay – no specific mention of studies or reports was made.
- It can be assumed that the agency position is to save the condor; however, no specific goals or objectives are outlined.

- The $50 million budget figure is mentioned but no detail as to what it would be used for is discussed.
- All the options in the BDD have the goal of "Saving the Condor." This testimony does not discuss any of the three outlined options.

10. **ADVOCACY DOCUMENT**

- **EXAMPLE –GOOD ADVOCACY DOCUMENT**

1 January 2013

Connie Condorson
U.S. Fish and Wildlife Service
2493 Condor Road, Suite B,
Condor Park, Los Angeles, CA 33333

Mike Michaelson
President, Friends of the California Condor
12344 Condor Way, Suite 400
Sacramento, CA 98765

Dear Mr. Michaelson,

The California condor population is currently at near-extinction levels. Current studies have indicated that the population has decreased from 410 in 2010 to 383 in 2012. Should this decline in population be allowed to continue, experts estimate that the species will become extinct within 10 years. This decline has resulted in various stakeholder requests that the government focus on whether the existing recovery strategy is the most effective in preventing further decline and possible extinction.

The U. S. Fish and Wildlife Service (FWS) are currently initiating a Captive Breeding program for the California condor. The FWS strategic objective is the following:

- Enact and promulgate statutes and regulations which prohibit the use of lead based ammunition and poison traps in California, Nevada, Arizona, Oregon and New Mexico.
- Limit the construction and use of wind energy facilities in the existing and planned condor habitats.
- Ban the use of harmful pesticides currently being used on vegetable and fruit farms in the condor's habitat.
- Expand the range of the protected area by an additional 15 miles in all directions.

As a champion of the California condor recovery program, we seek your counsel and recommendations on this issue. The FWS is holding a symposium to discuss the proposal, and we request that you be a keynote speaker for the conference. In addition, the FWS requests a number of meetings with your organization to coordinate efforts between all stakeholders involved and reach a resolution favorable to all involved parties.

Respectfully yours,

Connie Condorson
Acting Regional Manager
Office of Environmental Review and Analysis

- **EXAMPLE – POOR ADVOCACY DOCUMENT**

1 January 2013
Mike Michaelson
President, Friends of the California Condor
12344 Condor Way, Suite 400
Sacramento, CA 98765

Mike,

It was good to chat to your staff recently regarding the ongoing California condor issue. As they have probably informed you, the U.S. FWS is seeking strategic partners to reach our goal for the condor. Your staff indicated that you would be interested. Let me know your feelings on this.

Best,
Connie Condorson
Acting Regional Manager
Office of Environmental Review and Analysis

CRITIQUE

The example above demonstrates a poorly written advocacy document:

- All correspondence within the government and with stakeholders is considered formal, no matter how well you may know the recipient. Never begin a letter with the person's first name.
- The California condor "issue" is mentioned but not expanded upon.
- Assumes that your staff has discussed this with the recipient.
- The letter is completely non-substantive.
- There is no outlined strategy, goals or objectives, or solutions to the "issue" mentioned.
- Assumes that the recipient is on your side and will support you.

11. CORRESPONDENCE

- ### EXAMPLE – GOOD CORRESPONDENCE

January 1, 2013

Connie Condorson
U.S. Fish and Wildlife Service
2493 Condor Road, Suite B,
Condor Park, Los Angeles, California 33333

Mr. George Washington
Assistant Secretary, Environmental Affairs, Pacific Region
U.S. Department of Interior
1849 C Street, N.W.
Washington DC 20240

Dear Mr. Washington,

Enclosed is the FY 2012 annual report on the California condor rehabilitation program as requested. The following briefly summarizes our key findings and recommendations.

The California condor recovery program has now been underway for over 20 years, and the program continues to make progress in several key areas. The overall population in the wild is increasing year-over-year, and the birds are expanding their nesting ranges. The number of breeding pairs has increased through this reporting period, and they have successfully hatched and fledged chicks each year.

However, the most significant issue currently affecting the California condor is exposure to lead contamination, which continues to affect the entire southwest population. Although voluntary efforts to reduce the use of lead ammunition in the California condor range may help to reduce exposure to lead contamination among these birds, the FWS agrees that further efforts to reduce the lead load available to scavenging birds are crucial for program success. Thus, we commend the Administration's decision to enforce strict lead ammunition laws for hunters in the California condor range.

Very Truly Yours,
Connie Condorson
Acting Regional Manager
Office of Environmental Review and Analysis

- ### EXAMPLE – POOR CORRESPONDENCE

Connie Condorson
U.S. Fish and Wildlife Service

2493 Condor Road, Suite B,
Condor Park, Los Angeles, California 33333

1 January, 2013

Mr. George Washington
Assistant Secretary, Environmental Affairs, Pacific Region
U.S. Department of Interior
1849 C Street, N.W.
Washington DC 20240

Dear Mr. Washington,
Following our recent meeting, here is my recommendation for the points discussed.

As you know, the Administration's position to repopulate is a presidential priority. As the program leader, the support of scientific conservation and federally endangered species stakeholders is a critical determinant of the manner in which recovery is accomplished. While most of the experts support captive breeding, there is still a great deal of controversy associated with whether there are policies which the Administration can implement that would increase the probability that breeding in the wild is the most viable approach.

Thus, I have decided to agree with your recommendations to move forward.

Yours sincerely,
Connie Condorson

CRITIQUE

The correspondence is poorly formatted and skips from topic to topic.

- There is no reference to the "points discussed". An Assistant Secretary has many issues to deal with and will not recall each and every meeting he or she has attended.
- The entire main paragraph is a run-on line. Correspondence of this kind should be short and concise.
- A number of issues with the program are referred to; however, no detail is provided.
- The recommendation is inadequate. While the program will be "moving forward" it fails to mention what option has been chosen to "move forward" with.

12. PRESS RELEASE

- EXAMPLE – GOOD PRESS RELEASE

June 20th, 2013
U.S. Fish and Wildlife Service Implements New Program to assist Endangered Species Using Captive Breeding

Contact:
Fred Topple
703-338-2337
fredtopple@fws.gov

Today, President Obama signed Executive Order 55503 outlining a new program aimed to protect a group of endangered birds called the California condors. The Fish and Wildlife Service will be implementing a program called California Condor Recovery Program or (CCR) to reestablish the condor's population. The program has a budget of $4.5 Million dollars and will focus on the captive breeding technique. This involves capturing the birds and encouraging reproduction. Since the condors are known to "double clutch" they have the potential to produce two eggs if the first one is removed.

By 1900, the condor population plummeted due to many factors including loss of habitat, a low reproductive rate, poisoning, and shooting. The condor was limited to southern California.

The condors maintained a strong population in southern California until hunting, predatory eggs encroachment, poisoning by cyanide traps set for coyotes, collisions with power lines, wind farm operations, general habitat degradation, and lead poisoning began to take a heavy toll on the population.

In response to the significantly diminished condor population the Condor Recovery Program's strategy focuses on:

- Increasing reproduction in captivity;
- The release of condors to the wild;
- Minimizing condor death factors;
- Maintain habitat for condor recovery; and
- Implementing condor information and education programs.

A primary objective of the recovery program is to take the condor species off of the endangered species list and work to downgrade it to a threatened species.

The goal is to have three separate populations of 150 birds, which sets a safety net for the birds. Estimated time for achieving this goal is 2020.

- To achieve that expectation, the plan is to establish two geographically separate populations, one in California and one in Arizona, each with 150 birds and at least 15 breeding pairs.
- As progress is made the number of release sites will grow.

- The captive breeding program will be led by the San Diego Wild Animal Park and Los Angeles Zoo.

- **EXAMPLE – POOR PRESS RELEASE**

July 27th, 2013

The Department of Interior issues 2013 Condor Report

The Department of Interior issued the 2013 Annual Condor Report recently. A complete copy of the report can be found on Interior's website.

CRITIQUE

The press release above does offer sufficient information that educates an audience. It does indicate what the Department has done, but it offers no other supportive information.

After reading a press release the reader should have knowledge of the following information:

- What the agency has chosen to do and why;
- When the stated action will take place and the duration of that action; and
- Who is involved both in the public and private sector.

Chapter 24

Glossary of Terms

Legal Terms[1]

Affidavit – A voluntary declaration of facts written down and sworn to by the declarant before an officer authorized to administer oaths, such as a notary public.

Admissibility – The quality or state of being allowed to be entered into evidence in a hearing, trial, or other proceeding.

Arraignment – The initial step in a criminal prosecution whereby the defendant is brought before the court to hear the charges and to enter a plea.

Assignment – The transfer of rights or property.

Basis – A fundamental principle; an underlying condition; the value assigned to a taxpayer's investment in property and used primarily for computing gain or loss from a transfer of the property.

Bequest – The act of giving property (usuual personal property) by will.

Corpus – The property for which a trustee is responsible; the trust principal.

[1] Garner, Bryan A. Black's Law Dictionary 8th Ed. (West Group, 2004).

Glossary of Terms

Decedent – A dead person, especially one who has died recently.

Dissolve – To dismiss challenges.

Due Diligence – Research and analysis of a company or organization done in preparation for a business transaction

Exhaust – To exercise all possible or reasonable courses of action.

Expedite – Hasten.

First-degree relative – Usually used in conjunction with state probate codes to determine who gets real and personal property of someone who has died without a will. The term, then, will be defined however the statute defines it. The term will probably mean relatives directly related to the person who has died, parents, siblings, children, etc.

Intestate – Of or relating to a person who has died without a valid will.

Interrogatories – Formal, written questions.

Merits – The elements or grounds of a claim or defense; the substantive considerations to be taken into account in deciding a case, as opposed to extraneous or technical points, esp., of procedure.

Novation – The act of substituting for an old obligation a new one that either replaces an existing obligation with a new obligation or replaces an original party with a new party.

Relief – Aid or assistance given to those in need, esp., financial aid provided by the state; the redress or benefit, esp., equitable in nature.

Remainder – A future interest arising in a third person — that is, someone other than the estate's creator, its initial holder, or the heirs of either — who is intended to take after the natural termination of the preceding estate.

Common Grammar[2]

Adjective – A word that modifies, quantifies, or otherwise describes a noun or pronoun.

Adverb – A word that modifies or otherwise qualifies a verb, adjective, or another adverb.

---

[2] Strunk, Willion Jr. and E.B. White, *The Elements of Style 4th Ed.* (Boston: Allyn and Bacon, 2000).

Articles – The words a, an, and the, which signal or introduce nouns. The definite article refers to a particular item. The indefinite articles a and an refer to a general item or one not already mentioned.

Bracket – Used to enclose interpolations that are not specifically a part of the original quotation.

Capitalization – The act or process of capitalizing.

Colon – A punctuation mark (:) used after a word introducing a quotation, an explanation, an example, or a series.

Comma – A punctuation mark (,) used to indicate a separation of ideas or of elements within the structure of a sentence.

Common Noun – A noun, such as a book, that can be preceded by the definite article and that represents on or all of the members of a class.

Conventions – Rules of standard English usage, capitalization, punctuation, paragraphing, and spelling.

Declarative Sentence – States an idea.

Ellipsis – Three periods in a row (...), and signifies that words or figures are missing.

Em Dash – A symbol (—) used in writing and printing to indicate a break in thought or sentence structure, to introduce a phrase added for emphasis, definition, or explanation, or to separate two clauses.

Exclamation – A word, phrase, or sentence spoken with great emotion or intensity.

Exclamation Point – The sign (!) used in writing after an exclamation.

Hyphen – A punctuation mark used both to join words and to separate syllables.

Intransitive Verb – A verb that does not take a direct object.

Noun – A word that names a person, place, thing, or idea. Most nouns have a plural and a possessive form.

Numeral – A word class consisting of words representing numbers.

Parentheses – A pair of signs ( ) used in writing to mark off an interjected explanatory or qualifying remark.

Part Of Speech - One of the eight classes of word in English: noun, verb, adjective, adverb, pronoun, preposition, conjunction and interjection.

Glossary of Terms

Period – The point or character (.) used to mark the end of a declarative sentence.

Plural – A grammatical number, typically referring to more than one of the referent in the real world.

Possessive – The case of nouns and pronouns that indicates ownership or possession.

Pronoun – Used as replacements or substitutes for nouns and noun phrases, and that have very general reference, as I, you, he, this, who, what.

Proper Noun – The name of a particular person, place, or thing. Proper nouns are capitalized. Common nouns name classes of people, places, or things and are not capitalized.

Punctuation – Visual sign which help a reader distinguish between words and sentences and help the reader understand the relationships between words.

Question Mark – A mark (?) indicating a question.

Quotation Marks – One of the marks used to indicate the beginning and end of a quotation.

Semicolon – A mark of punctuation (;) used to connect independent clauses and indicating a closer relationship between the clauses than a period does.
Singular – A singular form of words refers to one person, thing, or phenomenon.

Verb – A word or group of words that expresses the action or indicates the state of being of the subject.

Sentence Structure[3]

Adjectival Modifier –A word, phrase, or clause that acts as an adjective in qualifying the meaning of a noun or pronoun.

Adverbial Clause – A clause that functions as an adverb.

Adverbial Phrase – A phrase that functions as an adverb.

Agreement – The correspondence of a verb with its subject in person and number, and of a pronoun with its antecedent in person, number, and gender.

Antecedent – The noun to which a pronoun refers. A pronoun and a noun must agree in person, number, and gender.

---

[3] Strunk, Willion Jr. and E.B. White, *The Elements of Style 4th Ed.* (Boston: Allyn and Bacon, 2000).

322

Appositive – A noun or noun phrase that renames or adds identifying information to a noun it immediately follows.

Auxiliary Verb – A verb which supports and precedes the main verb of a sentence.
Case – The form of a noun or pronoun that reflects its grammatical function in a sentence as subject, object, or possessor.

Clause – A group of words containing a subject and its verb.

Complement – A word or phrase that completes the predicate. Subject complements complete linking verbs and rename or describe the subject. Object compliments complete transitive verbs by renaming or describing the direct object.

Complex Sentence – A sentence with an independent clause and at least one dependent clause.

Compound Sentence – Two or more independent clauses joined by a coordinating conjunction, a correlative conjunction, or a semicolon.

Compound Subject – Two or more simple subjects joined by a coordinating or correlative conjunction.

Conjunction – A word that joins words, phrases, clauses, or sentences. The coordinating conjunction and, but, or, nor, yet, so, for join grammatically equivalent elements. Correlative conjunctions (both, and; either, or; neither, nor) join the same kind of elements.

Correlative Expression – See conjunction.

Dependent Clause – A group of words that includes a subject and verb but is subordinate to an independent clause in a sentence. Dependent clauses begin with either a subordinating conjunction, such as if, because, since, or relative pronoun such as who, which, that.

Direct Object – A noun or pronoun that receives the action of a transitive verb.

Gerund – The -ing form of a verb that functions as a noun.

Imperative Sentence – Asks, requests, or commands someone to do something. An imperative sentence drops the subject.

Indefinite Pronoun – A pronoun that refers to an unspecified person or thing.

Independent Clause – A group of words with a subject and verb that can stand alone as a sentence.

Glossary of Terms

Indirect Object – A noun or pronoun that indicates to whom or for whom, to what or for what the action of the transitive verb is performed.

Infinitive/Split Infinitive – In the present tense, a verb phrase consisting of to followed by the base form of the word. A Split Infinitive occurs when one or more words are placed between to and the verb.

Linking Verb – A verb that joins the subject of a sentence to its complement.

Loose Sentence – A sentence that begins with the main idea and then attaches modifiers, qualifiers, and additional details.

Main Clause – An independent clause, which can stand alone as a grammatically complete sentence.

Modal Auxiliaries – Any of the verbs that combine with the main verb to express necessity (must), obligation (should), permission (may), probability (might), possibility (could), ability (can), or tentativeness (would).

Modal Verb – An auxiliary verb like can, may, must, which modifies the main verb and expresses possibility.

Nominative Pronoun – A pronoun that functions as a subject or a subject complement.

Number – A feature of nouns, pronouns, and a few verbs, referring to singular or plural. A subject and its corresponding verb must be consistent in number; a pronoun should agree in number with its antecedent.

Object – The noun or pronoun that completes a prepositional phrase or the meaning of a transitive verb.

Participial Phrase – A present or past participle with accompanying modifiers, objects, or complements.

Participle - The -ing and -ed forms of verbs.

Paragraph – A unit of meaning signaled by indenting the first word or by inserting a line space between sections of writing.

Periodic Sentence – A sentence that expresses the main idea at the end.

Phrase - A group of words not containing a subject and its verb.

Predicate – The verb and its related words in a clause or sentence. The predicate expresses what the subject does, experiences, or is.

Preposition – A word that relates its object (a noun, pronoun, or -ing verb form) to another word in the sentence.

Prepositional Phrase – A group of words consisting or a preposition, its object, and any of the object's modifiers.

Principal Verb – The predicating verb in a main clause or sentence.

Pronominal Possessive – Possessive pronouns such as hers, its, and theirs.

Relative Clause – A clause introduced by a relative pronoun, such as who, which, that, or by a relative adverb, such as where, when, why.

Relative Pronoun – A pronoun that connects a dependent clause to a main clause in a sentence.

Restrictive Term, Element, or Clause – A phrase or clause that limits the essential meaning of the sentence element it modifies or identifies.

Run-on-Sentence – A sentence of two or more independent clauses are joined without a conjunction or correct punctuation.

Sentence Fragment – A group of words that is not grammatically a complete sentence but is punctuated as one.

Simple Sentence – A sentence consisting of one main clause.

Subject – The noun or pronoun that indicates what a sentence is about, and which the principal verb of a sentence elaborates.

Subject/Verb-Agreement – Singular subjects need singular verbs; plural subjects need plural verbs.

Subordinate Clause – A clause dependent on the main clause in a sentence.

Syntax – The order or arrangement of words in a sentence. Syntax may exhibit parallelism (I came, I saw, I conquered), inversion (Whose woods these are I think I know), or other formal characteristics.

Tense - The form of a verb that shows us when the action or state happens (past, present, or future).

Transition – Words or phrases that help make smooth connections between parts of a text.

Transitive Verb – A verb that requires a direct object to complete its meaning.

Glossary of Terms

Verbal – A verb form that functions in a sentence as a noun, an adjective, or an adverb rather than a principal verb.

Common Style Considerations[4]

Active Voice – The voice used to indicate that the grammatical subject of the verb is performing the action.

Abbreviation – A shortened form of a word or expression.

Acronym – A word formed from the initial letters or groups of letter of words in a set phrase or series of words.

Ambiguity – Doubtfulness or uncertainty of meaning or intention.

Audience – The intended readers of a text.

Boldface – Designated or pertaining to a style of printing types in which letters are thicker than the base font to emphasize or separate different kinds of information.

Cliché – A trite or overused expression or idea.

Claim - Thesis or main point, especially in persuasive writing.

Clarity – Direct and unambiguous language used to reduce reader uncertainty.

Coherence – Unity in a text, usually as regards to content.

Colloquialism – A word or expression appropriate for informal conversation but not suitable for academic or business writing.

Connotation – The associated or secondary meaning of a word or express in addition to its explicit or primary meaning.

Contraction – A shortened form of a word or group of words.

Compound words – A union of two or more words, either with or without a hyphen, used to convey a unit idea that is not as clearly or quickly developed by the component words in unconnected succession.

Derivative – A variation on a word.

Edit – Preparing writing for final draft by checking spelling, punctuation, capitalization, usage, paragraph indentation, neatness, and legibility.

---

[4] Strunk, Willion Jr. and E.B. White, *The Elements of Style 4th Ed.* (Boston: Allyn and Bacon, 2000).

Emphasis – Distinction given to a particular set of information within a document for the purpose of alerting the author to the significance of the information.

Expository – Writing that explains an idea and informs the reader.

Fragment – A group of words which does not express a complete thought.

Italic – Designating or pertaining to a style of printing types in which letters usually slop to the right, patterned upon a compact manuscript hand, and used for emphasis, to separate different kinds of information, etc.

Modifier – A word or phrase that qualifies, describes, or limits the meaning of a word, phrase or clause.

Narrative – Presentation of a series of event in a purposeful sequence.

Nonrestrictive Modifier – A phrase or clause that does not limit or restrict the essential meaning of the element it modifies.

Passive Voice - In the passive voice, the subject receives the action of the verb.

Persuasive Writing – Writing that convinces the designated audience to support a point of view, make a decision, or take an action.

Positive Form – Direct and clear conveyance of information with minimal display of noncommittal language.

Revise/revision – The process of reworking written materials, which includes: considering changes in audience, purpose, focus, organization, style, and elaborating, emphasizing, clarifying, or simplifying text.

Summarize – Condense the main points using as few words as possible and written in own words.

Summary – Without the usual formalities; esp., without a jury "a summary trial."

Voice – The attribute of a verb that indicates whether its subject is active or passive.

Glossary of Terms
Unique Government Instruments[5]

White Papers/Policy Papers – Instruments used to educate and position deliberations about a new scientific or technological advance, or a policy shift.

Scientific Reports – Documents used by researchers to convey the findings associated with their research, to support or challenge previous ideas.

Base Documents – Instruments developed typically from existing white papers and scientific reports capturing the institutional and stakeholder perspective, both current and historical, and are used to generate all future documents regarding the issue.

Issue Papers – Documents used for the examination of an issue associated with a policy shift and the evaluation of the alternatives associated with the issue.

Decision Documents – Documents used to assess the logic and reasoning behind major decisions made by the Federal Government, as well as, weigh the expected impacts of those decisions.

Brief Memoranda – Documents that serve as communication tools for sharing information between employees within the Federal Government.

Executive Summaries – Instruments at the beginning of a document designed to convey a clear understanding of the context, subject matter, and conclusions of the document without requiring the reader to delve into the document's body.

Advocacy Documents – Documents used to influence a decision maker's viewpoint on an issue via presentation of ideas, proposals, and solutions to facilitate the decision-making process.

Budget Justifications – Documents used to explain the reasoning behind budgetary requests, the methodology for program pricing, and performance timelines.

Press Releases – Summary documents used to disseminate the facts about a policy, program, or decision to be reported by the media.

---

[5] Strunk, Willion Jr. and E.B. White, *The Elements of Style 4th Ed.* (Boston: Allyn and Bacon, 2000).